CONSCIENCE

CONSCIENCE

John Donnelly & Leonard Lyons, Ed's.

alba house

A DIVISION OF THE SOCIETY OF ST. PAUL
STATEN ISLAND, NEW YORK 10314

BJ
1471
D66

Library of Congress Cataloging in Publication Data

Donnelly, John, comp.
  Conscience.

  Includes bibliographical references.
  1.   Conscience.   I.   Lyons, Leonard, joint comp.
II.   Title.
BJ1471.D66   241'.1   72-6720
ISBN O-8189-0259-0

Designed, printed and bound in the U.S.A. by the Fathers and
Brothers of the Society of St. Paul as part of their communications apostolate.

PREFACE

"There is a superior principle of reflection or conscience in every man, which distinguishes between the internal principles of his heart, as well as his external actions: which passes judgment upon himself and them; pronounces determinately some actions to be in themselves just, right, good; others to be in themselves evil, wrong, unjust; which, without being consulted, without being advised with, magisterially exerts itself, and approves or condemns him, the doer of them accordingly...." Joseph Butler, SERMONS UPON HUMAN NATURE II.

IN much traditional philosophy the faculty of reason is referred to as an "inner light," capable of illuminating the path to Truth. If we were to be traditional, we might refer to conscience as an "inner voice," capable of directing us along the path of Virtue. "Follow reason," exhorts the epistemologist. "And let your conscience be your guide," the moralist adds. These convenient maxims, though they may see us through many a difficulty, generate almost as many problems as they resolve. The number of philosophical volumes which question the function, the reliability, and even the existence of reason is legion. Yet, analogous questions may be asked concerning the faculty of conscience: When does a man's conscience come into play? Should a man always do as his conscience directs or is it possible for a man to follow his conscience and yet do evil? Finally, is there a faculty of conscience or is conscience no more than conditioned fears of retribution? The present volume introduces philosophical discussions of these and associated problems with the hope of inspiring further work in this pressing area of moral concern.

ACKNOWLEDGMENTS

We would like to express our gratitude to all the authors and/or editors who have allowed us to reprint their papers in this collection of essays. The journals or books in which the articles originally appeared are as follows:

I. *Philosophy*, vol. 15 (1940). II. *Analysis*, vol. 7 (1940). III. *Ethics*, vol. 74 (1963-64). IV. *Mind*, vol. 72 (1963). V. *Philosophy*, vol. 41 (1966). VI *Philosophy*, vol. 30 (1955). *The Journal of Philosophy*, vol. 58 (1961). VIII. *The Journal of Philosophy*, vol. 60 (1963). IX. *Religious Studies*, vol. 8 (1972). X. *Proceedings of the Aristotelian Society*, vol. 64 (1963-64). XI. *Ethics*, (Baltimore: Penguin Books Inc., 1954), pp. 251-59. XII. *Rice University Studies*, vol. 51 (1965); also simultaneously published in *Insight and Vision* (ed.) K. Kolenda (San Antonio: Trinity University Press, 1966). XIII. *The Southern Journal of Philosophy*, vol. 8 (1970). XIV. *Ethics*, vol. 80 (1970).

We are also indebted to Joyce Donnelly whose secretarial skill has greatly facilitated the preparation of this volume.

Contents

PART I

THE MEANING OF "CONSCIENCE" AND "CONSCIENTIOUSNESS"

INTRODUCTION

ANY philosophical analysis must include a thorough and comprehensive discussion of the terms crucial to that analysis. A philosophical treatment of the conscience and its role in the moral life is no exception to the rule. In a classically analytic paper C. D. Broad elucidates the concepts of "conscience" and "conscientious action." First, he distinguishes a wider from a narrower sense of the term "conscience." In the wider sense to say that a man "has a conscience" means that he has the power of reflecting on the moral aspects of his own character and actions, that he has a disposition to respond with certain emotions (such as remorse or approval) to his own character and actions, and that he has a disposition to seek what he believes to be right or good and to avoid what he believes to be wrong or evil. Broad notes that it is difficult to conceive of a man who does not, at least ostensibly, have such characteristics. Further, he notes that to say a man "has a conscience" in this sense entails neither that the man subscribes to any particular set of ethical principles nor that any particular ethical theory is false. It seems in fact that to say a man "has a conscience" in this wider sense is simply to say, as it were, that the man *has* morals.

There are, Broad maintains, several narrower senses of "conscience," the most important of which depends upon a distinction between "teleological" and "non-teleological" obligation. A teleological obligation is a duty to increase the total amount of good and to decrease the total amount of evil in the world. The duty to be kind or the duty to maintain a pleasant disposition in normal circumstances may serve as mundane examples. (These duties are often spoken of collectively as the duty of Beneficence.) Yet men have other duties, non-teleological obligations, which do not derive from consideration of how much good is produced. For example, a man is obligated to keep his promises, to respect his parents, or to defend his country (in normal circumstances) without considering whether or not his actions are productive of the greatest possible balance of good over evil. Now a man may satisfy his teleological obligation simply by estimating the probable effects of the various actions open to him and by doing that action which produces the greatest possible balance of good over evil. The situation is different, however, in the case of non-teleological obligations. If a man is deliberating over whether to keep a promise of secrecy to a friend or whether, instead, to answer an important question truthfully, he will have no simple criterion (such as the "maximization of good") to consult. He must, it appears, simply "see" which of these obligations takes precedence. Broad claims that the term "conscience" often refers to this sort of moral discretion. In a narrower sense, then, to say that a man "has a conscience" is to say that he has the ability to recognize and adjudicate between non-teleological obligations. Broad argues that this sense of "having a conscience," unlike the wider sense, does have implications for certain ethical theories. Thus, he claims that the wider sense is more "convenient." Finally, Broad defines three types of "conscientious action" in terms of the wider and more convenient sense of "conscience."

In "Conscience and Moral Convictions," Gilbert Ryle examines a feature of the term "conscience" which Broad's analysis tacitly presupposes. "Conscience," Ryle claims, refers to a peculiarly private phenomenon. A man cannot have, for example, a guilty conscience over the actions of another man, but only over his own actions. Ryle explains this aspect of the conscience in terms of an "operative" notion of moral convictions. Part of having a moral conviction, Ryle argues, is acting in accordance with that conviction and encouraging others to do so. When a moral conviction takes the form of a judgment passed on the conduct of others, it cannot be "conduct-regulating." It is, in a sense, only academic. Now Ryle argues that the conscience functions particularly when there is a conflict between the "operative" acceptance of a rule and a strong inclination to violate that rule. He suggests that the conscience discerns what is obligatory during such a conflict. (Here Ryle seems to presuppose the narrower sense of "conscience" described by Broad.) Having a conscience, then, is applying a moral conviction to one's self in the face of a temptation to desert that conviction. Thus, a verdict of conscience is not merely verbal but consists, as well, in a disposition to act in accordance with that verdict. A man's conscience is *private* because part of having a conscience is acting in accordance with it. Finally, Ryle observes that there are many types of behavior (aside from moral behavior) in which a man experiences the inclination to violate a rule of conduct. Ryle argues that in each of these cases it is a man's *scruples* which adjudicate between his temptations and convictions. Thus, Ryle classifies "conscientiousness" as a special type of "scrupulousness."

Peter Fuss in his article entitled "Conscience" proposes an analysis of "conscience" and "conscientious action" which he claims avoids the difficulties of certain historical analyses. After arguing that the views of Butler, Mill, and Broad are inadequate, he suggests that an analysis of "conscience" be based on a distinction between moral cognition and moral behavior. The conscience, he claims, is a purely formal principle which establishes in the individual "a felt need or disposition to act in accordance with his (moral) knowledge or belief." According to this analysis a man does not *consult* his conscience in order to discover which of several possible actions he ought to perform, he rather *follows* his conscience ("acts conscientiously") by doing that which his intellect and sensitivity discern to be right or good.

I

Conscience and Conscientious Action

I shall begin by trying to describe what I understand by "conscience," in the widest sense of the word. I have no doubt that it is often used in certain narrower senses, which I shall indicate in due course. I think that failure to recognize this ambiguity often leads to misunderstandings and disputes which are mainly verbal.

All civilized languages which I know or have heard of contain adjectives like "right" and "wrong," "good" and "evil," or their equivalents. This shows that human beings from the earliest times have had certain experiences which they took to be cognitions of acts, intentions, motives, etc., as having certain characteristics, viz. *moral* ones, which can take opposed forms. Again, retrospection assures most of us that we too have had such experiences when we have contemplated certain actions, dispositions, or characters, whether our own, or those of other real people, or those of fictitious persons in novels or plays. I am not at present concerned with the question whether there really are moral characteristics and whether we really do cognize them. I am concerned only with the plain psychological and historical fact that most of us, and most of our human predecessors back into prehistoric times, have had experiences which they took to be cognitions of such characteristics in acts, dispositions, characters, etc. I shall call these experiences "ostensibly moral cognitions."

It is an equally plain psychological fact that, when a human being contemplates an action or disposition or character in which these moral characteristics seem to him to be present, he is liable to feel certain kinds of emotions which he would not otherwise feel. All languages have words like "remorse," "feeling of guilt," "feeling of obligation," "moral indignation," and so on;

and most of us know what such words indicate from our own experiences of such emotions. I propose to call these "morally directed emotions."

Here I must interpolate some remarks in order to ward off possible misunderstandings. We must notice that nothing ever has or could have *only* moral characteristics, any more than a word could have *only* meaning without any particular sound or visible form. Anything that has moral characteristics will also have certain non-moral ones; and, what is more, its moral characteristics will always depend upon certain of its non-moral ones. If I am told that a certain act was wrong, it is always sensible for me to ask: "Why? What *made* it wrong?" And the answer that I expect would be an indication of some characteristic which can be fully described and understood without the use of any moral term, e.g., that it was a refusal to return a borrowed article, that it was an intentionally misleading answer to a question, that it was an intentional infliction of unnecessary pain, and so on. I propose to call those non-moral characteristics on which moral characteristics depend "right-making," "good-making," and so on.

Now emotions may be and often are felt towards acts, experiences, etc., in respect of their non-moral characteristics. Suppose, e.g. that a friend grants me a favor unfairly at the expense of another person because he likes me and does not like him. I shall tend to view this act with a non-morally directed emotion of complaisance in respect of its non-moral characteristic of being an act of special love and favor towards myself. But I shall tend also to view it with a morally-directed emotion of disapproval in so far as it is an act of unfairness towards my rival. It is, I think, quite possible to feel a non-morally directed dislike for an act in respect of those very right-making characteristics which give it a rightness which calls forth one's moral approval. Our attitude towards certain acts of stern justice towards their sons by typical Roman fathers is of this mixed kind.

It follows from all this that we may often think that we are feeling an *unmixed* morally directed emotion, when what we are really feeling is a mixture of morally and non-morally directed emotion. And we may sometimes mistake a purely non-moral emotion, such as fear of discovery and punishment or malice, for a morally directed emotion, such as remorse or righteous indignation. But the possibility and even the frequency of such mistakes has no tendency to show that there are not specifically moral emotions. The very fact that we recognize that we are liable to make these mistakes, strongly suggests that there are specifically moral emotions.

Lastly, it is an equally plain psychological fact that the belief that a certain course of action would be right does exercise a certain attraction or compulsion on most people and thus provides them with a motive-component for doing it. Still more obvious is it that the belief that a certain course of action would be wrong exercises a certain repulsion or inhibition on most people and thus provides them with a motive-component against doing it. Sometimes every other feature in alternative A is such as would make one prefer it to B. To do A might benefit me and other people, and to do B might injure me and other people. But to do A would involve breaking a promise which I gave, after due consideration, to a person who is now dead and therefore cannot release me. If I believe that it is wrong to break a promise given under those conditions, this one feature in A may make me reject it and choose B. I am not at present considering such cases from an ethical point of view; all that I am concerned with here is the psychological fact that they happen and are perfectly familiar. All civilized languages have words like "ought," "duty," "obligation," etc. All these words refer to the fact that the supposed rightness of an action gives rise to a motive-component for doing it, and that the supposed wrongness of an action gives rise to a motive-component against doing it, and that these specifically *moral* motive-components may conflict with others which arise from one's belief about the non-moral characteristics of the action. I shall refer to these psychological facts as "moral motivation."

Here again we must notice that non-moral motive-components, based on the attractiveness or repulsiveness which an action derives from the non-moral characteristics which we believe it to have, will generally co-exist and co-operate with components of moral attraction and moral repulsion. In consequence of this a person may often think that he is being moved by purely moral motives when really his total motive for choosing or rejecting an alternative contains both moral and non-moral motive-components. And we may sometimes mistake a purely non-moral motive, such as desire for comfort or safety, for the moral motive of desire to do what is right as such. But the possibility and even frequency of such mistakes has no tendency to show that there is not moral motivation.

We may sum up these facts by saying that the vast majority of sane adult human beings are capable of ostensibly moral cognition, of morally directed emotion, and of moral motivation. Now every such person is also capable of *reflexive* cognition, i.e., of contemplating himself, his experiences, dispositions, intentions, motives, and actions, from various points of view. To say that a person "has a Conscience," when this phrase is used in its widest sense, is equivalent to asserting the following three closely connected propositions about him. (1) That he has and exercises the cognitive power of reflecting on his own past and future actions, and considering whether they are right or wrong; of reflecting on his own motives, intentions, emotions, dispositions, and character, and considering whether they are morally good or bad; and of reflecting on the relative moral value of various alternative ideals of character and conduct. (2) That he has and exercises the emotional disposition to feel certain peculiar emotions, such as remorse, feeling of guilt, moral approval, etc., towards himself and his own actions, dispositions, etc., in respect of the moral characteristics which he believes these to have. (3) That he has and exercises the conative disposition to seek what he believes to be good and to shun what he believes to be bad, as such, and to do what he believes to be right and avoid what he believes to be wrong, as such.

I propose to describe this as "the phenomenological sense" of the phrase "having a conscience." I think that the most skeptical of speculators about morals would hardly deny that most people nowadays and throughout the course of history have "had a conscience," in this phenomenological sense. Let us consider where ethical skepticism would be relevant to this question. The most radical form of skepticism would deny that adjectives like "right," "morally good," "obligatory," etc., really stand for characteristics. Its advocates would allege that sentences in which such words occur as grammatical predicates are really interjections or commands masquerading as statements about certain peculiar characteristics of actions, dispositions, persons, etc. If so, those experiences which seem to most people to be cognitions of moral characteristics cannot really be so; for there will be no such characteristics to be cognized. But it can hardly be denied that there are experiences which *seem* to be cognitions of moral characteristics. If there were not, it is impossible to see why moral sentences in all languages should have been couched in the indicative form with a moral adjective as grammatical predicate. So I do not think that such an ethical skeptic, if he knew his business, would attempt to deny that there are *ostensibly* moral cognitions, and this is all that is involved in the cognitive part of the definition of "having a conscience," in the phenomenological sense of that phrase.

If there are no ethical characteristics, it cannot be their presence in the actions, etc., which we contemplate, that moves our emotions. But that would not affect our definition. Granted that a person believes that there are moral characteristics, and believes that such and such of them are present in certain objects which he contemplates, there is no reason why this belief (however false or baseless it may be) should not evoke in him specifically moral emotions towards those objects. The ethical skeptic will, indeed, have to regard those emotions rather as a disbeliever in ghosts might regard the fear which a superstitious person would feel in a room which he believes to be haunted. But any reasonable person would admit that, even if ghosts do not exist, a specific kind of fear is felt by persons who believe in ghosts when they are in places which they believe to be haunted. What is more, a disbeliever in ghosts might himself feel such a fear in such circumstances, though he would judge it to be unreasonable. Similarly an ethical skeptic might himself continue to feel morally directed emotions, though he would have to regard them as unreasonable. And he should have no difficulty in admitting that most human beings do so. Therefore this kind of

ethical skeptic need not deny that the emotional condition for
having a conscience, in the phenomenological sense of that
phrase, is fulfilled by most people.

Precisely similar remarks apply to the question of moral
motivation. We are moved by our *beliefs* about the characteristics
of things, regardless of whether those beliefs be true or false,
well or ill-founded. Since it can hardly be denied that most
people believe themselves to be aware of moral characteristics
in the actions, dispositions, etc., which they contemplate, the
doctrine that all such beliefs are in principle mistaken is quite
consistent with the contention that most people are susceptible
to moral motivation.

An independent attack could, no doubt, be made on the
applicability of the second and third clauses in our definition
of "having a conscience." It might be contended that, whether we
cognize moral characteristics or not, our beliefs in the presence of
such characteristics never evoke any specific emotion and never
influence our actions. Our emotions, it might be said, are evoked
and our actions are influenced *only* by what we believe about
the *non-moral* characteristics of what we are contemplating. But
we proceed either to deceive ourselves or to try to deceive others
about the direction of our emotions and the nature of our
motives.

I think that this kind of skepticism is usually based on some
general theory of human action, such as psychological hedonism,
which would rule out the possibility of specifically moral emotion
and motivation. I need only say that all such general theories
rest on certain rather subtle verbal confusions, and may safely
be rejected. A more empirical basis for such skepticism is the
admitted mixture of non-moral emotions and motives with moral
ones, and the admitted possibility of mistaking one of the former
for one of the latter in any particular case. As I have already
said, it does not seem to me that the facts about mixture and
about mistakes and sophistications are adequate to support
the sweeping negative conclusions which have been based on
them, in face of the strong *prima facie* evidence for moral motivation and moral emotion.

I see no reason, then, to qualify my assertion that, in the

phenomenological sense of the phrase, practically every sane
adult human being "has a conscience," whatever may have been
the case with himself as an infant or with his prehistoric an-
cestors. Of course an individual may happen to live in an
environment in which his conscientious dispositions are hardly
ever excited or are constantly suppressed. They may then
atrophy or become warped, as any other set of dispositions would
be likely to do under similar circumstances.

We must now notice some important negative facts about
having a conscience, in the sense defined. (i) To say that a
person has a conscience, in this sense, neither entails nor excludes that this person holds any particular theory about the
nature of goodness or rightness or moral obligation. It neither
entails nor excludes that he holds any particular theory about
what makes good things good or right acts right. And it neither
entails nor excludes that he holds any particular theory about
the nature and sources of our moral knowledge and belief. A
plain man, with no theories on any of these subjects, can have
a conscience and act conscientiously. So too can persons who
hold the most varied theories on these points; a man can be a
conscientious Utilitarian, a conscientious Intuitionist, a conscientious Hegelian, or what not. All that is necessary is that
he shall believe that, in some way or other, he can form a reasonable opinion about the rightness or wrongness, goodness or
badness, of various courses open to him, and that his opinions
on such matters shall be capable of evoking his emotions and
influencing his decisions.

(ii) The fact that most people have consciences, in the
senses defined, does not, so far as I can see, establish or refute
any particular ethical theory. That is, of course, quite a different
point from the one which we have just been discussing. It is one
thing to say, e.g., that a person could equally well have a conscience whether he accepted or rejected Utilitarianism. It is quite
another thing to say that a person could equally well have a conscience whether Utilitarianism be true or false. I assert that,
on my definition of "having a conscience," both these statements
are true, and that they would be equally true if any other ethical
theory were substituted for Utilitarianism.

Now there is no doubt that the phrase "to have a conscience" has often been used in a narrower sense than this. I propose now to consider the more important of the narrower senses in which it has been used. In order to do this I must begin with a very brief account of the moral situation in which we appear *prima facie* to find ourselves. It is roughly as follows.

We seem to be under an obligation to do what we can to maintain and increase the amount of good and to diminish the amount of evil, of every kind, in the lives of other persons whom we can affect appreciably by our actions. Let us call this a "teleological obligation." *Prima facie* it seems that we have other obligations, not derivable from it, which limit it and may conflict with it; e.g., the mere fact that a person has made a promise seems to be enough to impose on him an obligation to keep it unless the promisee should release him. This obligation appears to be independent of any good that may be produced or evil that may be averted or diminished in òthers by keeping the promise. We seem to be under an obligation to keep it even when we have strong reason to believe that the consequences would be better for all concerned if we were to break it. Again, there seem to be non-teleological obligations which bear upon the direction and range of our teleological obligations. Granted that one has the duty to do good to others, it seems obvious to most people that a man has a more urgent duty to do good to his parents or his benefactors than to complete strangers.

Now there seem to be a number of non-teleological obligations, e.g., to answer questions truly, to keep one's promises, and so on. And they are liable to conflict, not only with our teleological obligation, but also with each other. E.g., a person may have made a certain promise and he may afterwards be asked a certain question. And it may be impossible to keep the promise and answer truly. In order to keep the promise he must tell a lie, and in order to answer truly he must break the promise. The only remaining alternative is to refuse to answer the question; but in many cases refusal to answer would, for all practical purposes, be equivalent to answering in a certain way and betraying a confidence which one had promised to keep.

Now there is an important epistemological difference between teleological and non-teleological obligations. Suppose I am in a situation where several alternative actions are open to me, and that I am trying to fulfill the teleological obligation to produce as much good or as little evil as I can in others. In order to discover my duty I shall have to consider elaborately the probable remote consequences of the various alternative courses of action. Now this involves a great deal of wholly *non-moral* reflexion on the properties of things, the dispositions of persons, the laws of nature, and so on. The conclusions of such reflections will generally be highly uncertain, and one's capacity to conduct them successfully will depend on the extent of one's knowledge about non-moral facts and the degree of one's capacity for reasoning about physical, psychological, social, economic, and political matters. The *moral* insight that is needed will be concerned only with estimating and comparing the goodness and badness of the consequences which one thinks it likely that the various alternative courses of action would produce. Suppose, on the other hand, I am in a situation where non-teleological obligations are predominant, such as truth-telling and promise-keeping. Then in most cases the ascertainment of the relevant non-moral facts its perfectly simple and straightforward and can be performed without any expert knowledge or technical skill and instruction. If one has made a promise and is asked a question, there is generally not the least difficulty in being certain as to what answers would be lies and what answers would be breaches of promise. Here, then, almost the whole of the cognition involved is specifically *moral*; it is concerned with seeing that making a promise, as such, imposes an obligation to keep it; that answering a question, as such, imposes an obligation to answer it truthfully; and with estimating the relative urgency of these two obligations in cases where they conflict.

It is not surprising, therefore, that many people should be inclined to use the word "conscience" in such a way that conscience, on its cognitive side, is confined to the task of intuiting non-teleological obligations and estimating their relative urgency.

Suppose we take "conscience" in this narrower sense. Then it will follow that, if Utilitarianism be true, no one has a conscience. For the essence of Utilitarianism is that there are no non-teleological obligations. And, if there are none, no one can intuit them and estimate their relative urgency; though non-Utilitarians may mistakenly think that they do so. According to the Utilitarian, what makes it obligatory to keep a promise is not the mere fact that the promise has been made. What makes it obligatory, when it is so, is that we are under the obligation to produce as much good and as little evil as possible by our actions, and that experience has shown that promise-keeping on the whole leads to better consequences than promise-breaking. And similar remarks apply, *mutatis mutandis,* to all the alleged non-teleological obligations.

I am not at present concerned to discuss the truth or falsity of Utilitarianism, so I will confine myself to the following three remarks.

(i) In deciding what he ought to do in any situation, a Utilitarian would have to consider carefully, not only what the consequences of various alternative actions would probably be, but also what kinds and amounts of good and evil would attach to each of these consequences if it were realized. It seems inconvenient to use the word "conscience" in such a way that intuition and comparison of *goods and evils* would not be a function of conscience, whilst intuition and comparison of *non-teleological obligations* would be so.

(ii) Suppose the Utilitarianism is false, and that there are non-teleological obligations. It can hardly be denied that there is *also* the teleological obligation to produce as much good and as little evil as one can. The mistake of Utilitarianism would be to hold that this is the *only* obligation, and to fail to see that there are others, equally fundamental, which limit it and may conflict with it. Truth-speaking and promise-keeping will be duties not reducible to beneficence, but beneficence will still be one duty among others. Therefore, in deciding what one ought to do in a given situation, it will often be necessary to consider the relative urgency of the teleological obligation of beneficence and certain non-teleological obligations, such as truth-telling and promise-keeping. In order to estimate the urgency of the obligation of beneficence it will be necessary to enter into precisely the same kind of calculations as Utilitarians consider to be necessary in every case, since this urgency will plainly depend on the nature and amount of good to be produced or evil to be averted by one's actions. It seems to me that it would be highly inconvenient to use the word "conscience" in such a way that it was part of the function of conscience to compare the urgency of various non-teleological obligations, but was no part of its functions to compare the urgency of non-teleological obligations with that of teleological ones or to compare that of two or more teleological ones with each other.

(iii) Nevertheless, the considerations which have now been brought to our notice do suggest that the following explanatory sentences should be added to our definition of "having a conscience." We must distingush between the *purely factual* and the *purely ethical* considerations which are involved in any attempt to decide what we ought to do in a given situation. Both factors enter in all cases. The purely factual elements are generally (though by no means always) obvious, even to quite ignorant and simple people, when only non-teleological obligations are in question; but, when teleological obligations have to be seriously considered, they may be highly complex and uncertain and may demand technical knowledge and skill of an advanced kind. Now conscience, as such, is concerned directly only with the purely ethical factors. The operation of forecasting the consequences of various alternative actions, as distinct from estimating the goodness or badness of these consequences, could be performed as well or better by a person who had no conscience. But, although this intellectual process cannot itself be assigned to conscience, it is an essential condition without which conscience cannot do its own proper work in situations of any complexity. A person who is trying to find out what he ought to do is not using his conscience properly if he fails to inform himself as fully and accurately as possible of all the relevant facts, or if he omits to apply his utmost care and skill to the task of forecasting the remote and the indirect consequences of the alternatives under consideration.

When the word "conscience" is used in such a way that conscience, in its cognitive aspect, is confined to intuiting and balancing non-teleological obligations, I shall say that it is used "in the intuitional sense." I have now tried to show that this is an inconveniently narrow sense. But the word is often used in senses which are even narrower than this, and I will now consider some of them.

It is held by some people that certain kinds of non-teleo-logical obligation are so urgent that a person ought not under any conceivable circumstances to do an action which would infringe any of them. This claim has been made, e.g., for the obligation to answer a question truthfully if at all. Now it seems to me that the word "conscience," and phrases which contain it, are often used in such a way as to imply that a person can-not have a conscience unless he holds this opinion, and that his conscience is in operation only on occasions when his action or his refusal to act is based on his belief that one of these unconditional obligations is involved. I should consider it most undesirable that the word should be used in this narrow way. For the opinion in question is almost certainly mistaken; and, even if it were true, it has been rejected by many people who, in any ordinary use of language, have been scrupulously con-scientious, such as John Stuart Mill. It would plainly be un-fortunate to use the word "conscience" in such a way that no one could be said to have a conscience unless he were mistaken on an important point of moral theory, and that no one could be said to be following his conscience except when he was under the influence of this delusion. The utmost that can be granted to the intuitionist is that we can see directly that cer-tain relationships, as such, impose certain component obligations on us, and that some of them are so urgent that any act which would conflict with any of these has a very strong tendency to be wrong. In certain cases this is true, not only of all the *actions* open to one, but also of the only remaining alternative, viz. *refusal to act*. If we care to say that, in such cases all the alternatives are wrong, we can do so; but we shall then have to admit that we ought to choose that alternative (be it one of the actions or refusal to act) which is the *least wrong*. And in complex cases there is not the faintest reason to believe that we have intuitive knowledge as to which one this is.

It remains to notice one further narrowing of the word "conscience." Sometimes it is used in such a way that a person would be said to be following his conscience only in so far as he bases his decision about what he ought to do on some alleged divine revelation. In many cases, I think, this amounts to little more than the previous usage decorated with theological frillings. The pronouncements of conscience about what is unconditionally wrong are regarded as, in some sense, the voice of God speaking in and to the individual; and so the agent can take them to be infallible without arrogating too much for himself. In other cases, however, the situation is quite different. Certain actions are regarded by the individual as unconditionally right or unconditionally wrong, not because he sees this for himself by direct inspection, but because he believes that God has given a ruling on the matter either in inspired writings or in the traditions of a divinely founded and directed church.

I will now leave the notion of conscience, and pass to that of a conscientious action. Conscience, as I have defined it, is a system of cognitive, emotional, and conative *dispositions,* and it is only when these dispositions are in operation that we have conscientious action.

The question whether an action is conscientious or not is mainly a question about the agent's motives in doing it. We must clear up the notion of motive a little before we can give a satisfactory definition of "conscientious action." Suppose that an agent is contemplating a certain possible course of action in a given situation. He will have various beliefs and expectations about its qualities, its relations, and its consequences, e.g., he may believe that it would be unpleasant to himself, that it would please his mother, and that it would be a breach of a promise made to his father, and so on. Some of these beliefs and expectations will attract him towards doing the action, some will repel him from doing it, and others may leave him unmoved. I call any belief about an action which attracts one towards doing it a "motive-component *for* the action," and any belief about it which repels one from doing it a "motive-component *against* the action." Suppose that a certain action is in fact chosen and performed. Then I say that the agent's "total motive *in* doing the action" was the resultant of all the motive-components for doing it and all the motive components against doing it. And I say that he did it *"because of"* the former, and *"in spite of"* the latter.

Now suppose that there were several components for doing a certain action, and several against doing it, and that it was in fact done because of the former and in spite of the latter. Let us call the former a, b, and c, and the latter, u, v, and w. Now consider, e.g., the component a. We can ask ourselves the following question about it. Would a have been sufficient, in the absence of b and c, to induce the agent to do this action in spite of the components u, v, and w against doing it? Or did the component a need to be supplemented by b or by c or by both in order to overcome the influence of u, v, and w? If and only if the first alternative is true, we can say that a was "a *sufficient* motive-component for doing the action." Next we can raise the following question. Would bc have been sufficient, in the absence of a, to induce the agent to do the action in spite of the components u, v, and w against doing it? Or did bc need to be supplemented by a in order to overcome the influence of u, v. and w? If, and only if, the second alternative is true, we can say that a was "a *necessary* motive-component for doing the action." Lastly, suppose that a had been the only component for doing the action. Then we could say that "the action was done *purely* from the motive a."

We can now apply these general considerations to the particular case of conscientious action. An action is conscientious if the following conditions are fulfilled. (i) The agent has reflected on the situation, the action, and the alternatives to it, in order to discover what is the right course. In this reflection he has tried his utmost to learn the relevant facts and to give each its due weight, he has exercised his judgment on them to the best of his ability, and he has striven to allow for all sources of bias. (ii) He has decided that, on the factual and ethical information available to him, the action in question is probably the most right or the least wrong of all those which are open to him. (iii) His belief that the action has this moral characteristic, together with his desire to do what is right as such, was either (*a*) the *only* motive-component for doing it, or (*b*) a *sufficient and necessary* motive-component for doing it. If the first alternative is fulfilled, we can say that his action was "*purely* conscientious." If the second is fulfilled, we can say that it was "*predominantly* conscientious." The following would be an example of a predominantly conscientious action. Suppose that a person, after reflection, decides that the right action for him is to undertake military service. Suppose that the two motive-components which induce him to undertake this action, in spite of fear, love of comfort, etc., are his belief that it is right, together with his desire to do what is right as such, and his dislike of being thought cowardly by his friends. Then the action is predominantly conscientious if (*a*) his desire to do what is right, as such, *would* have sufficed to overcome his fear and his love of comfort even in the absence of his dislike of being thought cowardly, whilst (*b*) his dislike of being thought cowardly *would not* have sufficed to overcome those motive-components in the absence of his desire to do what is right, as such. In such a case we can say that the non-conscientious component for doing the action which the agent believes to be right is indeed present but is superfluous and insufficient. It would be absurd to refuse to call the action "conscientious" merely because a superfluous and insufficient non-conscientious motive-component for doing it happened to co-exist with the sufficient and necessary conscientious motive-component for doing it.

We come now to a much difficult and doubtful case. Suppose that the agent's belief that the action is right, together with his desire to do what is right as such, is sufficient, but not necessary, to induce him to do it, in spite of the components against doing it. This would be illustrated by our old example if we varied it in the following way. We must now suppose that the agent's dislike of being thought cowardly *would* have sufficed to overcome his fear and his love of comfort and *would* have induced him to choose the course of action which he believes to be right, even if his belief that it is right and his desire to do what is right, as such, had been absent. The situation may be described as follows. The non-conscientious motive-component for doing the action is still superfluous; but now we must say that the conscientious component for doing it is equally superfluous. Each is sufficient, and therefore neither individually is necessary; all that is necessary is that one or other of them should be present. If you confine your attention to the *sufficiency* of the conscientious motive-component, you will be inclined to say that the action *is* conscientious; if you attend only to the *superfluity* of this component, you will be inclined to say that it is *not* conscientious.

We pass now to another difficult and doubtful case. Suppose now that the agent's belief that the action is right, together with his desire to do what is right as such, is necessary but not sufficient to induce him to do it in spite of the components against doing it. This would be illustrated by the following modification of our old example. We must now suppose (*a*) that the agent's belief that it is right for him to undertake military service, together with his desire to do what is right as such, would not have sufficed, in the absence of his dislike of being thought cowardly to overcome his fear and his love of comfort; and (*b*) that the latter motive-component, in the absence of the former, would also not have sufficed to overcome his fear and his love of comfort. Each of the two motive-components for doing the action is now necessary, and therefore neither of them individually is sufficient. If you confine your attention to the *indispensability* of the conscientious motive-component, you will be inclined to say that the action *is* conscientious; if you attend only to its *insufficiency*, you will be inclined to say that it is *not* conscientious.

I will group together purely and predominantly conscientious actions, in the sense defined above, under the name of "*fully conscientious actions;*" and I will group together the two doubtful cases, which we have just been discussing, under the name of "*semi-conscientious* actions." The two kinds of these can then be distinguished as (i) actions in which the conscientious motive-component is sufficient but superfluous, and (ii) actions in which the conscientious motive-component is indispensable but inadequate.

If a person does an act which he believes to be less right or more wrong than some other act open to him at the time, he does it in spite of his desire to do what is right, as such. Any action of this kind may be called "*contra-conscientious*."

It is plain that a great many of our deliberate actions are neither fully conscientious, nor semi-conscientious, nor contra-conscientious; for many are done without considering them and the alternatives to them from the standpoint of rightness and wrongness. Such actions may be called "*non-conscientious*." A non-conscientious action may be such that, if the agent had considered it and the alternatives to it from the standpoint of rightness and wrongness, he would have judged it to be the most right or the least wrong of the alternatives open to him. And it may be that he would then have done it for that reason alone or for that reason combined with others which are superfluous and insufficient. If both these conditions are fulfilled, we may say that this non-conscientious action was "*potentially* conscientious." In a similar way we could define the statement that a certain non-conscientious act was "*potentially* contra-conscientious."

I have now completed the task of analysis and definition, and I will conclude my paper with a few remarks about conscientious action, as defined above. (1) There is a very important sense of "ought" in which it is true to say that a person ought always to do that alternative which he believes, at the time when he has to act, to be the most right or the least wrong of all those that are open to him. (There are, undoubtedly, other senses of "ought" in which this would not be true; but we are not concerned with them here.) For this sense, of "ought" to be applicable it does not matter how ignorant or deluded the agent may be about the relevant facts, how incompetent he may be to make reasonable inferences from them, nor how crazy or perverted his judgments about right and wrong, good and evil, may be. But, the more fully this is admitted, the more obvious does the following complementary fact become. The most right or the least wrong act open to other individuals or to a society, in certain cases, may be to prevent a conscientious individual from doing certain acts which he ought, in this sense, to do, and to try to compel him to do certain acts which he ought, in this sense, to refrain from doing. Moreover, if other individuals or the authorities in a society honestly believe that the most right or the least wrong action open to them is to treat a certain conscientious individual in this way, then they *ought*, in the very same sense, to do so. What is sauce for the conscientious goose is sauce for the conscientious ganders who are his neighbors or his governors. This fact is often obscured because many people inadvertently or dishonestly confine their attention to cases, such as the trial of Socrates or of Christ, in which subsequent generations have held that the individual was, not only conscientious, but also correct in his ethical opinions, whilst the tribunal which condemned him was either not conscientious or was mistaken in its ethical opinions. It may be salutary for such persons to widen their purview by envisaging the case of a high-minded Indian civilian conscientiously securing the capture and execution of a high-minded Thug for conscientiously practicing murder.

(2) It is sometimes said that, when an individual sets up his conscience against the general opinion of his society or of mankind, he is claiming "moral infallibility." If he knows his business, he is doing nothing of the kind. In order for it to be his duty, in the present sense, to do a certain alternative, all that is necessary is that he should think it *probable*, after considering the question to the best of his ability, that this alternative is more right or less wrong than any of the others which are open to him. Since he has to enact one of the alternatives, it does not matter in the least whether this probability is high or low. Nor does it matter whether the difference in rightness or wrongness is great or small. In considering the question, it is his duty to give full weight to the fact that most members of his society or most of the human race have formed a certain opinion about it. If he is a wise man, he will attach very great weight to this fact. But if, in spite of having done so, he comes to a contrary opinion, he ought, in the present sense, to act upon it, no matter how far short of complete conviction his opinion may fall.

(3) The last remark that I have to make is this. A *purely* conscientious action, in the sense defined above, must be a very rare event. It is hardly credible, e.g., that either undertaking

or refusing military service could be a purely conscientious act, in that sense; for everyone fears death and wounds and everyone dislikes to be thought cowardly.

Now the definitions of "predominantly conscientious" acts, and of the two kinds of "semi-conscientious" acts, all have the following peculiarity. They all involve the notion of what *would* have happened if certain conditions had been other than they in fact were. This notion of the consequences of unfulfilled conditions always enters whenever the question of sufficiency and dispensability is raised. It follows that an individual can seldom be rationally justified in feeling a very strong conviction that an action of his was conscientious; for, in order to decide this question, he has to form an opinion as to how he would have acted in the *absence* of certain motive-components which were in fact *present*. It seems to me that *a fortiori* it must be almost impossible for anyone to decide rationally as to whether another person's action is conscientious or not.

If I am right in this, the Tribunals have been given a task which is, from the nature of the case, incapable of being satisfactorily performed. This, so far as it goes, is a strong ground against allowing exemption from military service on grounds of conscience and against setting up Tribunals at all. There are, no doubt, other reasons which point in the opposite direction; and Parliament has decided that, in the present state of public opinion in England, the balance of advantage is in favor of allowing exemption on such grounds, and has therefore set up Tribunals to consider claims. It only remains for us to watch with sympathy and interest the efforts of these well-meaning men to deal with questions to which God alone can know the answer.

II

Conscience and Moral Convictions

GILBERT RYLE

IN discussing the conflict between Moral Sense theories of ethical knowledge (or conviction) and intellectual theories like those of Kant and Price, I struck a point which was new to me. I had always vaguely supposed that "Conscience" is ordinarily used to signify any sort of knowledge or conviction about what is right and wrong. So that *any* verdict about the rightness or wrongness either of a particular type of conduct or of a particular piece of conduct could be called a verdict of "Conscience." I had also supposed that "conscience" was too vague and equivocal a word to enjoy any definite syntax.

But then I noticed that "conscience" is *not* used in this way. We limit the verdicts of conscience to judgments about the rightness or wrongness of the acts only of the owner of that conscience. It is absurd to say, "My conscience says that *you* ought to do this or ought not to have done that." Judgments about the morality of other people's behavior would not be called verdicts of conscience. If asked to advise someone else on a moral point, I could not without absurdity say that I must consult my conscience. Nor, if someone else misbehaves, can *my* conscience be said to disapprove. Conscience is a *private* monitor.

True, I can set myself to imagine moral problems. I can consider how my conscience would react if I were in your shoes, doing what you have done, or meditate doing. I can say, "I could not do so and so with a clear conscience, so you ought not to do it." But I can't say, "*My conscience* won't be clear if *you* do it." What, then, is the difference between conscience and moral conviction which makes it absurd to regard the verdicts of my conscience as co-extensive with my moral convictions? Why can *my* conscience pass judgment only on *my* actions?

Originally, it appears, "conscience" generally connoted "self-knowledge" or "self-consciousness." Introspection would be an activity of "conscientia," whether the objects of the introspection were or were not subjects of moral predicates. With the Reformation, if not earlier, self-inspection was supposed to be the direct discovery of the requirements of God. And "Conscience" began to have the narrower meaning of the knowledge by self-inspection of *my* duties and faults. Butler links conscience very closely to "reflection" (in Locke's sense) which is equivalent to introspection. But why should any moral convictions apply differently to me, just because direct inspection by me is restricted to *my* thoughts, motives and resolves?

Certainly, I can't know directly how you feel or what you think, but I can often know well enough by inference. And in reading a novel I can know all about the motives and desires of the characters, for the novelist tells me them. Yet, though I know all about you, or about the hero of the novel, I can't say that my conscience approves or disapproves either of your conduct or of his. Conversely, introspection or self-inspection are not sources of infallible knowledge. I can misdescribe, to myself, without dishonesty, my own motives. I may, e.g., fail to find "Schadenfreude" in my "serves him right" attitudes, though it is there.

So the difference cannot derive from that between my having *knowledge* of myself and only *opinions* about other people. If God is omniscient it would still be absurd to say that *his* conscience chided me for my behavior.

At this point it looks tempting to go back and say (with the Moral Sensationalists) that, after all, my moral verdicts about myself do record special (moral) sense-perceptions, while my moral verdicts about others, involving as they do both generalizations of rules and inferential imputation of motives, dispositions, etc., are intellectual and rational. But this will not do. My particular verdicts of conscience are applications of general rules, imperatives or codes. My conscience says, "You aren't being *honest*" and this involves understanding both what being honest is, and that it is a general desideratum. (It is like one's prompt recognition that what one is saying is bad grammar, i.e., is a breach of a general rule. The facts that the recognition is prompt and may be unarticulated do not entail that we have a "grammatical sense.")

I suggest that the solution of the puzzle, which, I think, is a genuine one about the syntax of "conscience" and of "moral conviction," is in this direction. What is it to *have* a moral conviction? Or, what is it to *have* principles? At first, we begin by saying that it is to know or be convinced that some general proposition is true or that some universal imperative is right, or wise. But what are the public tests of whether a person really knows or is really convinced of so and so? They are, I think, the following:

(1) That he *utters* it regularly, relevantly and without hesitation.

(2) That other things which he says regularly, relevantly and unhesitatingly, presuppose it.

(3) That he is ready or eager to try to persuade other people of it and to dissuade them of what is inconsistent with it.

(4) That he regularly and readily behaves in accordance with it, on occasions when it is relevant.

(5) That when he does not behave in accordance with it, he feels guilty, resolves to reform, etc.

We are inclined to say that (1) and (2) show that he intellectually accepts the principle; he thinks e.g., that honesty is desirable: that (4) and (5) show that he is honest or pretty honest, and that (3) shows something between the two, namely, that he admires or respects honesty. And we should also be inclined to say that (1) and (2) taken *alone* show that he is not *really* convinced; the principle is a part of his intellectual furniture but not of his real nature. His acceptance of it is academic. It is not operative on his volitions, emotions and behavior. But this is rather fishy. For it sets up a queer fence between thinking, feeling and willing; as if being a man of principle (say, being honest) differs from acknowledging honesty by the irruption of some new faculty, called will or feeling, which can accept principles, only not in the way in which thought does so. But thinking, e.g., believing, is an aspect of character or nature. The difference between not feeling qualms of doubt and not hesitating in bodily action is not a hard and fast line. *Saying* readily and *doing* readily seem to be related as species to genus, not as coordinate species of a higher genus. Talking to oneself or aloud is behaving. So there seems to be a sense in which *real* acceptance of a principle (does not lead to, but) *is* being disposed to behave in accordance with it. To "know" a rule of conduct *is* to be regulated in one's conduct. To know *properly* the rules of grammar is to be able to talk correctly, to correct mistakes and to wince at those of others. A man's party manners show whether he "knows" the rules of etiquette; his ability to cite *Etiquette for Gentlemen* does not.

Supposing it conceded that sometimes appropriate behavior is part of what we *mean* by certitude or acceptance of a proposition, let us label as "operative" the knowledge or conviction which manifests itself in the disposition to behave—in *all* sorts of behavior, including "thinking"—in accordance with the principle which is said to be known or accepted. To be disposed to behave in a certain way in certain circumstances is to be prone or inclined to do so. Other things being equal a person with a certain disposition will probably behave in the given way; that is what the word "disposition" means.

Now if someone has operatively accepted a certain principle, but other things are not equal, i.e., he experiences some contrary impulse, there will not only exist a conflict between the temptation and the abstract principle; there will be actually experienced a conflict between the temptation and the disposition which is the operatively accepted principle. He will feel a tension because he *is* the two tendencies to act which are in conflict. "It goes against the grain." And these two tendencies, with their conflict, are visible on self-inspection or inferrible from what he can introspect. His knowledge or conviction of the principle is not an external censor but an internal competitor. His knowledge how he should behave does not *cause* but is a nisus to behaving in that way, but it is a *felt* nisus only when it is impeded.

But in passing verdicts on the conduct of others, our conviction, so to speak, cannot be more than academic. For me to believe that you should do so and so can be only to pronounce and perhaps to try to persuade; in the full sense of "operative" my conviction about your duty cannot be operative, for it cannot issue in the required behavior. (The desire to punish, rebuke and reform seems to be a response to the inoperativeness of merely finding fault.)

Or, alternatively, my application of a principle to you can take the form only of a verdict or of advice or exhortation, with perhaps subsequent reproof or punishment. But my application of my principle to me can take the form of doing what I should. In this sense conscience is never a merely verdict-passing faculty, it is a conduct regulating faculty. Its exercise is behaving or trying to behave and not describing or recommending. We credit conscience with *authority* as well as with knowledge. That is, we use the word "conscience" for those moral convictions which issue not in verdicts but in behaving or trying to behave. So it is a tautology that my conscience cannot direct the behavior of someone else.

This has analogies elsewhere. In a certain sense, I, having read the text books and been a spectator, know how to swim; that is, I know what actions people must take to progress in a desired direction in the water, with the nostrils clear of the water. But no-one would say that I really know how to swim or that I have swimming-skill, unless when I do it myself I usually succeed. And it would be absurd to say that I have skill or expertness in the swimming of others, though in the academic sense of the word "know" I may know just what mistakes they are making. The proper manifestations of my skill are my performances and not mere directions to others. And the proper manifestations of my conscience are in my good conduct, or reluctance to behave ill or remorse afterwards and resolutions to reform. Conscience is not something other than, prior to or posterior to moral convictions; it is having those convictions in an operative degree, i.e., being disposed to behave accordingly. And it is active or calls for attention when this disposition is balked by some contrary inclination. Conscience has nothing to say when the really honest man is asked a question and when he has no temptation to deceive. He then tells the truth as he signs his name, without considering what to do or why he should do it or how to get himself to do it. Conscience is awake only when there is such a conflict. The test for the existence of such a conflict is the occurrence of attention to the problem of what is to be done. Pangs or qualms of conscience can occur only when I am both disposed to act in one way and disposed to act in another and when one of these dispositions is an operative moral principle. (And this "can... only" is logical and not causal.) Wondering what to do is a manifestation of a balked disposition to act; if it was not balked I would act as I am disposed to act for that is what "disposed" means. Consulting my conscience entails attending introspectively to my conflicting dispositions to act. Hence I cannot (logically) consult my conscience about what you are to do. Having a conscience to "consult" is having a (partially) operative moral conviction.

Now there are convictions of rules of conduct other than moral ones. So they should in parallel circumstances engender naggings, commands, etc., parallel to those of conscience. Is this so?

1. *Rules of Prudence.* I have learned from experience, doctors, hearsay, etc., that it is bad for me not to have a regular allowance of sleep each night. I know that I shall feel "like death" tomorrow afternoon if I do not have at least seven hours of sleep. And I do habitually go to bed at 12, say, to be called at 8, without thinking of the effects of not doing so. "Midnight is my bedtime" is the only thought that usually occurs to me if any thought occurs to me at all. Now, suppose, I am halfway through an exciting detective story at midnight. So I want to read on, and I am disposed to go to bed at "my bedtime." I do not feel guilty, but I find myself making excuses and promises for the future. Or, I tell myself that tomorrow afternoon is disengaged so I can sleep then. So I do attend to factors in the situation similar to those which are considered in questions of conscience. In certain of their uses, words like "discretion" and "caution" resemble "conscience." In the sense, e.g., in which my discretion guides my actions it cannot guide yours. To be cau-

tious, provident, etc., is not just to acknowledge or enunciate certain propositions which may be true for everyone; it is to be disposed to live cautiously, providently, etc., which though it includes such acknowledging and enunciating does not reduce to them.

2. *Rules of Etiquette, fashion and social decorum.* "We dress for dinner at Christ Church." When we do this, the "done" thing, we do not generally consider the utilities or aesthetic amenities of the practice. We just dress—i.e., it is a habit—but one which is actualized not only in dressing, but also in feeling surprised if a colleague dines in day clothes, in stopping teaching some time before dinner, etc. Our acceptance of the convention is manifested primarily by our behaving regularly and unquestioningly in accordance with it. Sometimes I am prevented from dressing. Then, while dining in mufti, I feel uncomfortable (though not guilty or imprudent). My sense of decorum, which is not, of course, a new mode of sense perception, nags gently. And in the sense in which I am punctilious about my own dinner uniform I cannot be punctilious about that of other people; I can be only noticing about them or critical of them.

3. *Rules of arithmetic.* The accurate computer regularly observes the rules of addition, subtraction, multiplication and division. And observance of them is not manifested in a special momentary act of acknowledging them, declaring them or teaching them, but in all his acts of accurate computation. His grasp of the rules is his ability and skill in working in accordance with them. He does not begin each morning's work by reciting an arithmetical creed. In a certain sense of "think" he never thinks of the rules. In another sense of the word, however, he is thinking of the rules all the time; for he is continually applying them correctly and skillfully. The rules are now *habits* of operating. But his accuracy, flair or scrupulousness governs only his own computations. He cannot have a flair about the calculations of other people, though he knows the rules which they should keep and how these rules apply to their particular problems. But this knowledge is "academic" while flair is practical.

The former issues at most in behests and criticisms; the latter in accurate calculations. To know *operatively* the rules is to know how to calculate, i.e., to be able to calculate correctly, swiftly and without fatigue. The fact that many good mathematical teachers are bad mathematicians brings out these two opposing senses of "knowing mathematics." Is there anything in this field analogous to either the questions or commands of conscience? I think there is. If a computer happens to know the answer which he expects to arrive at, e.g., from reading a pass book, he may through laziness or wishful thinking run too hastily through a column of figures and then, even though by accident his answer is correct, he feels a sense of guilt about his steps, and is inclined to go over them again more carefully. This is especially so when he gets to an answer which for some reason *must* be wrong. To locate and correct a mistake requires a special act of attention to what, say, certain figures do and do *not* add up to. His ordinary scrupulousness does not normally require the occurrence of actual scruples. But sometimes he has actually to feel scruples, which he would not feel unless he were dispositionally scrupulous, and on a given occasion has not been scrupulous enough. God would calculate (if at all) with 100% scrupulousness and 0% scruples. Similarly, he would always do the right thing and would never wonder what he ought to do. He would never consult his conscience and would never have pangs of conscience.

It might be said that having scruples, though they will be scruples of different sorts, is common to all cases where *real* acceptance of rules or principles is the being disposed to behave in a certain way, but where this disposition is balked of its normal actualization by some special temptation or interruption. It is like trying to mis-spell one's own signature when writing one's own name has become an automatic habit. One *can* do it, but there is a resistance. One may compare also the practiced cyclist trying to control a tricycle. His normal responses, e.g., in turning or in tilting are balked by the abnormal situation. He knows (academically) what to do, but does not *really*, i.e., operatively know how to do it. But as cycling well does not involve acknowledging or being able to cite laws of dynamics, one can scarcely speak of cycling scrupulously. Roughly, *this* sort of habit is a reflex and not an observance.

Conscience, then, is one species, among others, of scrupulousness; and scrupulousness is the operative acceptance of a rule or principle which consists in the disposition to behave, in all modes of behavior, including saying to oneself and others, teaching, chiding, etc., in accordance with the rule. Scruples, whether of conscience or of any other species of scrupulousness, occur only when the normal actualization of the disposition is impeded or balked. And they, too, are only a special way in which the disposition is actualized, viz. when it cannot be *normally* actualized. The reason why my conscience is not spoken of as either judging or commanding other people is the same as the reason why, in general, a man can be described as scrupulous only about his own acts, namely, that full operative acceptance of the rule can (logically) take the form only of conducting oneself in accordance with the rule. Your actions can't (logically) be exercises of or exhibit *my* skill, readiness, capacity, enthusiasm, etc.

This answer to the original puzzle will, of course, provoke the objection that it denies the hallowed distinctions between cognition, emotion and volition. For I am saying that in one sense, and a very important sense, of the word my being "convinced" of something or my "knowing" it do not *cause* but *consist* in my tending to feel certain feelings and to enact certain actions. It will be said that a thought may *engender* dispositions to feel and to act, but that these dispositions are not the causes of themselves.

I reply: (1) Then must it also be said that when I think in words, my saying so and so to myself is the *effect* of the thinking and not a constituent of it, that I first think and then tell myself what I have thought? But then I must think also what to tell myself and how to tell it; and this thinking must also have its own articulation which must in its turn be premeditated and so on.... Thinking *is* talking sensibly, but then why should it not equally be *behaving* sensibly?

(2) The present view, that among the criteria (*not* the symptoms) of belief and knowledge are dispositions to feel cer-

tain emotions and perform certain actions does not entail that "thinking" "feeling" and "doing" are synonymous. It is still necessary to distinguish impulsive, reflex and automatic from intelligent, careful, purposive, deliberate and scrupulous actions; and silly from sensible, careless from careful, deliberate from unpremeditated, behavior. Similarly, feeling indignant, shocked, awed, amused, thwarted, respectfully differ from feeling uneasy, angry, or sleepy. Only rational beings in rational states of mind (i.e., not drunk, in a panic, or infantile) can (logically) feel the former, while animals and infants can feel the latter. Was Kant's obscure doctrine about "Practical Reason" something like this view, and Aristotle's φϱόνησις which manifests itself sometimes in *acting* from premises and which is internally connected with ἠΘικὴ ἀϱετή? What do we mean by "judicious behavior," "scrupulous conduct," "skillful or careful action"? They can't mean "acting in consequence of certain 'sententious thinking' "; for we can also say that the choice and control of the sentences in which we think when we think "sententiously" can be judicious and careful. Nor could the alleged causal connections between thinking and doing (or feeling) have been discovered by the people who speak of "judicious behavior" as an effect of "sententious thinking," for whatever trained psychologists may do, the plain man cannot find the pure thinkings which are to be inductively correlated with the supposedly resultant actions or feelings. So his use of phrases like "judicious behavior" do not signify instances of such correlations.

I have not tried to show what the differences are between conscience and other sorts of scrupulousness. That is not my present puzzle. Nor have I tried to list all the varieties of conduct which can be described as "scrupulous." There are plenty of others besides those mentioned; those, e.g., of good discipline in the Army and Navy, observance of Committee and Parliamentary procedure, keeping to the principles of good chess, bridge, grammar, strategy, style, prosody, and of the Judge adhering to the rules of admissible evidence. None of these adherences is "mere" acknowledgment of general truths or imperatives. They are fully adopted in habitual observance and in feeling scruples about breaking the habits.

III

Conscience

PETER FUSS

In many quarters, conscience has been, and is still, regarded as the very marrow of the moral life. Yet in the history of moral philosophy the phenomenon of conscience has received surprisingly little attention. Apart from Bishop Butler, who made conscience the central concept of his ethical theory, few moral philosophers have attempted a careful analysis of it. The major contention of the present essay is a negative one: whatever else conscience may be, it is not a faculty or source of moral knowledge. The first part of the essay is devoted to a critical examination of what three moral philosophers, Bishop Butler, J. S. Mill, and C. D. Broad, had to say about conscience. The second part, more constructive in tenor, ventures a theory as to what conscience really is.

I

Bishop Butler characterized moral conscience by two well-known and, one supposes, deliberately paradoxical phrases: it is "a sentiment of the understanding," "a perception of the heart." [1] These descriptions neatly straddle the question as to whether conscience is a faculty of reason or a faculty of sense or sentiment. For Butler, conscience seems to be a combination of cognitive faculty, affording knowledge of what is right and wrong (whether intuitively or not is not quite clear), and emotive faculty, registering feelings of obligation, remorse, etc., (thus the familiar "pangs of conscience").

seemingly self-contrad- ictory

pertaining to the mind

---

1. Joseph Butler, "A Dissertation upon the Nature of Virtue," in *Five Sermons* (New York: Liberal Arts Press, 1950), p. 82.

powers of the mind.   *supplying*

How does conscience guide us? Butler answers that any man reflecting in a calm and cool hour simply knows what is right and wrong. If he will but let his conscience speak, it will tell him what, from a moral point of view, he needs to know. However, it does not speak in general rules or formulas. Hence Butler seems to subscribe to a form of what Henry Sidgwick has called "perceptual intuitionism."

Why obey conscience? Because it is a law of my nature, Butler answers. It carries its own authority with it. The question, "Why should I obey my conscience?" is virtually equivalent to the question, "Why ought I do what I ought to do?" No further justification of the validity of conscience's dictates is possible or necessary. Our passions may have greater power, but conscience has supreme authority. "Had it strength, as it has right; had it power, as it has manifest authority, it would absolutely govern the world." [2] Thus it affords, as C. D. Broad has put it, a conclusive reason for acting in accordance with its dictates. [3]

That Butler's theory of conscience is untenable seems indicated by the following considerations.

1. The familiar facts about conflicting dictates of conscience cast doubt on the claim that conscience can be accepted as supreme moral authority. There are chiefly two groups of such facts. (a) The consciences of various individuals in various cultures are found to conflict. This being the case, a rational decision to accept the claims of one as against another of these conflicting consciences must be based on appeal to something other than the consciences in question. (b) The conscience of any one individual is sometimes found to issue conflicting dictates at different times. Once again we are faced with the problem of deciding which of these dictates, if any, is to be accepted as morally authoritative. An appeal to something other than the conflicting dictates themselves seems requisite. Now Butler does not tell us how to distinguish legitimate from spurious

---

2. *Ibid.*, p. 41.
3. *Five Types of Ethical Theory* (New York: Humanities Press, 1951), p. 78.

*not genuine,
authentic,
or good*

claims of conscience in either case. On his view, indeed, it seems as though there could not be such a thing as a spurious dictate of conscience. Since conscience is the supreme moral authority, its dictates must be authentic and legitimate by definition. Counterfeit claims must then stem from some other source. But that brings us to our second point.

2. On psychological grounds it is extremely difficult to distinguish authentic "pangs of conscience" from feelings not generally regarded as moral, such as feelings of guilt or shame at having violated rules of propriety, custom, or etiquette. But the mere fact that the question can arise as to whether a given impulse is really the voice of an infallible conscience or something else indicates that this question cannot be decided, as apparently it must on Butler's view, by appeal to conscience itself.

3. More important, it is not clear how the dictates of conscience can be *justified* by appeal to conscience itself. Even if we assume for the moment the existence of an internally consistent, interpersonally uniform, and readily distinguishable faculty of moral conscience, it would still be proper to ask what warrants our obedience to its dictates. The only reason Butler offers us is that conscience is the supreme law of human nature, carrying its own authority with it. But this is not a reason at all. For it either begs the question at issue (why is it the supreme authority?) or it presents us with an irrelevant piece of factual information (man is so constituted that . . .) which cannot furnish us with a morally justifying reason for anything.

Butler writes: "let any plain honest man, before he engages in any course of action, ask himself, Is this I am going about right, or is it wrong? Is it good, or is it evil? I do not in the least doubt but that this question would be answered agreeably to truth and virtue, by almost any fair man in almost any circumstance." [4] From this passage it is clear that Butler does not, and probably cannot, answer the objections just stated. Who are the exceptional men and what are the exceptional circumstances? Are they to be discounted just because they are ex-

---

4. Butler, *op. cit.*, p. 45.

ceptional, or do they impugn the universality and uniformity of conscience's dictates? How are we to understand "agreeably to truth and virtue"? If that means "in conformity with conscience," then we must ask *whose* conscience. The argument would either be circular, seeking to justify the dictates of some conscience by pointing out that they are the dictates of the conscience, or it would be self-refuting, in showing that this conscience is legitimated as the supreme ethical principle because it is in conformity with some still higher ethical principle, "truth and virtue."

II

For a more consistently emotivistic conception of conscience, let us look at John Stuart Mill's *Utilitarianism*. In chapter iii he writes:

> The internal sanction of duty, whatever our standard of duty may be, is one and the same—a feeling in our own mind; a pain, more or less intense, attendant on violation of duty, which in properly cultivated moral natures rises, in the more serious cases, into shrinking from it as an impossibility. This feeling, when disinterested and connecting itself with the pure idea of duty, and not with some particular form of it, or with any of the merely accessory circumstances, is the essence of conscience; though in that complex phenomenon as it actually exists, the simple fact is in general all encrusted over with collateral associations derived from sympathy, from love, and still more from fear; from all the forms of religious feeling; from the recollections of childhood and of all our past life; from self-esteem, desire of the esteem of others, and occasionally even self-abasement .... Its binding force, however, consists in the existence of a mass of feeling which must be broken through in order to do what violates our standard of right, and which, if we do nevertheless violate that standard, will probably have to be encountered afterwards in the form of remorse.[5]

Apart from the often-repeated criticism that Mill in general confused moral binding force with psychological determination

---

5. *Utilitarianism* (New York: Liberal Arts Press, 1957), p. 36.

or moving appeal, two comments about his particular conception of conscience are in order.

1. Mill acknowledges, rightly, that conscience is a "complex phenomenon" and that it is difficult to extract the "essence" of conscience from the "collateral associations" and "accessory circumstances" with which it is incrusted and surrounded. But this is merely another way of saying that the authentic voice of conscience is difficult if not impossible to distinguish from other "voices"—be they moral, immoral, or amoral; religious, cultural, or social. Since Mill did not appeal to conscience as the highest tribunal of moral judgment, however, he is not compelled, as is Butler, to resolve the difficulty at hand.

2. Mill would have us understand that conscience is an affective response to a deliberate willed action fulfilling or violating our duty as we conceive it to be. But would it not be more accurate to say that conscience *occasions* feelings of remorse and guilt, approval and esteem, than to say that conscience *is* these feelings? If conscience *is* a feeling of guilt, approbation, etc., then not only is it not a faculty or source of moral knowledge, it is not even a faculty or source of distinctively *moral* sentiments; for, as Mills points out, the sentiments in question are often occasioned by, or have reference to, non-moral states of affairs. Finally, we might note that on Mill's view conscience is merely reflexive; it has no active moral role at all. On this account, the phrase "dictates of conscience" is left with no intelligible meaning.

III

Turning now to C. D. Broad, we find him asserting that conscience has a threefold nature: cognitive, affective, and conative. According to Broad, to say that a person has a conscience means, in the wide sense:

(1) That he has and exercises the cognitive power of reflecting on his own past and future actions, and considering whether they are right or wrong; or reflecting on his own motives, intentions, emotions, dispositions,

and character, and considering whether they are morally good or bad . . . .
(2) That he has and exercises the emotional disposition to feel certain
peculiar emotions, such as remorse, feeling of guilt, moral approval, etc.,
towards himself and his own actions, dispositions, etc., in respect of the
moral characteristics which he believes these to have.
(3) That he has and exercises the conative disposition to seek what
he believes to be good and to shun what he believes to be bad, as such,
and do what he believes to be right and avoid what he believes to be
wrong, as such.[6]

This, according to Broad, is the "phenomenological sense" of
the phrase "having a conscience." He asks us to note that to say
someone has a conscience neither entails nor excludes his holding any particular ethical theory concerning the nature of goodness, rightness, obligation, etc. Moreover, the fact, if it be a
fact, that most people have consciences neither establishes nor
refutes any particular ethical theory. It is clear that Broad accepts
the threefold analysis of conscience given above, for he writes:
"Conscience, as I have defined it, is a system of cognitive, emotional, and conative dispositions, and it is only when these
dispositions are in operation that we have conscientious action."[7]

It should be pointed out at once that so comprehensive a
definition of conscience renders it virtually equivalent to the
individual's moral nature as a whole. Included in this notion
of conscience is what we commonly understand and distinguish
by the expressions moral knowledge or moral belief, moral
deliberation, moral feeling, and moral striving. In spite of
Broad's insistence to the contrary, it is very dubious that so
wide a characterization of conscience accurately expresses the
phenomenological facts. Even the man in the street is inclined,
at least on reflection, to make more careful distinctions than that.
But let us examine Broad's definition in greater detail.

Against the notion that conscience is a cognitive disposition,
the following objections, in addition to the ones brought previously against Butler, may be raised.

6. "Conscience and Conscientious Action," P. 8.
7. *Ibid.*, p. 17.

1. Precisely what is to be understood by a "cognitive disposition"? If by "disposition" is meant "inclination," then conscience is more properly called a conative disposition. If "disposition" means "tendency," as Broad seems to intend, then he is failing to note the distinction between actual moral discernment on the one hand, and a mere tendency to have such discernments on the other.

2. In his definition of conscience, Broad quite properly confines its scope of reference to the agent's own actions, motives, intentions, character, etc. But moral obligation and value, and their negative correlates, are commonly thought to be discernible in the actions and characters of other persons as well as in our own, and perhaps even more clearly in others than in ourselves. It is difficult to see why, *as such,* a faculty of or disposition to cognition should have an exclusively first-personal reference.

3. It is a familiar fact of moral experience that conscience operates exclusively with reference to concrete situations. But our moral cognitions have reference to general principles as well as to concrete situations. Conscience could therefore at most be one part or aspect of moral cognition. When we recall the facts alluded to in the preceding objection, the question remains why conscience, if it is a source of moral knowledge even in the restricted sense of being limited to knowledge of concrete situations, concerns itself exclusively with concrete situations in which the agent is actively involved.

4. Broad's contention that his definition of conscience does not constitute a commitment to any particular ethical theory cannot go unquestioned. Major ethical theories such as intuitionism, naturalism, utilitarianism, self-realizationism, and emotivism involve theoretical commitments both in regard to what we cognize morally, if anything, and how we do so. Thus, if, as we have argued above, moral conscience functions exclusively by reference to concrete situations, even if it is a source of moral knowledge, that knowledge is of moral particulars and not of moral universals. The claim that conscience is the faculty of moral knowledge, therefore, may very well commit its proponent to

what Sidgwick distinguishes as "perceptual intuitionism" as opposed to "dogmatic intuitionism."

Broad himself subscribes to the view that conscience is, among other things, the disposition to *see* that making a promise as such imposes an obligation to keep it, that answering questions as such imposes an obligation to tell the truth, etc.—and moreover it involves estimating the relative urgency of two or more obligations in cases where they conflict.[8] Broad adds that conscience should be understood widely enough to allow for the intuition and comparison of goods and evils as one of its functions as well. Thus Broad is prepared to accommodate the claims of deontological intuitionism and of teleological utilitarianism to his theory of conscience. But to accommodate the claims of rival ethical theories is not the same thing as to stand neutral with respect to them. Besides, Broad's own leaning toward deontological intuitionism is clearly in evidence throughout the essay.

Broad's definitions of the emotive and conative aspects of conscience are much more plausible than is that of its alleged cognitive aspect. But a remark concerning each is in order. The propriety of defining conscience as an emotive faculty or disposition hinges on whether we want to say that conscience occasions such feelings as guilt, remorse, approval, etc., or that it is constituted by these peculiar feelings. Broad, like Mill, seems to take the latter position. But the former view, as indicated in the section on Mill, has greater plausibility. If conscience merely occasions these feelings there is no reason to ascribe to it as such an emotive aspect or character.

The view that conscience is a conative disposition to seek what one believes good and to shun what one believes bad, and to do what one believes right and avoid wrong, *as such*, seems to me the most promising characterization of conscience thus far encountered. (The view of conscience which I shall propose presently is rather similar to this one of Broad's). But it should be observed that this definition of conscience is in conflict with

---

8. *Ibid.*, p. 13.

Broad's cognitive definition. If conscience is at one and the same time a source of moral knowledge or belief and a disposition to act on that knowledge or belief, Broad will be as hard put as was Socrates to explain *akrasia*, the well-known phenomenon of weakness of will whereby it is just the failure to act on what we know or believe to be right that occasions the feelings of guilt or remorse commonly associated with conscience.

To conclude our examination of Broad, then, it seems evident that his threefold definition of conscience is unacceptable. This definition may express in capsule form what it means to be moral in general, but in offering it as a definition of moral conscience in particular Broad both fails to do justice to the phenomenology of moral experience to which he himself appeals, and offers us an internally inconsistent and semantically confused theory.

IV

I would like at this point to propose a theory of moral conscience that attempts at once to meet the objections discussed above and to square with the generally accepted phenomenological descriptions of conscience. The distinctive role of conscience in the moral life is to establish a general sense of moral obligation in the individual's consciousness. It does this by constituting a certain relation between the individual's moral knowledge or belief and his action. Namely, it establishes in the moral agent a felt need or disposition to act in accordance with his knowledge or belief, giving him a sense of personal integrity when he does so as best he can, and a corresponding sense of inner failure, frustration, or guilt when, through some fault of his own, he fails to do so.

On this analysis, it is clear that conscience is not in any usual sense a faculty or source of moral knowledge. Of itself it does not tell the agent what is right or wrong, good or evil, either in individual concrete instances or as a matter of principle. Nevertheless, on this view conscience could be regarded as a source of moral knowledge in one, somewhat extended sense. It could be said, namely, that conscience affords one the "existential knowledge" (more properly, the existential conviction) that he is under obligation to do what he knows to be right and to pursue what he judges to be good. It should be noted, however, that such "knowledge" is purely formal or procedural, not substantive knowledge of what specific action or type of action is right or wrong, what specific object or type of object or state of affairs is good or evil. Moreover, if one is asked to justify the claim of conscience that one must act in accordance with what he knows or believes, an appeal to conscience itself will not provide such a justification. A decisive reason in favor of obeying the one "dictate" of conscience we have specified, if such a reason be available at all, must come from some source other than conscience itself.

Furthermore, conscience is not an affective moral faculty or disposition in any usual sense. It does not constitute some specific moral feeling such as benevolence, sympathy, or just desert. However, it does give rise to feelings of personal integrity, self-esteem, etc., when its "voice" as above described is heeded, and to feelings of personal disintegration, remorse, etc., when it is not heeded.

Finally, conscience is not a conative faculty or disposition in any substantive sense—that is, it does not as such move the agent to pursue this or that object of value or to perform this or that morally worthy act. However, it does constitute the disposition to integrate or harmonize moral knowledge or belief with the appropriate moral action.

The theory of conscience here proposed is more easily accommodated to the phenomenology of conscience than are the more traditional theories examined previously. It does justice to the familiar facts concerning the "relativity" of conscience, while at the same time it is able to render these facts intelligible. On the present theory, it is not conscience itself that is relative interpersonally and intrapersonally; instead, what conscience relates is relative. My conscience may "dictate" different or even inconsistent courses of action at different times either because what I know or believe I know to be morally right or good may and often does change, or because my estimation of what course of action will best implement my moral knowledge or belief may and often does change. Needless to say, the "dictates" of several consciences may be expected to vary all the more, for much the same reasons. Although conscience as such is invariable in its one *actual* dictate—Act in accordance with your moral knowledge or belief—the dictates of conscience will *appear* to vary endlessly, since both of the terms conscience relates, namely, knowledge or belief concerning what is good and right and knowledge or belief concerning the appropriate actions, will vary within and between individual agents.

It is the appearance of endlessly varying dictates of conscience that is probably responsible for much of the confusion in past theories of conscience. I have been urging that conscience properly regarded delivers no substantive moral dictates at all—that what it "dictates" is a purely formal relation between what we know or believe and what we are to do, namely, consistency between the former and the latter. But conscience, like any other human faculty or disposition, is subject to the phenomena of habituation. We frequently understand by a conscientious moral agent someone who not only acts consistently with what he knows or believes to be right, but who has developed his moral character to such a point that it has become "second nature" for him to behave in accordance with recognizable moral patterns. He may be so convinced of the rightness, say, of acting justly or benevolently that it is virtually unthinkable for him to do otherwise. His conscience, while in itself concerned only with a purely formal relation between his knowledge and his action, readily takes on the coloring of what it is that he knows and what action he deems appropriate accordingly. Hence it is not surprising that he comes to believe that his conscience delivers itself of substantive as well as of procedural dictates. Lacking the philosophical sophistication needed to make careful distinctions, he is given to calling the entire process of moral investigation, deliberation, decision, and their affective consequences by the name of conscience. But after all there is little harm in it: his everyday moral concerns do not require careful theoretical distinctions. The moral philosopher, on the other hand, is concerned with the precise nature of conscience; he fails to make the necessary distinctions at his peril.

v

The present theory conforms with and renders intelligible other peculiar phenomena of conscience as well. It explains why a man's conscience may not "bother" him when he is thoroughly convinced of the rightness of his action even though most or even all other men disagree or disapprove. Conscience has no socially determined content. Thus a given individual may know or think he knows some moral truth, in accordance with which he feels obliged to act, which none of his fellow men shares. On the other hand, my theory explains why a man's conscience may not disturb him when, in spite of disapproval on the part of outsiders, he continues to act in ways approved by the group or community to which he belongs. Conscience has no innate content either. Thus a given individual may know or believe only those moral principles to which those around him adhere. His "conscience" may then appear dismayingly impervious to the appeal of moral principles deemed higher, better, or more enlightened by anyone less limited or less parochial. What is at fault in such cases is, of course, not the man's conscience but his lack of moral insight or capacity for moral growth. The function of conscience, as we have been urging, is limited to specifying a formal relation of terms: knowledge (or belief) and action. It cannot be expected to transcend the limitations of the terms which it is its sole function to relate.

A possible corollary of the theory proposed is that there is no such thing as a "strong" or "weak" conscience, or a more or less enlightened or developed conscience. Conscience as such is simply the felt disposition to act in accordance with what we know or believe. The qualitative intensity of this disposition may very well be uniform among several individuals and within each individual, even though, as is obviously the case, men differ in both respects in the degree of their conscientiousness. Conscience is but one of the "voices" competing in the economy of the human psychic makeup. It may well be that conscience always "tells" me with the same urgency to do as I know, but (a) I may be doubtful that I really know, and hence unsure that I must act at all; (b) I may at times find my desire overwhelming my sense of obligation (as Butler recognized when he contrasted conscience's supreme authority with its relative power among our conflicting dispositions); and (c) I may, through weakness or perversity of will, tip the scales in moral deliberation in favor of rationalizing away what I know or believe to be morally right, or allow my impulses to get the better of my moral reason. The "voice" of conscience, then, can be suppressed or repressed; but the difficulty of stifling it altogether attests to the likelihood that the pressure of other dispositions rather than its own qualitative inconstancy lies behind the pervasive variations in degrees of conscientiousness among and within moral agents.

By the same token, it is a misnomer to speak of a more or less enlightened or developed conscience. Intellect is what is more or less enlightened, and moral character as a whole is what is more or less developed. The development of moral character, in turn, has to do with the informed tendency (a function of knowing and willing) to give our various impulses, dispositions, etc., their proper due and to act accordingly. Our varying degree of success and failure in so doing does not militate against the notion that the "voice" of conscience may be the only constant in the economy of the human makeup.

This analysis has the added virtue of avoiding the tendency, as in Butler and in Broad, to make of conscience a two- or even three-headed monster, at once cognitive and emotive, or even cognitive-emotive-conative. We have reason and emotions, will and impulses, we desire and we deliberate. None of these dispositions and faculties, singly or in any mysterious combination, is to be identified with conscience. The role of conscience is purely and simply to "enforce" our moral knowledge or belief with a tendency to act in accordance with what we know or believe. So regarded, it is a function of unification or integration, and thereby accounts for our sense of integrity, of wholeness when we act as we know we ought. It is "*con-scientia*"—with or accompanying or abetting (moral) knowledge, disposing us to be and to do what we think.

VI

The theory of conscience I am proposing sheds considerable light, I believe, on one of the most baffling phenomena of recent times: the moral dispositions of the Nazi war criminals, and, in particular, those of Adolf Eichmann as they were revealed during the sensational trial in Israel. Hannah Arendt, in her brilliant and controversial account of the Eichmann trials,[9] points out that Eichmann's attitude and behavior toward the Jews underwent a radical change near the end of the war. Earlier, Eichmann had played an important role in helping to organize the massive emigration of Jews from Germany and German-occupied territory. By comparison with what he did later, his actions at the beginning of the war, while hardly commendable, were relatively humane. But when Hitler ordered the wholesale implementation of the "Final Solution" (the extermination of the Jews), Eichmann, for whom an order by Hitler was at the same time supreme law of the land, quickly found himself able to adjust his "conscience" to what he was undertaking. In this moral reversal, Miss Arendt reports, he was abetted by the eagerness and zeal with which the men he respected and looked up to—both his more cultivated and better-educated superiors and many influential Jewish leaders—carried out Hitler's order. Miss Arendt writes: "He did not need to 'close his ears to the voice of his conscience,' as the judgment has it, not because he had none, but because his conscience spoke with a 'respectable voice,' with the voice of respectable society around him." [10]

Eichmann's "conscience" in fact, was so scrupulous that it tolerated no exceptions to the law, even when that law was

---

9. *Eichmann in Jerusalem* (New York: Viking Press, 1963).
10. *Ibid.*, pp. 111-12.

genocide. Miss Arendt records that he did in fact make several exceptions (he helped a half-Jewish cousin and, at the request of his uncle, a Viennese Jewish couple)—but that his conscience nagged him for it to such a point that he felt obliged to "confess his sins" (his own phrase) to his superiors. Whereas this rigor in the exercise of his Satanic duties condemned him in the eyes of his judges as much as did anything else, in his own eyes, Miss Arendt reveals, it is precisely what justified him. It constituted proof that he had always done his duty scrupulously, that he had always acted against his inclinations, whether these were selfish or sentimental. His well-meaning judges, Miss Arendt points out, were simply unable to believe that Eichmann was not motivated by fanatical hatred of Jews, and that he had not perjured himself when he claimed that he had simply obeyed orders. In point of fact, she writes, "the sad but very uncomfortable truth of the matter probably was that it was not his fanaticism but his very conscience that prompted Eichmann to adopt his uncompromising attitude during the last year of the war, as it had prompted him to move in the opposite direction for a short time three years before." [11]

The evidence compels Miss Arendt to say that the appeal to an "unambiguous voice of conscience" or a "general sentiment of humanity" is not only question-begging but indicative of a pervasive inability to grasp what is perhaps the most striking moral phenomenon of our day: the possibility of a wholesale inversion of moral consciousness. Whereas we are accustomed to believing that "Thou shalt not kill" is an invariable dictate of conscience, the law of Hitler's Germany appears to have had the power to change the voice of conscience to dictate: "Thou shalt kill." And whereas most of us have obeyed the traditional dictate in spite of occasional murderous natural desires and inclinations, those under Hitler must frequently have been tempted *not* to murder, rob, and betray, *not* to become accomplices to these crimes. "But, God knows," Miss

---

11. *Ibid.*, p. 131.

Arendt concludes, "they had learned how to resist temptation."[12]

In the face of this testimony from an insightful and informed witness, can there be any further question that conscience as such is not a source or faculty of moral knowledge? The phenomenon of Eichmann is, after all, merely the most dramatic illustration of the futility of appealing to conscience for what conscience of itself cannot deliver: sound moral judgment and correct moral sentiment. We must look elsewhere if we are to discover adequate criteria and adequate justifying principles for the latter. Josiah Royce once said: "ethical doctrine must tell us why, if the devil's conscience approves of the devil's acts, as it may well do, the devil's conscience is nevertheless in the wrong."[13] In terms of the theory I have been defending, Royce's point could be restated as follows: "if the devil believes that genocide is morally right, and if his conscience thereupon tells him (as on my view it must) that he is under obligation to act accordingly, the moral philosopher who appeals to the devil's conscience to rectify the situation is under a gross misapprehension."

In conclusion, it is worth emphasizing that acceptance of the theory of conscience here proposed does not commit one to any particular ethical theory concerning the meaning of moral terms, the nature of moral obligation or value, or the justification of moral principles. A Socrates or a Kant, a rationalist or an emotivist, an intuitionist or a moral skeptic, a self-realizationist or a utilitarian could maintain such a view of conscience without having to modify his ethical theories in any way. For these theories, if I am right, do not concern the nature of moral conscience in the first place.

12. *Ibid.*, p. 134.
13. *The Religious Aspect of Philosophy* (New York: Harper & Row, 1958), p. 57.

PART II

THE EXISTENCE OF CONSCIENCE

INTRODUCTION

THE colloquial contexts in which the term "conscience" appears, such as "You ought to follow your conscience" or "Have you no conscience?" or "It is to be decided by conscience," readily suggest that the term refers to some unique entity. Most men quite naturally suppose that there is in fact some such entity, some faculty, of moral significance to which this term refers. Yet, considering the central role which the conscience is alleged to play in the moral life, it is not surprising that there are philosophers who greet this natural supposition of the existence of conscience with skepticism. Is it not possible, they wonder, that the conscience is really nothing more than a convenient moral myth, or a set of psychological reactions, or simply the pressure of cultural *mores*?

J. F. M. Hunter in an article entitled "Conscience" questions the existence of a faculty of conscience which answers to our pre-philosophical conception of it. Our pre-philosophical notion of "conscience," according to Hunter, is that of an agency which produces conscious feeling of a moral sort, which informs us what ought to be done in a particular situation and encourages us to act accordingly, and which provides the sole infallible moral tribunal. Hunter argues that there is no way to establish that the conscience is responsible for these activities, since the term "conscience" purports to refer to a "logically hidden" or "private" entity. In using conscience-terminology we are not literally describing the operation of some agency. We are, instead, expressing ourselves by means of a well-known "story." Hunter compares "My conscience is bothering me" with "Santa Claus was good to me this year": the meaning in both cases is perfectly clear, but there is no reason to suppose that the entity allegedly referred to exists.

In "Freud's Theory of Moral Conscience," David H. Jones examines Freud's contention that the phenomenon of moral conscience is explained by the theory of the superego. Freud claimed that the mechanism of the superego converts anxiety into the sense of guilt which characterizes conscience. Jones argues that Freud failed to distinguish adequately between *guilt,* a conscious and moral affect, and *anxiety,* an unconscious and undifferentiated affect. Peculiarly moral feelings, such as guilt and remorse must be explained by consciously held beliefs relevant to the agent's situation and actions. When a man has a "bad conscience," for example, he knows what is bothering him and what he can do (or could have done) about it. A man's moral conscience is produced by his beliefs about his (moral) condition, whereas the superego is produced by an unconscious and object-less fear, which involves no beliefs whatsoever.

In "The Notion of Conscience," Austin Duncan-Jones examines the conception of the faculty of conscience which derives from Bishop Butler and analyzes the grounds for the skepticism to which it has given rise. He claims that Butler's notion of "conscience," as the capacity for reflecting with approval or disapproval upon human character and actions, is open to three distinct interpretations. First, conscience may be understood on a "rational" model as the power of reason applied to the subject matter of morals. Second, conscience may be understood on a "perceptual" model as a unique moral sense by which a man might "perceive" what he ought or ought not to do in a particular situation. Upon both of these models the conscience is construed as an innate faculty, much like the faculties of reason and perception themselves. Finally, conscience may be understood on an "emotional" model as a distinctive type of moral feeling or sentiment. Now feelings or sentiments, it is commonly claimed, are not innate but are molded by the family, the society, or one's psychological predispositions. It is this relativistic notion of "conscience," fostered by (cultural) anthropology and psychoanalysis, which leads to doubts about the existence of conscience (and, of course, about its reliability).

Duncan-Jones argues that neither the results of anthropology nor the results of psychoanalysis entail the unreliability, much less the non-existence, of the conscience. In fact, he claims that an understanding of the derivation of our moral inclinations (an understanding which anthropology and psychoanalysis increase) is a valuable asset in reflecting critically upon our character and actions. Such reflection, he adds, may appropriately be called "consultations of conscience."

Conscience

J. F. M. HUNTER

IF, as we say, there is such a thing as conscience, in the sense (which we need not yet endorse), very roughly of a piece of mental equipment which tells us authoritatively what is the right thing to do from time to time, then moral philosophy ought to have no other positive advice to offer than simply "Do what your conscience advises," "Always let your conscience be your guide," etc., and if moral philosophers had any *practical* function other than re-iterating such exhortations, it would take the form, not of discovering what in particular conscience would recommend, but of finding ways and means of unclouding people's consciences, or of inducing people to take their consciences seriously. The reason why philosophers, if they agreed that there were consciences in the above sense, could not proceed to offer positive moral advice, or set up supreme moral principles, or anything of the kind, is that to do this would be to usurp the supposed authority of conscience—to invite people to consult, not their conscience but a philosophical theory. And while it is conceivable that, if philosophers did their work well, the two counsels should in every case coincide, still any codification of the deliverances of conscience is, if set up as an independent guide, a limitation on conscience's authority: preventing it from being inconsistent with itself, from adapting to individual cases, branching out in new directions, or whatever else it might see fit to do.

For this, as well as for other reasons which we shall see later, it is worth investigating whether "there is such a thing as" conscience: if there were, it would on the one hand endow with perennial urgency the advice of Jimminy Cricket, and on the other, settle in a negative but very definite way a number of problems about the nature of a moral philosopher's job.

A

What exactly do we want to know when we ask whether there is such a thing as conscience? What seems to be required is a definition of conscience sufficiently illuminating to enable us to have a look and see, and to identify what we see as being or not being an authentic instance of conscience. But there is something very odd about the thought of first writing down a definition of conscience, saying, "This is what consciences are. If we find anything like this, then there are consciences, and if not, not,"—and then after due investigation concluding that in fact there were none. In such a case, what grounds could we have for thinking that we were working with the one true definition of conscience?

Not an insoluble paradox, this: there is no Santa Claus, but we can give a fairly detailed account of the man, of where he lives, what he wears, how his belly shakes, what he does, and what his information and attitude is concerning the moral behavior of the younger generation. People are inclined to say "Of course there is a Santa Claus. It's your Dad. (Or the spirit of good will, or even the idea of him which exists in people's minds.)" In saying such things, they are trading on parts of the familiar notion of the fellow, while ignoring other and equally important parts. (Santa and Dad both produce gifts at Christmas, and so far Dad qualifies; but Dad is not a sprightly elf living at the North Pole. Similarly the *idea* of Santa Claus qualifies and much more fully; but the idea does not exist at the North Pole, or have a belly which shakes in an interesting way when it laughs.)

Though we use the term "conscience" extensively in ordinary speech, the specifications of the concept *conscience* are not as clear to us as are those of Santa Claus, but we can perhaps piece together these specifications by taking a series of assertions parallel to "Of course there's a Santa Claus, it's . . . ," and seeing in each case what parts of the concept of conscience it trades on, and what parts, if any, it ignores. We will at the same time be discovering whether, or in what senses, "there is such a thing."

I

Almost anyone would be likely to say that for his part he knows very well that he has a conscience: it bothers him. Different people would perhaps report different forms of moral torment (nagging or wheedling voices, tweaks, twinges, even gongs or lights), but the experience of moral torment of whatever description would be identified with, rather than treated as evidence of, having a conscience. This is like saying, "Of course there is a Santa Claus. Don't gifts appear on the Christmas tree?" ("To say that there is a Santa Claus means that gifts appear at an appropriate time on Christmas trees.")

We have seen the defectiveness of this proof in the Santa Claus case, but it might be said that with conscience it is different: that when a person reports that his conscience has been bothering him, he is alluding to nothing more than the occurrence of certain tweaks, twinges, inner voices or other similar mental disturbances—he makes no representations about any agency producing these disturbances. If this is the case, our language is more colorful than we may at first appreciate: to say "my conscience is bothering me" is similar in form to saying "my creditors are bothering me," and while in the former case there is supposed only to be me and my botherment, the latter case embraces three elements, me, my creditors and the angry letters, legal writs or other methods of harassment. Our language, that is to say, suggests that there is something corresponding to the creditors, some agency producing the botherment which we feel. But language is colorful, and while we can readily produce our creditors for philosophic inspection, we are hard put to it to produce our conscience, in the parallel sense. One could still say, therefore, that all that is intended to be reported by "my conscience is bothering me" is my being bothered in a characteristic way.

There is, however, something disquieting about saying that the existence of conscience is proven in this way. It proves too little of what it suggests. It would set some crowds roaring and throwing up their sweaty night caps, while concealing from them the emptiness of the victory which they celebrated. The crowds who would roar, and indeed those who would sulk, are not misled merely by the parallelism between being bothered by conscience and being bothered by creditors: (*a*) In the days when the idea of conscience played a large role in Protestant theology, it was supposed to be the voice of God within us, and this idea still lingers; (*b*) other uses of the term "conscience" suggests even more strongly that it is an agency producing the well known forms of inner distress, and (*c*) most people are in any case sufficiently satisfied with the doctrine that every event has a cause, to be anxious to ascribe some cause to the mental events in question, and conscience appears, at least to the unsophisticated, to play the role nicely.

In amplification of (*b*): (i) To speak of "a man without a conscience" seems fairly clearly to say that one man lacks a piece of equipment which other people possess (like a man without a pineal gland), rather than just that he fails to hear voices which harass other people, though this is certainly part of what is meant; (ii) To say "He sincerely thinks he did the right thing, but his conscience is obscured by grief," is to conceive a case where there are no voices, but there is a conscience: what can this be but an agency which *would* produce voices, etc., under more advantageous conditions?—and (iii) "Your conscience would tell you if you would but listen" is like "(ii)" in that it presupposes the absence for the moment of voices;— and it also attempts to ascribe moral authenticity to conscience, since it could be expanded to read "Such and such is right, and since conscience knows what is right, it will tell you, etc." On the principles of ordinary armchair psychology, to explain the *authenticity* which is conceived to attach to conscience's deliverances, it is necessary to suppose a specially designed piece of equipment. If it were the case that consciences were conceived only to give us advice purporting to be moral, without regard to whether it was necessarily *good* advice, we could explain its troublesome ways as the effect of memory, habit, indoctrination or even whimsy. But none of these will suffice to account for the supposed authenticity. Whether one's upbringing will produce a sound moral attitude will depend on the upbringing, among other things. We therefore need some explanatory entity which is specifically designed to be right about moral questions, and this, as Aquinas might have said, had other things not been so unequal, all men call conscience.

Concerning (c): There are well-known difficulties about assigning causes to mental events, some of which we shall see later, and some of which can be seen in the above paragraph. Conscience appears there, not as the actually discovered cause of a type of mental event, but as a very sketchily conceived set of conditions which would have to be fulfilled before we could say we had discovered the cause. We think: There must be some piece of mental equipment which is somehow so constituted as to infallibly know what's what morally, and to be able to tell us what it knows under appropriate circumstances. Yet we could not quite say what a piece of mental equipment is in general; we have no idea how such equipment would have to be constituted in order to be morally infallible, nor by what mechanisms it would communicate its enlightenment to us. This is not to mention the special complications which arise when we ask questions like, "If we have a built-in infallible guide, how is it that we make so many mistakes?" ("Well, you see, when we make a mistake it's not really our conscience speaking: it's something we *take* to be our conscience.") "But how is conscience prevented from speaking, if it's there all the while, quietly knowing what's what? Is it lazy? Or forgetful?" "No, that's not it; it is just one of the facts about it that it can be obscured by all kinds of things like desire, grief, self-righteousness, etc." "How is it, though, that you can have two people equally afflicted by desire and such things, one of whose consciences continues to function nicely, while the other founders?" "Well conscience itself can become sick. When this happens it doesn't cease to know, but it loses its capacity to make itself felt, just as people do when they are sick." And so forth: the defender of conscience is forced under questioning to draw a more and more complicated and implausible picture of the workings of the device.

But regardless of how unsatisfactory the concept of conscience may be, in these and lots of other ways, the important point remains that it is used as an explanatory concept. We think of conscience as a behind-the-scenes piece of equipment, so designed as to be morally infallible, and causing certain characteristic manifestations in our conscious life; and therefore it will not do to say "Of course conscience exists: it bothers me."

II

There are some ways, over and above those which have incidentally appeared in the above discussion, in which it might be claimed that we have indirect or inferential knowledge of the existence of conscience.

The first is the wonderful case of the man who said "I know I have a conscience because it always tells me what is right." Such a remark might not be altogether laughable if (a) it were more carefully phrased, (b) there were some clear mark by which the deliverances of conscience could be identified among all the clamor of inner voices, etc., which we hear, (c) there were some independent way of knowing the authenticity of the deliverances so identified, and (d) we could assume that there must in every case be a cause adequate to explain given effects.

Not to spoil the fun by attempting any revision of the terms of the demonstration, let us go on to (b). We are able to identify a voice or a piece of handwriting as belonging to a given person whether or not he is at the moment in evidence, because he is sometimes present, and by seeing him write and then examining his writing knowing it to be his, we can notice certain things about it by which we can identify further pieces of handwriting as his or not his. But God's handwriting, given that no one ever saw Him with pen in hand, would be considerably more difficult to identify as such; and conscience, being never itself present to us, but speaking as from behind an eternally locked door, behind which there might be also, for all we know, mimics and other assorted miscreants, is in this respect in a class with God, and not with ordinary acquaintances. How then would we identify its voice? "It wheedles and whines," one might say, or "Speaks in stentorian tones," or more generally "There is a repeated inner experience which has a characteristic mark or set of marks by which it is recognizable and clearly distinguishable from all other inner experiences." Setting aside the question whether anyone enjoys or suffers such an experience, we might agree that this at least is what would be required, for the argument to have any force. We now have it that there is a voice, or something, distinguishable from all others by certain marks, and this voice gives only authentic moral advice, and since there is no other way of explaining such a thing, we must conclude that conscience exists, since conscience is conceived as the behind-the-scenes owner of just such a voice.

But (c) how do we know that the content of these deliverances is authentic moral advice? On the general theory of conscience, one would think the answer would have to be "Because our conscience tells us," since conscience is supposed to be the sole authority on moral questions. Such a reply might carry some weight if the situation were akin to one in which the truth of a report is accepted on the basis of the reputation of the reporter for insight and integrity; and in some ways it is just like this, because conscience has exactly such a reputation. The difference of course is that the reporter case works only where we have direct evidence of authorship, on which evidence the truth of the report is accepted, while in the conscience case the truth of what corresponds to the report *is* our evidence of authorship, i.e., if we think a piece of inner advice is good, we think it must be delivered by conscience—we never experience conscience itself in the process of giving advice.

One could not say either, that because the advice was rendered by the voice having the characteristic marks, it must be authentic advice and therefore the voice of conscience, because unless it is already given that there is an agency dispensing sound moral advice, there is not the least reason to suppose that any set of voices identifiable as one voice will necessarily voice the moral truth.

There remain the two tests of self-consistency and consistency with the conscientious views of other people. The use of either of these tests, it should be noted, is inconsistent with regarding conscience as the moral authority, because it externally imposes a requirement of consistency; and it also raises tiresome empirical questions about whether anyone, *if* they experienced a set of inner voices recognizable as one voice, would ever find its deliverances to be either self-consistent or consistent with the moral views of other people. And if these difficulties are set aside, others remain. What kind of consistency is required, and why? Is conscience consistent only if it regularly recommends similar things in similar circumstances, or is it enough if one is able plausibly to rationalize away apparent inconsistencies? e.g., by saying "yes, I punched him in the nose, but it was for his own good." The acceptance of the former would make conscience, and thereby morality narrower and less progressive than many people would like to have it, while the latter alternative, allowing scope as it does for the exercise of our ingenuity, is not likely to provide a test sufficiently clear for the purpose.

Summing up, it appears that if it is the case that it is conscience which informs us what is right, it is extremely doubtful whether we could have any way independent of the operation of conscience of identifying moral knowledge; and since such independent identification is required by the present proof, the proof fails.

But for what illumination it may provide, let us consider the fourth condition of the argument (*d*): In the ordinary way, when we hear a voice, for example, we are very loath to think that it is not produced by some agency, whether a person, a radio, gramophone, or anything else which we know is able to produce that sort of sound. If we hear a shout as we walk along the street, and looking around see only a dog, we are very upset until we find a child behind a bush, a friend waving from a window, etc. When we hear inner voices, we may be inclined to insist that they should be similarly explainable. In most such cases, as where I inwardly hear the voice of my dear old grandmother, we are content with an explanation like the association of ideas, e.g., if there is just now a smell of fresh-baked bread; but, suppose that never having seen or read "Hamlet," I inwardly hear a long speech beginning "To be or not to be . . . ." This is like the conscience case as above conceived, in that for no naturally explainable reason, what an inner voice said turned out to be exactly right. I might explain this by saying that I was a re-incarnation of Shakespeare himself, or of some Shakespearean scholar, or by saying that somehow I had foreknowledge of my first acquaintance with "Hamlet." These explanations would share two characteristics: (i) They are such that if true they would account for what was to be explained; Shakespeare or a Shakespearean scholar could no doubt recite to himself Hamlet's soliloquy; and if I could somehow pre-experience my first attendance at a performance of "Hamlet," I might very well hear the soliloquy just as I did hear it inwardly: and (ii) they are very unlikely ever to be shown to be true, and therefore, to feel any temptation to accept either explanation is to be moved more by the need of an explanation, than by sober consideration of what if anything will do that job. Explanations employing conscience are similar to these, yet more unsatisfactory in one important way: where the ideas of re-incarnation and of foreknowledge represent imaginable, if unlikely, states of affairs which as such are distinguishable from the idea of explaining the occurrence of the soliloquy, in the conscience case no distinction seems drawable between the idea of explaining and the explanation. To the question, "How is it that I am able to know what's what morally?" the answer is given in effect, "By virtue of having the ability to know what's what morally." Or in other words, to say "Conscience must exist because only so could we explain the having of moral knowledge," as the present proof argued, is not different from saying "There must be an explanation of moral knowledge because otherwise it would not be explainable," and this is not different from saying nothing.

A second indirect or inferential argument is Butler's briefly mentioned point that "without being consulted, without being advised with, [conscience] magisterially exerts itself." (*Sermon* II "Upon Human Nature.") (Did he mean to say "asserts" itself?) How weighty were Butler's actual intentions in mentioning this is not an important question: the words themselves are capable of arguing that our moral anxiety is not just an ordinary constituent of human nature, but has a way or a purpose or a life of its own, and therefore some quite distinct explanatory entity must be supposed to account for it. The point one supposes is that if one had to consult and advise with one's conscience to get any "exertion" out of it, it would be very difficult to distinguish such interludes from cases where one wonders within oneself what to do, and eventually decides—interludes which do not urgently invite a fancy psychology; but since advice appears unsolicited, and one may add contrary often to what one would like, it must flow from some distinct source or agency—it must be, not simply another of my moods, but like another person assigned to watch over me. It is perhaps as if we were listening to the sound track of a film, a track in which there was little distinction between the tone qualities of the voices, and in which no names were used, and trying to find out how many characters there were in the play. Some such sequences might be entirely consistent with the view that there was only one person and he was talking to himself as he went about his affairs. But if there was sometimes a stern order given suddenly, or if strongly critical remarks appeared without prompting, we would have every reason to think that there were at least two characters.

Such analogies are probably the source of whatever plausibility this kind of point has. When we are listening to a film track, we have every reason to suppose that the voices we hear are the voices of characters, that there is some definite number of them, that they are sufficiently like other people we know that we can say, for example, that it would simply never happen that one person would say *those* two things, or the person who said *this* would be more likely than any of the others to have said *this*. It is the availability of such assumptions which makes the film track game playable, as well, of course, as the possibility of chalking up scores by running the film through in its complete form. But none of these conditions seems clearly to hold in the rational psychology game. We do not know that in general mental voices are spoken by psychological entities, nor that there must be a definite number of such entities, nor that such entities are in general such that no one entity would behave in both this and that way, or that the entity which did this would be likely also to do that, etc. As a game, this kind of psychology might be excellent fun, and the impossibility of scoring might be used in such a way that it added to the fun; but there is surely not the least reason to think it is a game which teaches us anything about minds, except of course, what sorts of thing amuse and confuse them.

III

"Of course we have a conscience: it's the such and such region of the brain." Neurophysiological investigations have perhaps not advanced to the point where anyone has ventured to say this, but suppose that under some kind of anaesthetic which would leave a person conscious, electrodes or something could be hooked up to various areas of the brain, whereupon the patient was regaled with tales of sin and crime, courage and justice, or perhaps was neddled about his mistresses or the conduct of his business affairs, and suppose it was found in a number of such experiments that the same area of the brain became greatly agitated, while other parts were not disturbed more than could be accounted for by the memories, associations, desires, fears, etc., which were incidentally incurred by the terms of the experiment. Could we not then say that that area of the brain was the conscience, and that we did indeed have consciences? If the patient reported that his conscience bothered him during parts of the experiment, and if conscience is conceived as the cause of such botherment, what more could be required?

A difficulty, perhaps not insuperable, in such a proof is that when we say conscience has been bothering us, what we are attempting to communicate is (or concerns) botherment of a specific kind: we have been upset, not by grief, not by business worries, not by fears, headaches or hallucinations, but by moral worries. Without being specific, we are saying that we have had a lot of thoughts of the same type as "I wonder whether I should have . . . ?" "What a cad I was to . . . !" "How can I make amends for . . . ?", etc.

If instead of "my conscience has been bothering me" we said "my xyz area has been bothering me," we would be saying less, in that while we would be saying we had been bothered, we would not be saying we had been bothered in a specific way; and we would also be saying more, in that we would be volunteering a piece of medical information entirely absent from the former locution, and having a very different sort of interest. It might be that in time, as knowledge of the xyz area spread, this difficulty would largely disappear. "My kidneys have been bothering me" is now quite illuminating regarding what sort of aches and pains I have been having, and may have replaced some such expression as "I've got the malmseys" after it was discovered that the malmseys were caused by kidney malfunctioning. But there would remain anomalous features: my kidneys bother me when they are functioning badly, but my conscience, when it is functioning well: kidney symptoms one regards simply as a vexation, but one is not concerned so much about the unpleasantness of conscience symptoms as about the moral imputation which they represent; and while we cure a kidney ailment by going to work on the kidneys, a "conscience ailment" is "cured" by tackling whatever one is conscientiously bothered about, by apologizing, by making amends, by doing what one has been resisting doing. Except in abnormal cases—there is such a thing as an over-active conscience, which may have to be treated in a way more like the way we treat kidneys.

A more serious difficulty perhaps is that the xyz area, though as the discovered cause of our moral botherment it so far qualifies nicely as an instance of a conscience, fails to qualify, at least as far as the terms of the hypothesis specify, as a case of something which is so constituted as to know what's what morally. It becomes agitated when confronted with moral questions; but this in itself neither shows that it knows the correct attitude to take to these questions nor explains by means of what ingenious design its moral knowledge, if such it has, is guaranteed. So far, therefore, we have not found a way of showing that conscience in the full sense exists.

Suppose however that a very long series of moral problems was posed to the patient, to which in every case he gave the right solution, and his pondering the problems and giving the solutions was accompanied by agitation primarily in the xyz region, and suppose further, if you like, that if he made mistakes, these were accompanied by activity in other regions: would this tend to show that the xyz region was morally infallible?

Given that we knew independently how to check these solutions, no doubt one could answer affirmatively: it would be like testing a new design of adding machine, and when it did all the operations required of it to perfection, we could call it infallible. But the story about conscience is that it is the unique source of our moral knowledge: that if anything is so morally, e.g., if drinking is sin, it is so because conscience so declares. We could therefore check the solutions only if they were known to be either the deliverances of the patient's conscience, or, perhaps, in accordance with the deliverances of other people's consciences. But since we have not yet ascertained in our experiment whether *any* consciences exist, we can have no proper means of checking the solutions.

Two difficulties in this criticism may be suggested: (*a*) It is not so certain that conscience is conceived as the sole source of moral knowledge: it might be like an adding machine, which will do in its own way jobs which can be done just as well in a whole lot of other ways; (*b*) In any case, why would it not serve the purpose of checking solutions if the deliverances of everyone's xyz areas concurred?

To take the latter difficulty first: if the deliverances of everyone's xyz area concurred, it would be a very remarkable fact of human nature, but it would not in itself show that the content of such agreement was moral knowledge. If by some revelation we knew that we indeed have consciences as standard equipment, and knew that they would tell us the moral truth, but did not know in particular what this truth would be or which part of our standard equipment was our conscience, then given the other information we have supposed it would be a highly probable inference that the xyz area was the conscience, and that its deliverances were moral knowledge. But such a revelation is just what, when we are trying to prove the existence of conscience, we suppose ourselves not to have; and without it the required conclusion cannot be drawn.

Is it then, to come to the earlier difficulty, so certain that conscience is conceived as the sole source of moral knowledge? There are some uses of the term which however distasteful they may be would make no sense on any other interpretation—for example, what may be called the argument-stopper use. Discussions of what should be done are sometimes abruptly terminated by one of the parties saying things like "I don't care. My conscience tells me thus and so, and therefore any further discussion of the matter is either a waste of time or will result in sophistry and sin." Here at the very least a verdict of conscience is taken as more conclusive than any moral argument; and indeed rational discussion in such a context would commonly be thought to have nothing to do with genuine moral verdicts. It is the same with the persuasive use already alluded to. To say "I can only appeal to your conscience to see ..." is loaded with insinuation; but it would not do the job assigned it, were conscience not conceived, not just as one of the ways, but as the only way of settling moral questions.

It will not do to reject this point on the ground that these uses are objectionable, concerning which more later. It remains the case that the concept of conscience is such as to make them possible; and if we wish to stamp them out, this is more properly done by elucidating their unsavoriness than by tampering with the concept of conscience.

The demonstration here has so far been considered mainly from a conceptual point of view—the question has been "Does what the experiment discovers tally with what is conceived under the concept of conscience?" Lest this method appear too facile, we might briefly look at one or two of the mechanical difficulties in the experimental process itself. We must of course overlook any difficulties there may be in setting up the experiment at all—in examining a man's brain while he is conscious, detecting activity in the brain cells and correlating it with what he is conscious of.

There would be mechanical difficulties in the fact that the patient's paying attention to and reporting of his conscientious tremors would set up patterns of cerebral activity either not present or not prominent in ordinary cases of being troubled by conscience. A doubt would arise therefore as to whether the xyz area were not the brain's introspecting equipment. A similar, if more complicated problem would arise from the combined facts that (a) there are presumably at all times all kinds of activity in the brain cells, arising from sounds, smells, hopes, memories, suspicions, etc., (b) granting what it was suggested we ought not here to grant, that we know independently what is right and wrong morally, most people would produce correct verdicts on some of the matters posed them in the experiment, but incorrect ones on others, and (c) (shall I say it?) our conscience is supposed to be there functioning always, "If we would but listen," regardless of what we take to be its deliverances from time to time. The problem arising from (a) of picking out the cerebral agitations which were specifically producing moral manifestations would be immeasurably complicated by the (b) factor. We would not know whether to connect mistakes with activities of the wrong areas, like the fearing, imagining, desiring, etc., areas, all of which according to (a) would be active anyway, or whether to connect them with a malfunctioning of what we took to be the right area; and if we took the latter course we would not know how to detect, in purely neurological terms, a malfunctioning. Discovering that, for example, some of our grey matter has turned green is not like uncovering a dirty spark plug, because we can explain why the latter will make a car wheeze and sputter, while we have (as yet?) not the least notion why green matter should not produce judgments as acceptable as grey. But these difficulties pale beside (c), if the point is granted, because where the main tool of the investigation has been the discovery of correlations between brain agitations and contents of consciousness, if (c) is granted then there are very often brain agitations with no corresponding awareness.

As always with so-called mechanical difficulties, however, one can say that they are just difficulties, that with sufficient care and ingenuity there is no evident reason why they should not be overcome—identifying, for example, the brain's introspective parts or functions by carrying on separate experiments in introspection, devising ways of allowing for this, discounting that, explaining why green cells are not as good at moral decisions as grey ones, etc. Indeed if we assume (and why not?) that our brains are causally responsible directly or indirectly for everything we are aware of, it could not fail to be the case that we have a conscience, in the sense of a cerebral cause of the moral discomfiture, etc., we experience. But when it turns out to be as easy as this we see more clearly that the question whether we have consciences is not simply or primarily a problem in neuro-physiological explanation. We can be fairly confident *a priori* that anything we actually experience is explainable. But conscience is a concept including a lot more, as we have seen, than just the notion of an explanation of a type of experience; and it is from the further complexities of the concept that the difficulties arise.

IV

"Of course we have a conscience: it's our super-ego." Where the last argument consisted in outlining a programme for discovering conscience, the present case rests on some actual findings of the science of psychology, and so far may appear more promising. The story, in case it is unfamiliar, is very roughly that our psyche is divisible into three main parts—the unconscious, which includes desires, wishes, fears, anxieties and quirks, of which we are not ordinarily aware and which we would not confess to ourselves, but which affect our behavior in many and often devious ways: slips of the tongue, lapses of memory, shrinking from situations which we can see no reason for shrinking from, etc.; the ego, which is the set of our everyday purposes, plans, thoughts, desires, fears, tastes, etc., and the super-ego, which assumes a role of authority over the ego analogous to that of parent over child, and which represents all our tendencies to be stern with ourselves—to be careful, diligent, self-critical, remorseful, abstemious, etc.

The popular literature on the parts of the psyche tends to personify them, sometimes in a very colorful way, rather than regarding them as classificatory concepts. Walter Hollitscher [1] says: "In [melancholia] the most remarkable characteristic is the way in which the super-ego treats the ego. [The melancholiac's]

---

1. Sigmund Freud, An Introduction (Oxford Univ. Press, 1947), p. 72.

super-ego becomes a veritable tartar. It abuses, maltreats and humiliates the ego, threatens it with the direst punishments...." But when the pressure is off, "The ego gives itself up to triumph and ecstacy, as though the super-ego had been overthrown or merged with itself."

We need not attempt any settlement, either of the question of the general soundness of psychiatric theory, or of the logical status of its working concepts. If "super-ego" is simply a term used to designate a certain type of conscious manifestation, then the argument here is indistinguishable from our first proof, in which it was said, "Of course we have a conscience: it bothers us." But if "super-ego" stands for some behind-the-scenes force or entity producing this type of manifestation, then we can consider the question, "*If* psychologists have indeed discovered such an entity, have they thereby discovered that we have consciences?"

The points to be made here turn out to be all versions of points already made in discussing the earlier demonstrations, and can therefore be set out briefly.

(i) To say "My super-ego has been bothering me" does not convey the same information or express the same attitudes as "My conscience has been bothering me": (*a*) While the latter does, the former does not specifically assert that the worries are of a moral kind; (*b*) when one reports conscientious botherment it is understood that the distress is not regarded merely as a nuisance; while when we report super-ego botherment, no matter how doggedly the super-ego may persist in its activities, they are seen now with scientific detachment, as analogous to being bothered by bunions, a thing which, no matter how painful it may be, need not trouble one's conscience. Can one say, "The machinations of the super-ego need not trouble one's conscience"?

(ii) Try also substituting "super-ego" for "conscience" in the following sentences:

X is a man without a conscience.
It is a question of conscience.

His conscience won the day and he married the girl.
Always let your conscience be your guide.

(iii) Conscience is conceived as being morally infallible;
but there is nothing in the bewildering accounts of the origin
of the super-ego which gives us any grounds for thinking that
it is acting on authentic moral insight. It gets its authoritarian
attitude, we are told, from a process known as identification
with the father, or presumably with anyone who plays a like
role in one's life, regardless, mysteriously, of whether such person is an authoritarian type; but where it gets the ideals, or
whatever you would call them, concerning which it exercises
this attitude, is never very clear. If they too, as one might at
first expect, are derived from the parent, then whether they are
sound ideals will depend on what sort of a person the parent
is; but if they are gathered up from here and there, as on
reflection seems more likely, then their soundness will depend
partly on what is available here and there, partly on the kind
of discrimination which has been used or the kind of causes
which have been operative in the gathering up process.

In sum, the differences of meaning in uses of "conscience"
and "super-ego" show that we conceive them differently; and in
particular the conception of conscience as a source of genuine
moral knowledge not only is not, but could not be, instantiated
by the super-ego—whether or not it is true what they say about
the super-ego.

What we appear so far to have discovered may be set out
under two general heads.

(i) The senses in which conscience does and does not exist.
(a) Clearly we do experience botherment about matters conceived to be or purporting to be moral, and if conscience is
identical with such botherment, then it undoubtedly exists. But
most of our talk is as if conscience is not the botherment itself
but at least the agency causing the botherment. (b) In this
revised sense it is fairly certain that conscience in the sense
of some part or parts of the brain which have the job of nagging, chiding, wheedling, etc., exists; and (c) it is as clear
and certain as the findings of Freudian psychology that some

probably non-physical explanatory entity which could be in part identified with conscience exists. But conscience seems to be conceived, not merely as an explanatory entity, but as one which knows what's what morally, and there appears no prospect of either of the latter two explanatory systems accounting for this feature of it. (*d*) A sort of vicious circle is encountered in any attempt to justify a theory that conscience as a knowing entity exists, owing to the fact that it seems to be conceived as the sole source of moral knowledge, and there is therefore no independent method of checking its deliverances. (*e*) For this and other reasons the so-called inferential argument that, whether we can actually discover one or not, there must be consciences, fails. (*f*) In general, the existence of conscience in a sense full enough to account for all the uses of the term is unproven; but on the other hand, perhaps, its non-existence is equally not known.

(ii) The conception of conscience may be pieced together as follows: It is an agency causing certain conscious manifestations of a moral kind, and having the dual function of informing us what is right where we do not already know and of encouraging us on all occasions to act accordingly. Not only is it so constituted as to be morally infallible, but it is the sole source of moral knowledge. It is such that its effect can be obscured in consciousness by all sorts of psychological eventualities, but it is not itself distorted by such circumstances, and if it is there at all it is never completely inaccessible. There is some confusion as to whether we are all equipped with such a device ("If you had any conscience at all you would see . . ." could be, since no one likes to admit he lacks admired equipment, just a wicked persuasive tactic); and also, it must be admitted, about whether there are grades of conscience; "He has the conscience of a pygmy."

B

Our conclusions concerning the existence of conscience suggest the following problem: in view of the doubtfulness of its existence on the one hand, and the apparent confidence in its existence presupposed by so many of our uses, on the other, ought we to purify our speech by ceasing to use the term, thereby eradicating the confusions and false or doubtful beliefs which its use engenders, or is there some way of understanding the logical machinery involved, which will have the same effect while allowing us to carry on using the term?

The first point to be made surely, is that there are a number of things we want to say, which are handled very conveniently by the use of the term "conscience," and often not nearly so neatly and unpretentiously in any other way, and that therefore there should be no serious question of forswearing the word. If events have occurred such as would ordinarily occasion me to say "My conscience has been bothering me," not only is it graceless, instead of this locution, to describe the events in detail, but it switches the interest from the moral question to the pathos of my torment; while on the other hand most *general* characterizations we can think of sound pretentious, or disengaged, or are lean in content, or misleading. We could say "I have been bothered about the morality of my personal behavior," and this is perhaps the nearest equivalent; but it is colorless, slightly cumbersome, and does not specifically express, as the other way of putting it does, the continued acceptance of our involvement in the conscientious worries.

If there is no question of abandoning the conscience terminology, then the job is to find an understanding of the way it works which will dissolve the problems which its use so strongly suggests. It should be plain from what has been worked out about the content of the concept of conscience, as well as from the discussion of conscience's "existence," that in the ordinary way people using the term cannot be literally reporting or describing the behavior of such an agency. Whether a conscience is an area of the brain, a super-ego or an even more recondite phenomenon, we are not in a position to make reports on it itself. We cannot report, for example, that it turns green when it is a question of money, red when it is sex, and pink when it is politics, or that, oddly enough, it is very active when not on the job, but still and small when at work. Therefore the basic *sense* of our ordinary uses, what we are trying to convey or express, must be intelligible in terms of common experience; and we must be if anything using a fancy if not fanciful notion to express a plain meaning. We are doing, that is to say, the kind of thing we do when we say "Santa Claus was very good to me this year," or that a man with legs amputated does when he says his bunions are troubling him. What one means in the former case is that one received many fine gifts at Christmas; but to say this one trades on the public notion of Santa Claus as a giver of gifts at Christmas—without either meaning or being taken to mean that Santa Claus actually provided them. We mean: "What I found on Christmas morn was the kind of thing one *would* find if there were a Santa Claus, and if he was well disposed toward one." Similarly in the other case, what the legless man means is that he has been suffering just the kind of sensation one would experience if one's bunions were troubling him.

In using the term "conscience," we do not assert or pre-suppose the existence of things of its description—we pre-suppose only that the description is well known, and that working from this description people will understand what we mean, what we are trying to say. Not every use of "conscience" will presuppose the whole story about it, and therefore the pattern of analysis need not be identical in every case; but there is usually nothing in our words themselves which clearly in-dicates which part of the conscience is paramount, and it is left to the good sense of an interpreter to decide what is and what is not intended. ("Santa Claus was very good to me this year" could [since Santa is supposed to be generous only to good boys and girls], logically be interpreted in part as boasting that I have been a very good boy, but it would not usually be so intended or taken.)

Let us take some uses of "conscience" and in each case set out first the "plain sense" of the locution, and then the way the conscience story is used to convey this sense.

"*My conscience has been bothering me*" says roughly that I have been bothered in a moral way, rather than a prudential, aesthetic or some other way, about my personal behavior, and not about the behavior of other people, or about anything else which may be a moral torment. On the suggested analysis this message is conveyed by inviting people to imagine how one would be bothered by a mental agency whose function it was to inform us what is right and encourage us to act accordingly, and then saying "That's the sort of way in which I've been bothered." This may seem not quite a good enough account in cases where the botherment concerns past behavior, since conscience is represented in our analysis essentially as a guide to present behavior, but (a) in most cases where we say conscience is bothering us, there is a question of doing something now—paying an overdue debt, apologizing, making amends, setting things right; and (b) in cases where there is no such question, e.g., if I reproach myself for wronging someone now dead, one can at least say that conscience is trying to prevent the recurrence of such misdemeanors by keeping us well reminded of our sinfulness.

"It's a question of conscience" is used in two rather different contexts: (i) To distinguish the given question from a prudential or some other kind of question, and suggest that it should be judged by moral criteria. "Why did you tell the truth about the events leading to the accident, when there were no witnesses and a different story could have saved you a lot of money?" "You don't understand: it's a question of conscience." There are overtones also of piety in this usage, derived from a permissible expansion of it into "It's a question of whether one has a conscience or not"—but the main purport of it is conveyed by saying that if questions were decided by agencies, it is the kind of question which would properly be decided by no other agency than the one for deciding moral questions. (ii) The expression may also be used to say "It's one of those moral questions which everyone must decide for himself"; and here it trades on a different part of the conscience story, the part which pictures each one of us as equipped with an unchallengeable moral authority, in which state of affairs it would be a clear moral transgression to prevent this authority from functioning in its own sublime way. There is some confusion in this usage, because it suggests that there are some moral questions which people are not to be allowed to decide for themselves, and this is inconsistent with the conscience story. But if we can, as this analysis claims, use the concept *conscience* without actually believing the conscience story, then there is no problem, because it is only inconsistencies in what we believe, or offer as a suggested belief, which are objectionable.

"A *man without a conscience*" is a man whose behavior lacks any semblance of concern about morality, and the expression trades on the conscience story by asking one to imagine a man who, in a world so constituted that only by having a conscience, i.e., an agency ... etc., could one behave virtuously, didn't have one. Poor soul, he would be utterly lacking in virtue and do good or bad things indifferently without a tremor, wouldn't he? This usage explains the shock which is commonly felt at any skepticism about the "existence" of conscience. If conscience doesn't exist, then we are all "without conscience," and utterly amoral. This inference, of course, only holds within the conscience framework, the literal truth of which is rejected by such skepticism.

"*I couldn't with a good conscience do that*" says that there would be moral objections to doing it which would weigh heavily with me. This usage is more difficult to fit into the pattern, because contrary to the standard specifications of the concept, it talks as if there are grades of conscience, and in this it is in a class with talk of a "clear" conscience. Generally speaking the usages carry the same meaning, but the adjectives are not always interchangeable: "I couldn't with a *clear* conscience do that" is all right, but "My conscience is clear" cannot be changed to "My conscience is good." They could, it would appear, be changed into variations of the "conscience bothering me" usage, and analyzed in the same way: i.e., "I couldn't with a good conscience do that" seems to be equivalent to "If I did that my conscience would bother me," and "my conscience is clear" seems equivalent to "My conscience is not bothering me," etc. One can only suggest that the explanation of the confusion here is that some ambivalence exists as to whether conscience is the voice itself which we hear, or the owner of the voice. It is presumably not the case that a good conscience, like a good child, is one which creates a minimum of fuss and trouble.

"A guilty conscience" and "a bad conscience" present similar difficulties. Like an English monarch, conscience can do no wrong, and therefore ought neither to feel guilty nor be pronounced guilty, one would think. Perhaps a guilty conscience is one which re-iterates verdicts of "Guilty!" But "bad conscience" is more difficult. It is certainly not one which recommends bad things; but neither can one happily say it is one which pronounces verdicts of "Bad!"—mainly because "bad" is not much used in this way. Once again one must reluctantly suggest that the prime reference here is not to the agency but to its effects in consciousness, and that "bad conscience" is like "bad apple": it is a state of consciousness concerning morals which figuratively smells.

The uses we have so far considered are all in a very general sense fact-stating, both in that they appear or purport to state facts about conscience, and in that the sense of them is to report or make clear either the speaker's moral beliefs or attitudes, or something which he regards as a plain moral fact, as in "a man without a conscience," and this, by and large, without tendentious overtones. There is also a whole range of uses which, whether or not they are explicitly so conceived by their users, have the effect of ordering, advising, persuading and insinuating, and these, mostly because they tend to be used in a fact-stating fashion, are more difficult to analyze.

"*Always let your conscience be your guide*" in fact seldom appears outside fables and fairy tales, but it is the kind of thing which fathers, Polonius-like, might urge upon their sons, and is to this extent worth considering. The sense of this advice is less than unmistakable. Does it say, "You know what is right. Do not fail to be guided by this knowledge"?—or is it "Always do what you sincerely believe to be right, i.e., whether it *is* right or not—and you at least cannot be accused of willful wrongdoing"? The former reading would follow most naturally from the conception of conscience as a source of moral knowledge, and would trade on this conception by using "conscience" in such a way as to presuppose that the hearer had one; we wouldn't tell a one-armed man to hold a chisel with both hands. But (*a*) our analysis has been attempting to avoid any pre-suppositions of the actual existence of conscience; (b) one would think that in the supposed circumstances the advice would be unnecessary, since conscience is conceived as an agency which itself contrives most diligently to be obeyed; and (c) there is in any case a vacuous quality about the advice—it is like saying "To act rightly, always do what is right." To this extent the latter reading seems recommended. However it is not nearly so clear how it is to be derived from the conscience story, unless it is that if we had consciences, one of the main ways of telling whether an inner voice we heard was indeed the voice of conscience would be the test of sincerity: if there were lurking doubt, or if it seemed that we were willfully and groundlessly ascribing the voice to conscience, it would to that extent be unlikely we were right. Some doubts about this reading arise, however: (a) the sincerity test is not a very prominent feature in the conscience story, and therefore the use of its machinery is perhaps an unduly indirect way of conveying such a meaning, and (b) it is in any case a doubtful, if not curious piece of advice. It is true that after an unfortunate deed has been done, if we think the doer of it was at least sincere, we do not blame him so much for his folly; but surely this cannot be converted into before-the-event advice. Before the event what we need is advice about what things should be done, not about how we can protect ourselves in advance from criticism, without regard to what we get done.

On one account of it, to summarize, "Always let your conscience be your guide" is vacuous advice, readily understood if one knows the conscience story but presupposing in a way which we would prefer to avoid the truth of that story; while on the other it is advice which might tell us something significant which we did not already know, but which is perverse, and not especially aptly conveyed by the conscience machinery. There let us leave the matter.

"My conscience has spoken and I can only act accordingly" falls uneasily even into the very rough classification of uses we are now considering, but it is persuasive at least in that it is used to persuade people that an issue is not further discussable. In this case it does not appear possible to assign a

meaning distinct from what it appears literally to say: it would lose its force if the speaker were not taken to be reporting his belief that his moral knowing agency had indeed magisterially exerted itself and pronounced a verdict, which could therefore not be tampered with. One could say that the sense of it is, "I am quite clear in my mind about it and I don't care to discuss it further," and that this is conveyed by the conscience machinery in the way suggested in the last sentence. But this will not quite do: in this reading one is merely declining to discuss the matter further, while the original way of putting it offers a knock-down justification of this refusal. One could logically be "quite clear in one's mind" about something, but still think it reasonable to consider it further, in case there were features of it one had overlooked; but one could not logically deem one's conscience to have spoken and still consider the matter discussable. We must therefore consider this use either as a willful sophistry playing on the hearer's assumed belief in the conscience doctrine, or as a sincere expression of the speaker's belief in the doctrine and its applicability to the given situation. If this is the case, then since our analysis goes on the principle that in using the word "conscience" we are using a fancy idea, the literal truth of which is irrelevant, to convey a plain meaning, we must either abandon the analysis, or show that there is something wrong with using the concept in this way. The spadework for the latter course has in fact already been done in the first part of the paper. To use "conscience" in such a way as to presuppose that things of that description exist is to have been misled by the suggestiveness of the conscience terminology. We do not know that consciences exist, and if we did, we would have no way of being sure—not as sure at any rate as the present locution requires—that any given inner manifestation was a deliverance of conscience. Situations similar to what this purports to be do occur: sheriffs and army privates can say, "The court (or the colonel) has so ordered, and I have no option but to obey." But no point is made by purporting to act on the orders of an imaginary court.

This is perhaps the place for a brief mention of "conscientious objectors." Do we not, in respecting the position of the con-

scientious objector, show our belief in the existence of conscience and in the inviolability of its ordinances? The answer
surely is that our ways with conscientious objectors follow, not
from an acceptance of the conscience doctrine, but from the
political principle of freedom of belief. It would be contrary
to this principle to force any one to fight in a war if he had
sincere moral objections to doing so, and we therefore examine
people on their beliefs, not with a view to finding out whether
they are in fact the edicts of conscience, but whether they are
sincerely held, and not excuses or rationalizations for selfishness,
cowardice, or other qualities not enjoying the protection of any
social principle. What then is the appropriateness of the conscience terminology? Probably not either the sincerity feature or
the if-it's-conscience-then-it's inviolable feature, but that the
force of the use of "conscience" is to say that it is or is conceived to be a moral, rather than any other kind of question.
A conscientious objector is an objector on moral grounds. It is
the same as in "conscientious botherment," which is botherment
of a moral, rather than any other kind; and the same as one
of the readings of "a question of conscience," which is a moral,
rather than any other kind of a question.

"If only you would heed your conscience you would see ..."
is another case where it does not appear possible to distinguish
between the sense of what is said and the method of conveying
that sense. One might try as a reading, "[The moral point to
be made] is so obvious that stubbornness, selfishness, confusion
or something must be concealing it from you," and this indeed
is part of what is insinuated. But where to this reading one
could reply "It is not obvious at all, and there are good reasons
for doubting it, for example ...," one could make no such reply
to "If you would only heed your conscience...," and in fact
the peculiar odium of the gambit is partly that there is no
reply possible which is such as directly to further the discussion
of the given moral issue. One can take the remark seriously,
stop in one's tracks and start listening for thin small voices;
one can boldly claim that heeding conscience is exactly what
one is doing: one can carp at the insinuations of confusion and
insincerity; one can embark on a philosophical discussion of

the whole question of conscience, or one can just ignore it. The first response, to which we will return, and also the last, are not replies, and with the others one is embarking on discussions which are not discussions of whether to do this or that. Therefore the remark, if it is not ignored, either introduces irrelevances into a moral discussion, or it induces one of the disputants to stop in his tracks and listen for inner moral direction. This is the response which is most naturally suggested, and it may therefore be worth some consideration.

If I stop and listen for my conscience, particularly listen to see if it says thus and so, I may hear nothing, I may hear a reiteration of the position I had been taking prior to this juncture in the discussion, or "thus and so," or something else. In the latter three cases the same problem will arise: is my conscience, and nothing else, the author of what I hear? In one case I may well suspect it is just me, being dogmatic about my position, in another, that of course I would hear "thus and so," because that is what I was listening for, and in the mind there is no way of distinguishing between what you listen for and what you hear; and in the third case I might or might not have positive grounds for suspicion—what I would not have is positive grounds for asserting conscience's authorship. Lastly if I hear nothing, taking the conscience doctrine seriously as I here am assumed to do, I can only conclude that either I have no conscience or it is in very bad shape, and from thence perhaps decide to accept the verdicts of people who are apparently more fortunate in this respect. With naive people therefore, "If you would listen to your conscience" is a powerful gambit. It may have a variety of different effects, but they are all advantageous to the user of the gambit. The victim will either convict himself of dogmatism and from thence be more susceptible to suggestion; hear "thus and so" and take it to be that thin small voice; hear something else, hesitate to ascribe it to conscience, and convict himself of confusion and inconsistency; or hear nothing and think himself a moral freak.

To sum up, this usage seems, contrary to our analysis, to presuppose the literal truth of the conscience doctrine, but is not a proper exception to the analysis, because it can be shown to be

a misuse, not only in that it presupposes what we have argued
not to be presupposable, but because it introduces irrelevances
into moral discussions, and it unfairly plays on the naivety of
people to deliver them into the hands of a dialectical adversary.

"His conscience failed him and he voted conservative" and
"The reason I am a socialist is that I have a conscience" are
dissimilar in that one would perhaps be less likely to be reporting
known facts such as inner botherment in one case than in the
other, but similar in that they are ways of expressing certi-
fication of the rightness or wrongness of forms of behavior. They
are like the very general class of uses we have latterly been
considering in that they lose their peculiar force when translated
into plainer terms. To say "It is wrong" or even "It is certainly
wrong to vote conservative" or "I am a socialist because I think
it immoral to be anything else," does not quite do the same
job, because the rightness or wrongness asserted, or even the
certainty asserted, is still the speaker's opinion, and as such
can be freely disagreed with, whereas one can no more disagree
with conscience than with God. If conscience speaks, it is
settled. In speaking this way, therefore, one is transferring
responsibility for the moral points to an agency other than oneself, and an agency which, being conceived as possessing infallible moral knowledge is unchallengeable. It is like saying,
as a national news magazine is fond of doing, "The wise money
had it, at week's end, that X would be defeated by a narrow
margin." It sounds like plain reporting of the views of people
who, being wise, command respect, and as such any obligation
of the editors to defend the forecast is denied—while in reality
it is the expression of the opinion of the editors, since "wise
money" is, perhaps not always, but here to be defined as any
money which supports the editorial forecast. It is perhaps true
that neither with "wise money" nor with "conscience" is anyone
deceived by this type of gambit; nevertheless only where the
conscience doctrine is accepted, or where it is believed that "the
wise money" can be ascertained independently of what it is
bet on, do such remarks have their intended effect. Otherwise
they are merely read as what they are but do not purport to be:
an evasion of responsibility for opinion, and in the conscience

case, an attempt to enforce acceptance of a point of morals.

To conclude, the question whether we should abandon the word "conscience," and if not whether we can reach an understanding of its ways which eliminates the difficulties suggested by its use, has been answered by saying that there are many things we want to say which are very aptly conveyed by this terminology, and often only awkwardly by any alternative way of speaking. These fall into the general category of non-aggressive communications, reporting certain sorts of occurrence, making clear what we mean or how we see things; and to say these things we seem to make use of the popular comprehension of the idea of a conscience, of what functions it would perform, what differences it would make if such things existed, etc., without asserting or presupposing that there are consciences. But there are other ways in which we sometimes use the term, generally speaking aggressive ways, which do not fit the analysis in that they work only to the extent that they presuppose the truth of parts of the conscience doctrine. These, however, can be shown independently of any question of what they presuppose, to be objectionable uses, and therefore not genuine exceptions to the suggested method of analysis. This seems further to recommend the abandonment of any belief or suspicion anyone might have about the "existence" of conscience.

To return to where we begin, the idea of conscience seems to determine the nature of a moral philosopher's work in no other way than by providing him with jobs of the kind we have just been doing.

V

Freud's Theory of Moral Conscience[1]

DAVID H. JONES

FREUD is often assumed to have given an explanation of how human beings acquire a morality, especially as it is manifested in the phenomenon of moral conscience. Freud himself certainly lends credence to such an interpretation of his theory, as the following passage testifies.

Psycho-analysis has been reproached time after time with ignoring the higher, moral, supra-personal side of human nature. The reproach is doubly unjust, both historically and methodologically.... But now that we have embarked on the analysis of the ego we can give an answer to all those whose moral sense has been shocked and who have complained that there must surely be a higher nature in man: "Very true," we say, "and here we have that higher nature, in this ego-ideal or super-ego, the representative of our relation to our parents. When we were little children we knew these higher natures, we admired them and feared them; and later we took them into ourselves." [2]

Moral philosophers can hardly afford to ignore a psychological theory which purports to explain the genesis and function of moral conscience in human beings. This is so because the fact

---

1. This paper is a summary of a doctoral dissertation, "Freud's Theory of Moral Conscience," presented to the Department of Philosophy at Harvard University. I wish to express my indebtedness to Professor Roderick Firth, my principal adviser for his encouragement and criticism. My debt to Professor John Rawls will be apparent to all who are familiar with his analysis of moral feelings.

2. Sigmund Freud, *The Ego and the Id* (New York: W. W. Norton & Co., Inc., 1961), p. 51. For a similar passage see *The New Introductory Lectures on Psychoanalysis* (New York: W. W. Norton & Co., Inc., 1933), p. 95. After the first reference to a work by Freud, I shall make all subsequent references to that work by citing in the text only the title and page numbers between parenthesis, e.g. "(*The Ego and the Id*, p. 5)."

that a person has a morality implies the possibility of his suffering from a bad conscience. And it is this latter phenomenon,
the experience of suffering from one's conscience, which Freud
purports to be explaining by means of his theory of the super-
ego.

In this paper I wish to argue that the claim that Freud has
explained the genesis and function of moral conscience in human
beings is false. The reason why the claim is false is a very simple
one: Freud is not talking about moral conscience in his theory
of the super-ego. What one finds upon a close examination of
Freud's theory is that he often used moral terminology ambiguously to describe and explain *non-moral* phenomena. In particular, Freud often spoke of *conscience, morality,* and *the feeling
of guilt,* when he was describing such non-moral phenomena as
the *operation of the super-ego, repression,* and the *feeling
of anxiety.* It is this ambiguous use of moral terminology (which
Freud himself explicitly recognized) which in large measure is
responsible for the erroneous interpretation of his theory of the
super-ego. This interpretation in turn has often obscured the
correct meaning of Freud's theory and its relevance to moral
philosophy.

It must, of course, be *shown* that Freud's theory of the
super-ego is not a correct account of the phenomenon of moral
conscience. Consequently, the task which occupies the remainder
of this paper is to show that the phenomena discussed in
Freud's theory of the super-ego must be distinguished from
the phenomena which constitute a bad moral conscience. A bad
moral conscience is constituted by such moral feelings as shame,
guilt, or remorse. In order to simplify the exposition I shall focus
attention on the moral feeling of guilt. The conclusions reached
with regard to the feeling of guilt are equally applicable to the
feelings of shame and remorse.

Why should the moral philosopher concern himself with the
phenomenon of bad conscience? The answer to such a question
must be given in terms of what it means to say that a person
is morally sincere, or that he has a morality. If it is admitted
that a person can be both morally sincere and *fail* to live up
to his morality, then there is implied the possibility of his

having a bad conscience. That is, the *moral sincerity* of a person will show itself in the phenomenon of bad conscience when he *fails* to live up to his moraltiy.

What does it mean to have a bad conscience? I have said that it means to feel ashamed of oneself, to feel guilty, or to feel remorse. Such moral feelings constitute the phenomenon of bad conscience.

One can state the foregoing considerations more formally as follows:

(1) If a person believes that he has done some act X, and (2) if he sincerely believes that X is morally wrong, and (3) if he lacks an excuse, justification, or explanation, which would exculpate his doing X, then (4) his moral sincerity shows itself in the moral feelings of shame, guilt, or remorse, whichever is appropriate. Note that I am using the expression "morally sincere" so that it does not mean the same as "morally good." I am assuming that being *perfectly* virtuous is not a necessary condition for attributing moral sincerity to a person. "I acted against my principles" is not a contradiction.

The notion of the phenomenon of bad conscience is conceptually tied, then, to the notion of a person's being morally sincere. Obviously the moral philosopher must consider seriously the merits of any psychological theory which purports to explain the various phenomena of conscience. For this reason it is mandatory that Freud's theory of the super-ego be given a thorough philosophic scrutiny.

The paper is divided into the following sections:

I. The Problem: Some Freudian Puzzles.
II. Freud's Theory of the Super-ego.
III. The Nature of Moral Feelings.
IV. Conclusion: Freud's Puzzles and Moral Theory.

I. THE PROBLEM: SOME FREUDIAN PUZZLES

In this section I wish to draw attention to some puzzling features of Freud's psycho-analytic theories concerning moral phenomena. Freud claimed that his metapsychological concepts, especially his notion of the super-ego, were derived from clinical observation and a deeper insight into the nature of man's psyche. If we review briefly some of Freud's assertions regarding the nature of morality and conscience, I believe we shall come to feel that something is wrong. In fact, these puzzling assertions constitute *prima facie* evidence of the correctness of my thesis that Freud has used moral terminology ambiguously, and that he is in fact talking about non-moral phenomena.

(a) One of the more puzzling features of Freud's theory, to which he often gives voice, is that man (individually and collectively) would be better off if he were less moral, that is, if he were less subject to his conscience. From the inception of his theory, Freud often spoke of the conscience as being something basically undesirable, and even unhealthy.[3] After he developed his ego-psychology, Freud began to speak of conscience fairly consistently in terms of what he took to be the primitive and anxiety-producing function of the super-ego.

It is remarkable that the more a man checks his aggressiveness towards the exterior the more severe—that is aggressive—he becomes in his ego ideal .... It is like a displacement, a turning round upon his own ego. But even ordinary normal morality has a harshly restraining, cruelly prohibiting quality. It is from this, indeed, that the conception arises of a higher being who deals out punishment inexorably. (*The Ego and the Id,* p. 73.)

(b) Freud took obvious delight in repeatedly asserting that it was only with the advent of psycho-analysis that an amazing fact had come to light: the more moral a man is, the more he suffers from his conscience. In discussing the obsessional neurotic, Freud states that

Something of this is present in every normal person. It is a remarkable fact that the more moral he is the more sensitive is his "conscience." It is just as though we could say that the healthier a man is, the more liable

---

3. Freud, "Mourning and Melancholia," *Collected Papers,* 5 vols., trans. Joan Riviere (London: Hogarth Press, 1949), IV, p. 157.

he is to contagions and to the effects of injuries. This is no doubt because conscience is itself a reaction-formation against the evil that is perceived in the id. The more the latter is suppressed the more active is the conscience. (*Collected Papers*, V, p. 157.)

This "insight" gained by Freud into the phenomenon of moral conscience does indeed sound startling, since our ordinary view of the matter is just the opposite; on the ordinary view it is when a man *fails* to live up to his morality that he suffers from his conscience, not when he *succeeds*. Nevertheless, Freud seems to be saying that the more a man lives up to his morality, the more he suffers from his conscience. It is obvious from the context that Freud intended that the analogy with physical health be taken seriously. Hence, a "sensitive" conscience must be understood as one which causes discomfort and suffering. I emphasize this only because it might be thought that Freud was making a quite different point, i.e., that a man with a more sensitive (insightful) moral sense would obviously be more likely to suffer from his conscience. A person with a more "sensitive" (insightful) conscience would be more likely to recognize a failure to live up to his explicitly recognized moral principles. This is not what Freud has in mind, since by hypothesis the obsessional neurotic would *not* fail to live up to his "morality," and hence he would not feel ashamed, guilty or remorseful. When Freud discusses such obsessional "morality" in the normal person with its attendant suffering, he is not referring to the *failure* to live up to one's morality and the attendant feelings of shame, guilt or remorse. What precisely *is* Freud talking about in such contexts? This is the question I wish to answer.

(c) Another feature of Freud's views which seem strange is his claim that the aim of psycho-analytic therapy is to reduce the power of the super-ego (conscience) over the ego (*The New Introductory Lectures*, p. 111). This feature of Freud's view of moral conscience follows from (a), the alleged undesirability of conscience. It must, of course, be borne in mind that Freud equates conscience with the operation of the super-ego. We shall consider the justification for this equation later in the paper. At this point we are merely taking note of the familiar

Freudian pronouncements concerning the suffering of so-called "hyper-moral" neurotics. In order to alleviate the suffering of such patients, the physician must strive to make them less moral! Pronouncements such as this could not fail to arouse the apprehensions of any decent layman who might venture into Freud's theory to find out what it is all about.

(d) Freud's postulation of the unconscious also plays an important part in his analysis of the phenomenon of moral conscience. For our purposes, the most important result of this is Freud's belief that a person can feel guilty and not know it, or, as Freud puts it, there is an "unconscious sense of guilt." [4] This implies that a person can be suffering from a bad conscience and not know it. While this might not sound odd to a person familiar with Freudian argot, it certainly seems to contradict our familiar notions concerning the phenomenon of moral conscience.

(e) Lastly, there is in Freud's theorizing a tendency to conflate and confuse feelings of quite disparate kinds. The most serious confusion arises from the failure to distinguish adequately and consistently between what I shall call *security feelings* (such as fear, anxiety and dread) and *moral feelings* (such as shame, guilt, and remorse) (*Collected Papers*, IV, pp. 53-59). If this distinction is not made, then it is also very likely that often there will be a failure to distinguish prudential conformity and neurotic compulsiveness, from morally sincere action. This certainly seems to happen in Freud's theory of the super-ego.

We may summarize (a) to (e) by noting that Freud often writes as if he were committed to the following conclusions concerning the phenomena of moral conscience and moral sincerity:

(a) Being moral and having a conscience are undesirable.
(b) The aim of therapy is to make a person less moral (i.e., less subject to his super-ego, his conscience).

---

4. Freud, *Civilization and Its Discontents* (New York: W. W. Norton and Co. Inc., 1962), p. 82.

(c) The more moral a man is, the more he suffers from his conscience (i.e., the more a man lives up to his morality, the more his conscience bothers him).

(d) A person may feel guilty and not know it (i.e., there is an unconscious sense of guilt).

(e) There is no need to distinguish prudential conformity and neurotic compulsiveness from moral sincerity.

II. FREUD'S THEORY OF THE SUPER-EGO

In this section I shall give an exposition of those aspects of Freud's metapsychology which are relevant to gaining an understanding of how he could come to make the puzzling assertions about conscience outlined in Section I. This will require detailed discussion of some of the features of Freud's developmental hypotheses concerning the origin and function of the super-ego. In the course of this exposition, it will also be necessary to pay some attention to Freud's explicit statements relating to the nature of feelings such as guilt and anxiety.

Freud's own account of his theory of the super-ego may profitably be consulted. In *The New Introductory Lectures on Psychoanalysis* (p. 84), Freud observes that

The ego can take itself as an object, it can treat itself like any other object, observe itself, criticize itself and do Heaven knows what besides with itself. In such a case one part of the ego stands over against the other. The ego can, then, be split; it splits when it performs many of its functions, at least for the time being. The parts can afterwards join up again.

Freud then shifts his attention to one such function, the function of self-observation. He takes this function to be a necessary condition for the phenomenon of conscience.

There is hardly anything that we separate off from our ego so regularly as our conscience and so easily set over against it. I feel a temptation to do something which promises to bring me pleasure, into doing something against which the voice of my conscience has protested, and after I have done it my conscience punishes me with painful reproaches, and makes me feel remorse for it. I might simply say that the function I am beginning to distinguish within the ego is the conscience; but it is more prudent to keep that function as a separate entity and assume that conscience is one of its activities, and that the self-observation which is necessary as a preliminary to the judicial aspect of conscience is another. And since the process of recognizing a thing as a separate entity involves giving it a name of its own. I will hence-forth call this function in the ego the "super-ego." (*ibid.*, p. 86.)

In order to gain an adequate understanding of the *origin* and *function* of the super-ego, we must also consider four familiar and important Freudian concepts: The *Oedipus complex,* the process of *identification, repression,* and the *aggressive instincts.*

The *Oedipus complex,* according to Freud, is a stage in the normal "sexual" development of human beings. Briefly, it is the young child's erotic and affectionate attachment to the parent of the opposite sex, with a corresponding ambivalence of hate, fear, and admiration for the parent of the same sex. Though there are supposed to be wide variations in the process, Freud usually speaks of the Oedipus complex and its demolition by the process of identification in terms of the *male* child with a *positive* identification (*The Ego and the Id,* pp. 46-49). What is *identification?* It is, in the type of relation being considered, the striving of the boy to be like his father. Freud describes the origin of the Oedipus complex as growing out of the situation in which the young boy's erotic attachment to the mother and his "primary identification" with the father come into conflict (*The Ego and the Id,* pp. 46-47). According to Freud, in overcoming this threatening incestuous situation, the boy develops the rudiments of a conscience. In addition to the anxiety and tension produced by the ambivalence of his relation to his father, the child is also motivated to alter the Oedipus situation because of the unconscious fear of castration. It should be emphasized that Freud looks behind the scenes for unconscious psychic factors to explain the origin of conscience. The child develops a conscience in order to avoid emotional distress.

The way in which the Oedipus complex is overcome and the super-ego (conscience) is established is by means of a dual process consisting of *selective* identification with the father and a repression of the incestuous id impulses (*The Ego and the Id,* p. 49). There should be no mistaking Freud's conception of the nature of the process of repression which brings about the origin of conscience. *Repression* is a process automatically activated, and *wholly unconscious,* by which the ego avoids pain and distress, according to Freud. The young child's ego "sees" (because it is governed by the "reality principle") that the id impulses, incestuous in nature, will lead to pain (castration) and hence the id impulses are repressed (*Collected Papers,* IV, pp. 13-21). There is here no deliberation, reasoning or choice; there is only the bare "perception" by the ego of the threat of pain and distress. All the rest is automatic and unconscious, according to Freud (*Collected Papers,* IV, pp. 84-97).

We have now to consider Freud's view of how the super-ego functions once it has been formed, and how this functioning is supposed to explain what Freud wished to call the "morality" of the individual. As we have seen from another quotation, it was Freud's purpose to explain the "harshly restraining, cruelly prohibiting quality" which he believed characterizes "ordinary normal morality."

Freud believed that the punitiveness of the super-ego could be explained by the existence of the *aggressive instincts.*[5] He warned that as long as the child conforms through fear of an *objective* nature or a *real* threat of punishment, one should not speak of conscience, nor of the super-ego.

It is only later that the secondary situation arises, which we are far too ready to consider as the normal state of affairs; the external restrictions are introjected, so that the super-ego takes the place of the parental function, and henceforth observes, guides, and threatens the ego in just the same way as the parents acted to the child before. The super-ego seems to have made a one-sided selection, and to have chosen only the harshness and severity of the parents, their preventive and punitive function, while their loving care is not taken up and continued by it. (*The New Introductory Lectures,* pp. 89-90.)

---

5. Freud, *Beyond the Pleasure Principle* (London: Hogarth Press, 1961).

It is important to note that, for Freud, the only difference between the person who has a conscience on the one hand, and the prudential conformist who acts out of fear on the other, is to be found in the fact that conscience consists of *internalized threats* and *fears* to which the ego now unconsciously and unwittingly conforms. The aggressive impulses, which cannot safely be acted upon, now are "borrowed" by the super-ego in its function as the constant monitor of the ego (*ibid.*, p. 151).

We are now in a position to look somewhat more closely at some of Freud's puzzles concerning the nature and function of moral conscience with which we began. Recall that Freud often is found asserting that being moral and having a conscience are undesirable (and even neurotic), and that the aim of psycho-analytic therapy is to make the ego more independent of the super-ego. In addition, Freud often asserted that the more moral a man is, the more he suffers from his conscience.

It is of crucial importance that we consider Freud's description of the suffering and distress which he wished to ascribe to the morality of the individual. I shall argue that the feelings to which he referred are *not* moral feelings such as shame, guilt, and remorse. On the contrary, it will be found that Freud was referring to some form of *anxiety* (conceived of, in most cases, as being due to unconscious factors).

Let us look at what Freud actually said about the suffering caused by being "moral," that is, the suffering caused by the super-ego. He employed terms ordinarily used in moral discourse, and I shall focus attention on four locutions containing such terms: (a) "moral anxiety," (b) "the affect of guilt," (c) "the unconscious sense of guilt" or "the need for punishment."

(a) *Moral anxiety* (*Gewissensangst*).[6] The importance of

---

6. It will become apparent that my choice of the expression "moral anxiety" as the focus of attention is rather arbitrary, since Freud uses "tension between the ego and the super-ego," "anxiety of conscience," and "fear of the super-ego" in such a way that they are interchangeable. Freud's translators render the German *Gewissensangst* by both "moral anxiety" and "normal anxiety." See Freud, *Gesammelte Schriften* (12 vols.), Vienna, 1924-1934.

anxiety in Freud's theory is related to his view that the acquisition of morality is primarily the dual process of repressing dangerous id impulses (instincts) and instituting the super-ego which is invested with the energy of the aggressive instincts. Freud described the plight of the ego in rather melodramatic terms.

The poor ego has a still harder time of it; it has to serve three harsh masters, and has to do its best to reconcile the claims and demands of all three . . . . When the ego is forced to acknowledge its weakness, it breaks out into anxiety: reality anxiety in the face of the external world, normal [moral] anxiety in the face of the super-ego, and neurotic anxiety in the face of the strength of the passions in the id. (*The New Introductory Lectures,* pp. 108-110.)

Freud holds that the object of moral anxiety is not the external danger, such as the threat of castration or the loss of love (since these arouse objective anxiety, i.e., fear). Rather the object of moral anxiety is the danger of a *reappearance* of an earlier traumatic factor, "a condition of tense excitation, which is felt as pain, and which cannot be mastered by discharge" (*The New Introductory Lectures,* p. 129). The prototype of such a traumatic factor is experienced by the human organism at birth. However, Freud held that there are many other occasions when it may occur, such as during the period of "dependence in early childhood, the danger of castration in the phallic phase; and finally, fear of the super-ego which occupies a special position, in the period of latency" (*ibid.,* p. 122).

How then does moral (normal) anxiety operate? Freud's answer is perhaps too ingenious.

In the case of repression . . . the impulse is still part of the id, and the ego feels weak. In such a contingency, the ego calls to its aid a technique which is, at bottom, identical with normal thinking. Thinking is an experimental dealing in small quantities of energy, just as a general moves miniature figures about over a map before setting his troops in motion. In this way, the ego anticipates the satisfaction of some questionable impulse, and enables it to reproduce the painful feelings which are attached to the beginning of the dreaded danger-situation. Thereupon the automatic mechanism of the pleasure-pain principle is brought into play and carries through the repression of the dangerous impulse. (*Ibid.,* p. 124.)

Freud calls this function of the ego the "experimental cathexis" or danger-signal. It must be emphasized that in this process (just as in all repression) nothing like the presence of conscious deliberation or consideration of prudential reasons by the person is envisaged by Freud. Much less are there any moral reasons which could be called the person's motives for behaving "morally." The entire process is unconscious (in the pre-conscious part of the mind) (*ibid.*, p. 125).

Thus, *moral anxiety is an unconscious variety of anxiety* activated by completely unconscious "mechanisms." These mechanisms are related to the history of dangers, threats and conscious anxieties which the individual has encountered in attempting to gratify id impulses which were later successfully repressed. In many individuals who have a strengthened ego, these early experiences no longer pose as great a threat, but Freud seems to have held that no one is ever completely independent of his super-ego (*ibid.*, p. 123).

We may begin to see that moral anxiety is not a moral feeling associated with the ordinary phenomenon of bad conscience. For it is consistent with Freud's use of moral terms to say that (1) a person has *succeeded* in behaving "morally" (he has automatically acted at the behest of the dictates of his super-ego and in accordance with character traits which are reaction-formations), and at the same time hold that (2) nevertheless this person suffers moral anxiety (signals of danger) in the process. When Freud used such expressions as "tension between the ego and super-ego," "moral anxiety," and "dread of the super-ego" he was referring to anxiety which *causes* the person to behave in accordance with the pain-pleasure principle. It is precisely because the ego's use of moral anxiety has been successful that the person has conformed to the patterns of behavior to which his past experience has unconsciously conditioned him.

The moral feelings of shame, guilt and remorse, however, are appropriate only when a person has *failed* to do what he *consciously believes* is unworthy, wrong and immoral, not when he has automatically complied with unconscious threats.

With the foregoing considerations in mind we may now dispel

the air of paradox from Freud's assertion that "the more moral
a person is, the more he suffers from his conscience." For by
"suffering from his conscience" Freud did not mean anything like
"feels ashamed and guilty." Freud was not talking about a bad
conscience in the moral sense, but about an efficient "good"
conscience in the psychoanalytic sense. He seems to have had in
mind a model of the super-ego as a constant monitor of the
ego's every wish, impulse and fantasy. The super-ego (conscience) makes the person suffer anxiety (though perhaps only
preconsciously) in order to successfully keep him from satisfying his instinctual impulses.

(b) *The Sense of Guilt* (*Schuldbewusstsein* or *Schuldgefühl*).⁷ Freud quite explicitly held an affect-theory of feelings.
To understand this theory it will be necessary to consider briefly
some of Freud's assumptions concerning the biological and
neurological foundations of feelings.

Freud conceived of an instinct as being ultimately a somatic
process which may find representation in consciousness. Every
instinctual impulse may reach consciousness not only as an
idea, but also as an affect (*Collected Papers*, IV, p. 91). An
affect, according to Freud, is a combination or concatenation
of kinesthetic and proprioceptive sensations.⁸ He also seems to
have held that there are many different affects, each having "a
particular qualitative-tone," or dominant-note (*Collected Papers*,
IV, p. 92).

The most important affect, from the viewpoint of psychiatry,
is anxiety. Freud never went beyond bare generalities in his
attempts to *describe* the qualitative-tone of anxiety (*The New
Introductory Lectures*, pp. 113-114). Indeed, even though Freud
often mentioned the existence of affects with unique qualitative-
tones, he rarely went beyond the assertion that they exist. In

7. Both "Schuldbewusstsein" and "Schuldgefühl" were used by Freud
variously to refer to (a) the alleged affect of guilt, and (b) the unconscious
feeling of guilt or "Unbehagen" to which the title of *Civilization and Its
Discontent* refers. See Freud, *Gesammelte Schriften*.

8. Freud, *General Introduction to Psychoanalysis* (New York: Liveright
Publishing Corporation, 1935), trans. Joan Riviere, p. 343.

his later works he displayed a growing and understandable puzzlement concerning how one should proceed to study and classify affects. Sometimes Freud speculated that perhaps the qualitative-tones of different affects may be due to their different "origins" in the mental apparatus (*The Ego and the Id*, pp. 33-34). The favorite method which Freud employed to specify such an "origin" for an affect was, of course, to appeal to unconscious tensions and threats related to the individual's psychological development. Such a procedure was generally employed in order to account for the affect of anxiety which Freud believed to be caused by the "tension" between the ego and the super-ego. However, we must now ask ourselves how an *affect of guilt* could be identified by an appeal to its qualitative-tone, or by its "origin" in the unconscious.

Consider an example from Freud. In the course of the analysis of an obsessional neurotic, Freud explained to the patient why he was experiencing an "affect of guilt" which seems so foreign and exaggerated for the real situation.

> When there is a mésalliance, I began, between an affect and its ideational content (in this instance, between the intensity of self-reproach and the occasion for it), a layman will say that the affect is too great for the occasion—that it is exaggerated—and that consequently the inference following from the self-reproach (the inference, that is, that the patient is a criminal) is false. On the contrary the physician says "No. The affect is justified. The sense of guilt cannot itself be further criticized. But it belongs to another content, which is unknown (unconscious), and which requires to be looked for . . . ." (*Collected Papers*, III, pp. 313-314.)

The other "content" to which the affect belongs turns out to be (a few pages later) the repressed infantile death wish of the patient toward his father (for whose death some years later he now "blames" himself). The death wish, an aggressive impulse, is now turned upon the ego by the punitive super-ego (*ibid.*, pp. 316-319).

Now it is certain that while Freud did speak of an affect of guilt, he was actually referring to a *feeling of anxiety*. This interpretation of Freud's reference to an affect of guilt is justified, first, by his frequent equating of guilt and anxiety, and, secondly, by his even more frequent use of the expression "the sense of guilt," [9] which is not meant to refer to an affect with a peculiar guilty-quality, but to a feeling of illness.

Even in obsessional neurosis there are types of patients who are not aware of their sense of guilt, or who only feel it as a tormenting uneasiness, a kind of anxiety, if they are prevented from carrying out certain actions. Here perhaps we may be glad to have it pointed out that the sense of guilt is at the bottom nothing else but a topographical variety of anxiety; in its later phases it coincides completely with *fear of the super-ego.* (*Civilization and Its Discontents,* p. 82.)

In the previous section we have seen that this fear of the super-ego is what Freud called moral anxiety.

Freud expressed a similar interpretation of the sense of guilt present in what he called the "negative therapeutic reaction," that is, the clinical phenomenon presented by patients who resist recovery because of their unconscious need for punishment.

In the end we come to see that we are dealing with a "moral" factor, a sense of guilt, which is finding its satisfaction in the illness and refuses to give up the punishment of suffering. We shall be right in regarding this disheartening explanation as final. But as far as the patient is concerned this sense of guilt is dumb; it does not tell him he is guilty; he does not feel guilty, he feels ill. (*The Ego and the Id,* pp. 68-69.)

We may conclude that when Freud spoke of an affect of guilt, or the sense of guilt, he was actually referring to consciously experienced anxiety or distress which he, the *physician,* explained as due to an unconscious feeling of guilt or the need for punishment. Being the careful clinical observer that he was, Freud quite correctly pointed out that usch patients do not feel giulty, they only feel ill.

We have assumed that the feeling of guilt is not the same as the feeling of anxiety. This assumption will be argued for in the following section (Section III). At this juncture we need

---

9. Freud's translator renders both "Schuldbewusstsein" and "Schuldegefühl" by the English phrase "the sense of guilt."

only point out that it is the feeling of anxiety which constitutes what Freud calls the affect of guilt. Very likely "guilt" is employed in such a context only because Freud links it to the operation of the super-ego ("conscience"). We have already cast some doubt on his conception of the super-ego as an account of moral conscience. We shall now see that Freud's explanation of the nature of the unconscious feeling of guilt and the need for punishment also fails to make plausible his use of "guilt" in such expressions as "the sense of guilt."

(c) *Unconscious Guilt* or the *Need For Punishment.* That Freud was accustomed to speaking of the existence of *unconscious* feelings and affects can be seen in his earliest works. However, later he qualified the meaning of such an expression as "unconscious affect" by insisting that it refers only to a *disposition* to have certain consciously "perceived" affects in specifiable situations (*Collected Papers*, IV, pp. 110-111). Such a qualification was dictated in part by Freud's definition of an affect as a consciously perceived sensation or occurrent-feeling. Of course, the most important variety of unconscious affect for Freud is that which is being *repressed.* If a disposition to feel anxiety (for example) were repressed, psycho-analytic therapy would be required to actualize the disposition (so that the patient would come to feel conscious anxiety).

By far the most important of such repressed unconscious affects in Freud's theory is what he called the unconscious feeling (sense) of guilt (*Unbewusstes Schuldgefühl* or *Unbehagen*). It is the unconscious sense of guilt as a widespread phenomenon in the lives of modern men to which Freud referred in the title of *Civilization and Its Discontents.*

In view of his caveat concerning the dispositional nature of unconscious feelings, Freud introduced what he considered to be a less misleading characterization of the unconscious sense of guilt. It could, he said, more correctly be called a "need for punishment" (*Strafbedürfnis*) (*Collected Papers*, II, p. 163). Freud, however, did not abandon the alternative expression, "unconscious feeling of guilt," and one finds it throughout his works used interchangeably with "the need for punishment."

Let us look more closely at the phenomena which Freud

calls an unconscious feeling of guilt or the need for punishment. One such phenomenon is the negative therapeutic reaction which has already been discussed. Another kind of behavior which Freud attributes to the existence of an unconscious sense of guilt is what he calls "criminality from the sense of guilt" (*Collected Papers*, IV, pp. 318-346). Freud's discussion of this phenomenon also indicates the kind of need involved in the need for punishment. On Freud's view, a person may commit a crime in order to obtain mental relief or mitigation of a sense of oppression.

> ... such deeds are done precisely *because* they are forbidden, and because by carrying them out the doer enjoys a sense of mental relief. He suffered from an oppressive feeling of guilt, of which he did not know the origin, and after he had committed a misdeed the oppression was mitigated. The sense of guilt was at least in some way accounted for (*ibid.*, p. 342).

This passage is instructive in that Freud seems to be assuming the existence of a unique conscious affect of guilt. This assumption would make it plausible to say of the patient that he feels guilty but that he does not know why. However, in the immediately succeeding passage Freud makes it clear that, again, it is he, the *physician* who is attributing the feeling of guilt on the basis of other factors

> Paradoxical as it may sound, I must maintain that the sense of guilt was prior to the transgression, that it did not arise from this, but contrawise—the transgression from the sense of guilt. These persons we might justifiably describe as criminals from a sense of guilt. The pre-existence of the guilty feeling had of course to be demonstrated by a whole succession of other manifestations and effects (*ibid.*).

How do the transgression and the punishment bring relief from the unconscious sense of guilt? Freud's explanation of this point is not always clear; and where it is clear, it is unconvincing.[10]

---

10. For example, in *The Ego and the Id*, Freud states, "In many criminals, especially youthful ones, it is possible to detect a very powerful sense

Can we identify the phenomenon described by Freud as an unconscious feeling of guilt (the need for punishment) with the moral feeling of guilt? I think not. In the first place, a person who feels morally guilty does not need or seek punishment as an end in itself. If such a person seeks punishment at all, it is only as a means to, or a condition for, healing a breach in a moral relationship which his wrongdoing has damaged or destroyed. To feel guilty includes the dispositions to confess, to ask forgiveness, and to *accept* punishment as *deserved* or *justified*. Punishment may expiate a wrongdoing and thus relieve the feeling of guilt. But the end is the expiation, not the punishment.

This is not to deny that a person who feels deep moral guilt is depressed and suffers from "pangs" of conscience. But his suffering, unlike the anxiety which Freud discusses, is perfectly comprehensible to him and he knows what he must do to alleviate it. He must confess his wrongdoing, ask for forgiveness, make amends, accept whatever punishment may be involved, and so on. In addition, the person who feels moral guilt can explain his guilty feeling by referring to his belief that he has done some action for which he is responsible and which he believes is morally wrong. These reasons and belief are consciously entertained and known to him.

When we turn to Freud's psycho-analytic explanation of the unconscious feeling of guilt and the need for punishment, it becomes clear that he was discussing the anxiety due to the operation of the super-ego. The real (unconscious) "reasons" for the distress felt by the person are to be found in the history of the development of his super-ego. His present distress is due to the functioning of his punitive super-ego; he is said to

---

of guilt which existed before the crime, and therefore is not its result but its motive. It is as if it was a relief to be able to fasten this unconscious sense of guilt on to something real and immediate" (p. 71). This is not very plausible, but it is clear. The person who "suffers" from an unconscious sense of guilt is being punished by his super-ego. Such a person *needs* an objective, real punishment from the external world in order to make his suffering comprehensible, in a way which his neurotic, unconsciously caused suffering is not. The *relief* is supposedly obtained by finding an objective reference for an already present anxiety.

suffer from being too "moral." This is why Freud could say that the "guilt" (anxiety) was present *prior* to the transgression. As with the notion of moral anxiety, we must conclude that Freud was discussing only anxiety, not the moral feeling of guilt.

Thus we are left with the problem of deciding whether the feelings of anxiety and guilt are the same. Up to now I have merely assumed that they are not. In the next section I wish to present a general argument concerning the nature of moral feelings such as shame, guilt, and remorse. This argument is designed to show that none of these moral feelings is properly identified with the feeling of anxiety.

III. THE NATURE OF MORAL FEELINGS

I wish to argue that the moral feelings such as shame, guilt, and remorse are *generic dispositions* [11] and that the presence of these dispositions is explained by the *beliefs* and *interpretations* of the person of whom it is said that he feels shame, guilt or remorse. The most important result of this argument will be that neither the having of specific sensations and emotions, nor exhibiting certain kinds of behavior are necessary and sufficient for the correct attribution of one of these moral feelings. This conclusion will also establish the truth of the proposition for which I am arguing: The phenomenon of bad moral conscience is not constituted by objectless anxiety, unexplained tension, or dread nor by behavior to which such security feelings often give rise. A person is said to have a bad moral conscience because of his consciously entertained beliefs about himself and his situation, not because of the presence of specific sensations, occurrent-feelings or the presence of a disposition to certain kinds of behavior.

Many concepts which we have for characterizing human ex-

---

11. Gilbert Ryle, *The Concept of Mind* (New York: Barnes and Noble, Inc., 1949), p. 118. I shall adopt Ryle's distinction between disposition-feelings and occurrent-feelings for purpose of exposition.

perience and behavior are generic-disposition concepts. As Gilbert Ryle expresses it, they "signify abilities, tendencies or pronenesses to do, not things of one unique kind, but things of lots of different kinds" (*ibid.*). This is especially true of most of our *feeling* concepts. A person is said to *feel patriotic* not merely because it may be true that he tends to swell with pride when the national anthem is played, but also (perhaps) because he has a tendency to defend the foreign policy of his country when it is attacked, to buy government bonds, to fight inflation, and to volunteer for military service in time of war. Thus, many feeling-concepts include the notions of "feeling like doing" this, that, or the other kind of thing.

So it is that when we attribute the feeling of shame or the feeling of guilt to a person, we are attributing to him a highly generic, determinable disposition to do or to experience a number of different kinds of things. I shall use the feeling of guilt as the focus of my attention in what follows.

In attributing the feeling of guilt to a person, we thereby attribute to him a variety of *sub-dispositions* such as the disposition to have occurrent-feelings, sensations and "pangs" in specifiable situations, as well as the disposition to behave in certain ways out of typical motives. The presence of these sub-dispositions is made understandable by the consciously entertained beliefs which the person has about himself and his situation. He believes that he has actually performed some act which he sincerely believes is morally wrong and that he has no exculpating excuse or justification for having done so.

What kind of point is being made by asserting that these beliefs make the attribution of the sub-dispositions mentioned understandable and plausible? What I am suggesting (among other things) is that a person's "pangs" are not properly called *guilt*-feelings until and unless the beliefs of the person are assumed or known to be of the kind I have specified. For example, if Paul experiences unpleasant occurrent-feelings or sensations when confronted by Mary, there is no justification for asserting that he feels guilty unless it is assumed or known that he believes he has done something which he sincerely believes is morally wrong, and so on. That the confrontation with

Mary is the occasion for his "pangs" of guilt must be explained
by other factors. Perhaps she is the person whom Paul has
wronged. She may be known by Paul to hold certain moral principles, a fact which leads him to expect that she would hold
him in contempt if she knew of his wrongdoing, and so forth.
Of course, Paul may experience unpleasant occurrent-feelings
just by recalling vividly something he has done; there is no
need for a confrontation with another person. In either case,
the unpleasant sensations and occurrent-feelings are not properly
called *guilt*-feelings unless Paul believes that he has done
something which he sincerely believes is morally wrong, and so
forth. There is no way of specifying all of the situations in
which a person who feels guilty would be likely to actualize
the sub-disposition to have pangs of conscience, nor is there
any need for such a specification. In any particular case, the
attribution of a feeling of guilt would stand or fall with the
attribution of the beliefs of the person; the presence of these
beliefs is a *necessary* condition for the attribution of the moral
feeling of guilt.

In the same way, the presence of a disposition to exhibit certain kinds of behavior is correctly characterized as being due
to a feeling of guilt only if the person's beliefs are taken into
account. A person who feels guilty typically feels like confessing
his wrongdoing, asking forgiveness, accepting punishment as
justified and making amends. These are ways of relieving his
feeling of guilt, since they tend to re-establish a normal and
desirable moral relationship with another person or persons.[12]
His wrongdoing may have disrupted a moral relationship with
a respected authority, with the members of his immediate family,
with his fellow men in cooperative enterprises, or with his community as a whole by damaging an institution or practice. The
dispositions to action, along with the motives, which the many
kinds of wrongdoing give rise to, will vary accordingly. But

---

12. Varieties of moral relationships which can give rise to some cor-
responding varieties of guilt-feelings have been carefully analyzed by John
Rawls in his article "The Sense of Justice," *Philosophical Review*, LXXII,
July 1963, pp. 281-305.

these various kinds of guilt feeling are attributed on the basis of the beliefs which the person is assumed or known to have about the immorality of his conduct.

It must be emphasized that the presence of the dispositions to have occurrent-feelings, to exhibit the kinds of behavior for the typical motives cited, and the presence of the beliefs discussed above are not *criteria* by which one can infer that the person also possesses *another attribute,* the feeling of guilt. Rather, to feel guilty is just to be possessed of these dispositions and beliefs. The most important implication of this last consideration is that *the having or experiencing of an occurrent-feeling or sensation is neither a necessary nor a sufficient condition for attributing the feeling of guilt.* Thus, if anxiety is characterized as being objectless dread, felt tension or the presence of unpleasant occurrent-feelings, then the presence of anxiety is neither a necessary nor a sufficient condition for the attribution of a feeling of guilt.

The foregoing argument may seem to contradict the fact that we do say that a person *suffers* from feelings of guilt, and that the feeling of guilt is a *bad* feeling. This objection is answered by pointing out that the moral feelings of shame, guilt, and remorse do involve a *disposition* to have bad occurrent-feelings in a wide range of situations. The presence of such a disposition is a necessary condition for the attribution of the feeling of guilt. But, since it is only the presence of the *disposition* which is necessary, the actual presence of occurrent-feelings is neither necessary nor sufficient for attributing the feeling of guilt. Having granted that the presence of the disposition to have bad occurrent-feelings is a necessary condition for the attribution of the feeling of moral guilt, it must be remembered that it is not sufficient. For a person may have a disposition such that he would experience "pangs" of anxiety in all the situations in which it might be plausible to say that he feels "pangs" of guilt. It might be suspected that he does actually feel guilty. Yet, if he does not believe that he has done something morally wrong for which he is responsible (and so on), he can only correctly be described as feeling anxiety, not as feeling guilty.

The last consideration is important for assessing Freud's

theory of moral conscience. A neurotic may feel anxiety in a given situation where Freud (the physician) is prepared to explain the presence of the anxiety in terms of the unconscious. As we have seen, the person is said to feel ill, anxious, tense, and so on. It is in such situations that Freud speaks of *moral anxiety, a sense of guilt,* or the *need for punishment.* But the use of such expressions, borrowed from moral discourse, to describe the mere presence of anxiety, tension and dread is not legitimate, for, by hypothesis, there is nothing in the neurotics's beliefs (conscious or unconscious) which warrants the attribution of the feelings of guilt. The consciously experienced anxiety is explained by Freud in terms of his theory of the super-ego. But this is no justification for using the moral terminology, for we have seen that the super-ego is conceived of as being a constant monitor which prevents the ego from realizing dangerous id-impulses which have been repressed according to the pleasure-principle. And we have seen that neither the way in which the super-ego functions nor the process of repression involves any beliefs, moral or otherwise.

The correct view of the relationship between occurrent-feelings and the generic-disposition which is called the feeling of guilt seems to me to be as follows: the person himself *interprets* whatever occurrent-feelings and sensations he might experience as being "due to" his (generic-disposition) feeling of guilt. No matter what occurrent-feelings and sensations a person experiences, they can only be said to be *guilt*-feelings if the person himself *interprets* them in the light of his beliefs about himself and his situation. Of course, *others* may interpret his avowal of "bad" occurrent-feelings as referring to *guilt*-feelings if they attribute to him (correctly or not) the requisite beliefs. There is no mystery in this, since presumably the person himself would agree with this interpretation of his occurrent-feelings if he were asked about them, provided he really entertained the requisite beliefs. This is not the case with the anxiety-laden person who has a tyrannical super-ego. In the latter case, all that presumably can happen, according to Freud, is the undoing of the repressions by means of pains-taking psycho-analytic therapy. Such therapy would presumably bring to light factors related to past threats and dangers which have been operative on the unconscious level.

I have been assuming that there is no unique affect of guilt (with a specific qualitative-tone), the presence of which would justify the attribution of the feeling of guilt. The truth of this assumption is not essential to the main argument concerning the generic-dispositional nature of the feeling of guilt, since even if there were such a unique affect of guilt, it is still the case that the ordinary attribution of the feeling of guilt does not depend on the presence of any such presently experienced affect.

We can see why this is so if we ask ourselves how a person would learn to use the expression "feel guilty" correctly. A person learns how to use an expression correctly by noticing how people use it in characterizing themselves and others. The criteria for a person's having learned to use (for example) the expression "he feels guilty" will include his ability to explain the behavior of *others,* and to attribute to them the kinds of motives and beliefs which are considered essential to the feelings of guilt. So too, a person is said to know how to use "I feel guilty" correctly when he can interpret his *own* occurrent-feelings, behavior, and motives as being "due to" a feeling of guilt in the light of his moral beliefs. Of course, the person learns that others feel "bad" when they feel guilty, and he himself will often have experienced "pangs" of conscience when he has been correctly characterized as feeling guilty by others. But it is not necessary that he become adept at heeding and attending to his occurrent-feelings, sensations or affects in order for us to say that he knows how to use the expression "I feel guilty." For to learn the ordinary meaning of "I feel guilty" which I have been discussing, it is sufficient that a person acquire a social, linguistic skill which need not involve any phenomenological expertise whatsoever.

One can safely leave the phenomenological question open; whether or not there is a unique affect of guilt would leave the main argument untouched. If it were to be discovered that there are indeed unique guilt-feelings (affects), such a discovery could only amplify what we already mean by "feel guilty," and need not replace the ordinary, familiar meaning. This is so because the interest which human beings have in moral feelings depends to a much greater extent upon the dispositions to action which are intrinsic to them, rather than on the bare quality of the "pangs" suffered.

In any case, Freud is not warranted in speaking of a feeling of guilt on the basis of the presence of anxiety, tension or dread.

IV. CONCLUSION: FREUD'S PUZZLES AND MORAL THEORY

If the discussion of moral feeling in Section III is correct, then there seems little doubt that Freud often used moral-feeling terminology in an ambiguous way to describe such non-moral feelings as anxiety, tension, fear and dread. Freud explicitly admits this ambiguity in *Civilization and Its Discontents* (pp. 78-84), but his attempts at clarification seems to me to have failed. The effect of Freud's use of the moral-feeling terminology has been to blur, and even to obliterate, the distinction between moral feelings and security feelings. It is this confusion of security feelings with moral feelings which gives rise to what I have called Freud's puzzles concerning the phenomenon of moral conscience. I shall now reconsider these puzzles in the light of our discussion of the feeling of guilt in Section III.

(a) *Being moral and having a conscience are undesirable.* The psychological phenomena condemned by Freud are the anxiety, inhibition, and symptoms caused by the operation of what he called the super-ego. Freud certainly did not hold that it would be desirable if human beings developed *without* a super-ego, but he certainly felt that the effect of the super-ego could be, and ought to be, mitigated. He often and quite intentionally took the stance of the social and moral critic. His observations on the psychological "discontent" of civilized man, on the psychology of war, and on the need for reform in our sexual mores and for tolerance of socially controlled aggression attest to this. All these can be seen as landmarks on the tortuous

road leading man away from his reliance on irrational and op-
pressive psychological techniques for obtaining social stability.[13]
Such "morality" Freud judged to be undesirable.

Having granted all of this to Freud, we must reiterate that
being moral in the ordinary and familiar sense cannot be undesirable. For even if we suffer from a bad conscience and feel
guilty and ashamed when we do what we believe is wrong, it is
still desirable that we should be so constituted that we *are able*
to have a bad conscience. For we have seen that having a bad
conscience is the way in which one's moral sincerity evidences
itself when one fails to live up to one's morality.

Obviously, having a bad conscience and having the feelings
of shame and guilt are undesirable in one sense. No one would
recommend that people should deliberately do wrong *in order*
to suffer from a bad conscience. To actively seek oppportunities
to feel ashamed or to feel guilty is not a normal motivation, and
such behavior would call for an explanation. That is, in order
to understand why someone desires and actively seeks opportunities to feel ashamed and guilty, one must be able to attribute
some unusual or abnormal beliefs or needs to the person. Suffering from the "pangs" of conscience, feeling ashamed and guilty
are not desirable psychological states in themselves.

But neither is it desirable that a person should be without a
conscience, or that he should be shameless, or incapable of feeling guilty when he does wrong. We use the familiar expression
"You ought to feel ashamed," but we do not use it to mean
"Seek opportunities for self-abasement and the contempt of
others"! "You ought to feel ashamed" is properly directed to
a person who lacks insight and the appropriate feeling of shame
with regard to some shortcoming in his character of which it is
desirable that he feel ashamed. The person would be a better
person, one with more self-respect and pride in his moral worth,
and one motivated by a desire to do better in the future if he
were to feel ashamed instead of being indifferent and callous,

---

13. See " 'Civilized' Sexual Morality and Modern Nervousness," *C. P.*
II, pp. 76-99; "Thoughts on War and Death," C.P., IV, pp. 288-317;
"Why War," *C. P.*, V, pp. 273-287; and *Civilization and Its Discontents.*

as he now is. So, too, a person who feels guilty (and hence, a person who feels like confessing, asking forgiveness, accepting punishment, and making amends or restitution) is preferable to the unfeeling psychopath. This is only to make the point, previously mentioned, that it is more the *motives, dispositions, and actions* typical of the moral feeling which give evidence of the *moral sincerity* of the person, not so much the bad "pangs" and occurrent-feelings.

To the extent that it is desirable that a person should have the capacity to have a bad conscience, it is also desirable to be a morally sincere person. Being a moral person is not a state of disease; it is not a neurosis; and it is not something that needs to be treated or cured. This becomes clearer if we ask ourselves what is implied about the natural feelings and sentiments of a person who is capable of feeling shame and guilt. To be able to feel shame, a person must have a sense of proper pride, self-esteem and self-respect. For such a person there are limits to what are honorable and worthy ways of living one's life. To be able to feel guilty, a person must be capable of some form of fellow-feeling (love, affection, trust) or be committed to perpetuating institutions and practices shared with a community larger than himself (Rawls, *op. cit.*). Seeing man's capacity for morality as the outcome of such natural feelings as pride, love and trust certainly puts before us the prospect of a considerable degree of eventual moral agreement. This is not so when man's morality is erroneously construed as the result of a process of unconscious, irrational repression of antisocial impulses.

The contention that being a moral person is desirable and not a disease or neurosis should not be taken to imply that one cannot criticize the *content* (i.e., the values, principles, and ideals) of a person's morality. While it is desirable to be a moral person capable of suffering from a bad conscience, the person's moral *beliefs* are always open to scrutiny and evaluation. A person's morality may be based on prejudice, ignorance, and rationalization. Such a morality needs to be criticized and challenged, but the purpose of such criticism is to enable the person to adopt *new* moral values, principles or ideals. Obviously, no one is in a position to claim that only he has access to correct moral values, and that others must change their morality to fit his views. For this reason, the psycho-analyst or therapist should not confuse moral debate with therapy, even though in practice they are often very difficult to distinguish. The great danger is that genuine debates between two equal moral agents about moral principles will often be viewed by the psychiatrist as a contest between the rational doctor and the mentally-ill patient.

(b) *The aim of therapy is to make a person less moral (i.e., less subject to his super-ego, his conscience).* One can paraphrase this assertion and remain faithful to Freud's meaning by saying that the aim of therapy is to make a person less anxiety-laden, less inhibited, and less neurotic. This is precisely what Freud himself says much of the time. If he had not confused moral feelings and security feelings, he very likely would never have been tempted to formulate the more puzzling way of saying what he meant. One can even interpret Freud as envisaging the aim of therapy as an *increase* of those capacities which make possible moral sincerity and maturity. In Freudian terms, the goal of therapy is to see that the patient becomes more reality-oriented, with a greater capacity for love and trust; as a consequence, his actions will be dictated to a greater degree by the real demands of his social situation instead of by the need to avoid anxiety originated by the super-ego.

(c) *The more moral a man is, the more he suffers from his conscience (i.e., the more a man lives up to his morality, the more his conscience bothers him).* Once the proper translation of this assertion has been made, it becomes a tautology, but it also loses its paradoxicality. Hence, "The more a person suffers from anxiety due to the operation of his super-ego, the more he suffers from anxiety" is an analytic statement, and in this form Freud's puzzle disappears.

(d) *A person may feel guilty and not know it (i.e., there is an unconscious sense of guilt).* If the feeling of guilt is identified with anxiety, and if the psycho-analytic view of the cause of anxiety is accepted, then the assertion is indeed innocuous. For translated, (d) states that a person may experience anxiety and tension for the presence of which there is assumed to be a psycho-analytic explanation. However, I have criticized the view that the feeling of guilt is identical with the feeling of anxiety. If my criticism is justified, then one can never correctly attribute the feeling of guilt to a person on the basis of the presence of anxiety alone. In addition, I have criticized the appeal to the unconscious factors by which it is thought that the *physician* is warranted in speaking of an *unconscious* feeling of guilt, regardless of the patient's conscious beliefs. For the unconscious "reasons" appealed to do not fulfill the necessary condition that the person believe that he has done something which he sincerely believes is wrong, and so on. These criticisms are based on Freud's conception of what he erroneously called the unconscious feeling of guilt. I maintain that the history of the person's *repression* of dangerous id-impulses (instincts), however important it may be in explaining his present personality, does not account for that part of the person's psychology which enables him to think, feel, and act as a morally sincere person.[14]

(e) *There is no need to distinguish prudential conformity and neurotic compulsiveness from moral sincerity.* Freud does not anywhere explicitly assert this proposition, so far as I know. However, it is clearly implied by Freud's theory when it is not noticed that he used moral terms ambiguously in the way which I am criticizing. It should be recalled that I have adopted the expression "moral sincerity" to designate those beliefs,

---

14. There is a perfectly legitimate manner of speaking about an "unconscious" sense of guilt which both ordinary language and psychiatric usage often employ. I have in mind the situation in which the person is said to be unable to face up to his guilt, or that he is "running away" from his guilt. In such cases, the implication is that the person does actually *believe* that he has done something which is reprehensible, but that by rationalization or self-deception, he has avoided acknowledging his genuine moral guilt. By hypothesis, such a person does not yet feel guilty (hence the need to speak of "unconscious" or "unacknowledged" guilt), but he *would* feel guilty if he were to admit the belief that he has done something morally wrong. Such "unacknowledged" guilt must be distinguished from the phenomenon which Freud called the unconscious sense of guilt.

motives, feelings, and actions associated with having a morality.
I have focused attention on the motives, feelings, and beliefs
involved in the phenomenon of bad conscience, since it is
perhaps the most important criterion by which we ordinarily
distinguish moral from non-moral behavior.

I have tried to show that the "morality" which Freud discusses is the successful compliance of the ego with the dictates
of the super-ego brought about by automatic and unconscious
processes of repression and the production of anxiety. The
person with a "conscience" in the Freudian sense has merely
internalized threats and fears which are now self-administered,
so to speak. Where before there was the selfish, id-dominated
child, there is now the "moral," super-ego-dominated adult. So
far as I can discern, there is in such a conception of "morality"
nothing more than prudential conformity transformed into neurotic compulsiveness. However true it might be that this describes
accurately a good deal of the psychological development of
the human being, it is also just as true that it says little or
nothing about the capacity for moral sincerity. It might be
argued that the existence of something like the super-ego is a
necessary condition for development of the capacity for mature,
rational morality, and it is this claim which Freud seems, at
times, to be making. This weaker claim is not what I am challenging, although it could be challenged on different grounds.
What I am challenging is Freud's tendency to *reduce* morality
to what he calls the operation of the super-ego; that is, his
tendency to claim that morality is *nothing but* the psychological
phenomena which he describes and purports to explain.

It is with this purpose in mind that I have insisted upon
distinction between such moral feelings as shame, guilt and
remorse on the one hand, and security feelings such as anxiety,
fear, and dread on the other. Making this distinction enables
one to point out that Freud certainly does not explain the
phenomenon of bad conscience. A careful analysis of such other
moral phenomena as the feeling of obligation and conscientiousness would be needed to give a complete critique of Freud's
theory of moral conscience.

VI

The Notion of Conscience[1]

AUSTIN DUNCAN-JONES

I

NOWADAYS the word "conscience" has an old-fashioned, obsolete air. I shall try to guess at the reasons, and then I shall consider whether they are good reasons.

The traditional meaning of the word is well brought out in a famous passage of Butler's (*Dissertation on Virtue* I). "We have a capacity of reflecting upon actions and characters, and making them an object to our thought: and on doing this, we naturally and unavoidably approve some actions, under the peculiar view of their being virtuous and of good desert; and disapprove others, as vicious and of ill desert. That we have this moral approving and disapproving faculty, is certain from our experiencing it in ourselves, and recognizing it in each other. It appears from our exercising it unavoidably, in the approbation and disapprobation even of feigned characters: from the words *right* and *wrong*, *odious* and *amiable*, *base* and *worthy*, with many others of like signification in all languages applied to actions and characters: from the many written systems of morals which suppose it; since it cannot be imagined that all these authors, throughout all these treatises, had absolutely no meaning at all to their words, or a meaning merely chimerical: from our natural sense of gratitude, which implies a distinction between merely being the instrument of good, and intending it: from the like distinction every one makes between injury and mere harm, which Hobbes says, is peculiar to mankind; and between injury and just punishment, a distinction plainly natural, prior to the con-

---

1. The Bishop Butler Lecture on the Loveday Foundation, delivered in the University of Bristol on 19 March, 1954.

sideration of human laws. It is a manifest great part of common language, and of common behavior over the world, is formed upon supposition of such a moral faculty; whether called conscience, moral reason, moral sense, or divine reason; whether considered as a sentiment of the understanding, or as a perception of the heart; or, which seems the truth, as including both."

That there is something or other in most of mankind answering more or less to Butler's description seems probable. And Butler adroitly stands aside from the traditional controversies about the exact status of the moral faculty—the place it occupies in the general scheme of mental powers. But of those controversies I must say a little.

If we assume for the present that we recognize well enough the general feature of our minds to which Butler is referring, we find that there are three conventional doctrines about its exact nature: (1) that conscience is reason—the rational power of the mind exercised upon a particular subject-matter; (2) that conscience is something like a distinct mode of perception—a "moral sense"; (3) what is sometimes confused with the moral sense view, that conscience is a distinctive sentiment, or mode of feeling and desiring. Briefly, these are (1) the rational, (2) the perceptual, and (3) the emotional conception of conscience.

Conscience has often also been spoken of as a divine voice, a means by which God speaks directly to man: and this way of thinking is ancient, going back at least as far as Socrates' τὸ τοῦ Θεοῦ σημεῖον. But I do not think it need be regarded as an *alternative* conception of conscience; presumably it is a vivid metaphor, expressing the general relation between human and divine nature, and compatible with any of the three notions of conscience I have noticed.

These three notions, it will be obvious, are not mutually exclusive. I need not review their possible modes of combination, for my purpose is to consider reasons for being dissatisfied with them, or with at least two of them.

(1) By "reason" we mean the power to judge what grounds there are for accepting or rejecting a proposition. That includes, not only the making of inferences, but the apprehending of self-

evident or necessary propositions—"truths of reason." We usually assume that everyone who is not defective in some way
possesses this power in some degree or other: and that the possession of it does not depend on any particular type of environment. The reasoning part of the mind may, of course, be more
or less cultivated as a result of more or less favorable influences:
and conceivably in some highly inhibiting environment it might
not mature at all. If we suppose that the growth of a plant
may be more or less vigorous or stunted, according to stock
and soil and climate; but that its general pattern of growth
will always be the same—then we are assuming something similar
about human reasoning powers: that though they may vary a
great deal in degree of development, their form is essentially
the same in everyone (This is the kind of assumption Plato illustrated when he wrote the dialogue between Socrates and the
slave in his *Meno*).

There is a modern doctrine, that all so called "truths of
reason" are tautologies or analytic propositions. If that is true,
there must still be a distinct power of grasping tautologies: and
this power must either be innate—in the rather vague sense which
I have outlined—or acquired. And in fact—whatever our opinion
about the logical nature of truths of reason—we readily assume
that our power of grasping them is innate in the sense that,
as I have explained, the possession of it does not depend on any
particular type of environment.

Anyone who takes a rationalistic view of moral truths and
of conscience will probably reject that modern doctrine. And
he will hold that, if conscience finds out truths of reason, they
are general moral truths—general rules, or statements of ends
to be aimed at, or statements that certain general classes of
object are good or bad.

(2) The second theory was the moral sense theory. If conscience is perceptual it is concerned with individual situations:
it pronounces that a certain person, here and now, ought or
ought not to act in a specified manner—or that the act which
in fact he did was right or wrong. To think of conscience in this
way is to liken it to sight, hearing, and so on. We assume that a
certain range of perceptual powers is, with minor variations,

common to all normal people. A given person may lack a specific power, e.g., color vision, or all vision; tone hearing, or all hearing: and degrees of discrimination vary. But almost every person will have a fair number of those powers, with some degree of discrimination.

We also assume that these perceptual powers—and conscience if it resembles them—are innate, like our reasoning powers: we assume, that is, that possession of them does not depend on any particular type of environment—even though an inhibiting environment might prevent some power from maturing.

Rightly or wrongly, these assumptions that certain powers of the mind are innate seem to be bound up with another assumption—that they are on the whole *reliable*. This notion needs explaining. Of course, as everyone knows, we may make mistakes in reasoning; we may take a proposition to be self-evidently true when it is not; and we may misperceive. But I think what we assume is that, in the first place, more often than not we don't make those mistakes; and secondly, that by careful exercise of our faculties we can somehow make them correct their own errors. And anyhow, we have no other resources.

The common assumptions which I have been expounding may be false. I do not argue that they are true; but only that they are hard to get away from, plausible and not *patently* false.

If we hold that a certain power of the mind is on the whole reliable, that, of course, is not an *additional* reason for accepting its findings. I may judge that there are a certain number of people in this room, basing my estimate on what I can see. The general reliability of my perceptions is not a further reason, over and above my present perception, which backs up my estimate. The point is that there is no reason for *changing* our practice of relying on our own judgment.

I suggest, then, that if we regard a certain cognitive power as innate we also regard it as on the whole reliable. But if we regard it as not innate, we shall be ready to doubt whether it is reliable. If a certain feature of the mind is not innate, we assume it to be the product of circumstances—acting, of course, on innate dispositions; but innate dispositions which may develop in varied forms. We assume that if conscience is in that class it will be plastic, and highly responsive to outside influences: resembling our judgments of the sublime and beautiful, which vary so notoriously from age to age. And our doubts will be reinforced if we find that the causes of a certain cognitive power being what it is in a given individual are quite unconnected with any good reasons there might be for the propositions which he comes to accept. That, as I shall suggest shortly, is the position in which we now find ourselves when we contemplate the idea of conscience.

(3) The third kind of theory—that conscience is an emotion, or a tendency to feel and strive in a certain manner—is on a different footing. In that case what we arrive at, by consulting our consciences, does not consist of beliefs, which are presumably either true or false: and so the question whether conscience is reliable does not arise in the plain and obvious sense which it would bear if either of the other views of conscience were accepted.

I began by saying that the notion of conscience has an obsolete air. The reason is, of course, that we cease to think conscience important if we cease to think it reliable: and the assumption that it is reliable is very much out of fashion.

I think there are two main causes.

1. Anthropologists have shown—or seem to have shown—that there is almost endless diversity among the moral codes and rules which prevail in different societies: and that most individuals adopt as a matter of course the morality which prevails at the place and time at which they grow up.

In the sentences which immediately follow those which I have already quoted, Butler makes a claim which seems to us incredible. "Nor is it at all doubtful in the general, what course of action this faculty, or practical discerning power within us, approves and what it disapproves. For, as much as it has been disputed wherein virtue consists, or whatever ground for doubt there may be about particulars; yet, in general, there is in reality an universally acknowledged standard of it. It is that, which all ages and all countries have made profession of in public; it is that, which every man you meet puts on the show of: it is that, which the primary and fundamental laws of all civil constitutions over the face of the earth make it their business and endeavor to enforce the practice of upon mankind: namely, justice, veracity and regard to common good" (*D. on V.* 1.).

Admittedly the simple-minded interpretation of anthropological findings which I have given is open to question. It may be argued, and has been argued, that on certain matters, at least— murder, treachery, deceit, for instance—the amount of agreement between the moralities of dissimilar cultures is more striking than the divergence. It may also be argued that, when we find apparently incompatible precepts taught in different communities, they result from the applying of a common principle—e.g., the promotion of happiness—to diverse circumstances. I do not mean to reject these suggestions; but they are at least controvertible, and the opinion that there are genuine incompatibilities between moralities remains tenable and plausible. My purpose is, not to show that the considerations which have undermined the notion of conscience are irrefutable, but that they are at least worth taking seriously. If the findings of anthropologists are what I suggest, they lead to two conclusions about the nature of conscience. In the first place, conscience cannot be innate, in the sense that it cannot be a faculty which like color vision, or like the power of making simple inferences, appears in more or less the same form in all mature and normally developed people. Secondly, it cannot be reliable: and this follows, not only from its not being innate, but independently of any assumptions on that point, from the fact that different people's consciences deliver logically incompatible judgments.

2. Some psychologists, of whom Freud is the most celebrated, have claimed to show how the conscience of the individual is formed under the influence of his home and family. Here are some typical statements by Freud. "Conscience is no doubt something within us, but it has not been there from the beginning. In this sense it is the opposite of sexuality, which is certainly present from the very beginning of life, and is not a thing that only comes in later. But small children are notoriously amoral. They have no internal inhibitions against their pleasure-seeking impulses. The role which the super-ego undertakes later

in life is at first played by an external power, by parental authority. The influence of the parents dominates the child by granting proofs of affection and by threats of punishment, which, to the child, mean loss of love, and which must also be feared on their own account. This objective anxiety is the forerunner of the later moral anxiety; so long as the former is dominant one need not speak of super-ego or of conscience. It is only later that the secondary situation arises, which we are far too ready to regard as the normal state of affairs; the external restrictions are introjected, so that the super-ego takes the place of the parental function, and thenceforward observes, guides and threatens the ego in just the same way as the parents acted to the child before" (*New Intro. Lectures,* pp. 84-5). "Since it itself [the super-ego] can be traced back to the influence of parents, teachers and so on, we shall learn more of its significance if we turn our attention to these sources. In general, parents and similar authorities follow the dictates of their own super-egos in the upbringing of children. Whatever terms their ego may be on with their super-ego, in the education of the child they are severe and exacting. They have forgotten the difficulties of their own childhood, and are glad to be able to identify themselves fully at last with their own parents, who in their day subjected them to such severe restraints. The result is that the super-ego of the child is not really built up on the model of the parents, but on that of the parent's super-ego; it takes over the same content, it becomes the vehicle of tradition and of all the age-long values which have been handed down in this way from generation to generation" (*N.I.L.,* p. 90). An interesting anticipation of Freud's teaching on this point was W. K. Clifford's theory of the "tribal self." What Freud is expressing here is not a mere hypothesis, but a theory which is alleged to have overwhelming support from the clinical records of hundreds of cases. From this theory it appears to follow that the *content* of conscience—the precepts which an individual accepts—is derived from early impressions which vary a great deal from one person to another. There are, of course, innate tendencies or instincts upon which early training works: but they are almost indefinitely malleable, and may develop in almost opposite forms in different people. Moreover a primitive tendency may be deflected and distorted to such a degree that it becomes something like its own opposite. Freud has suggested, for instance, that "aggression" turned inwards may beget rigorous control of one's aggressive impulses (*N.I.L.*, pp. 136, 141-3).

In such doctrines as these, we find further support for the conclusion that conscience cannot be either innate or reliable. Not only do they support those conclusions, but they seem to offer an intelligible account of the way in which the conscience of the individual actually is manufactured by assignable influences.

If we accept such a doctrine as Freud's doctrine of the superego as a complete account of conscience, a further consequence follows. The process by which an individual is supposed to have imposed on himself a system of ideals and taboos strikes us as irrational: his morality is ill founded, and might as well be abandoned. It is not at all easy to say what "irrational" means in this connection. For moral philosophers are still disagreed as to the sense, if any, in which a system of morality might be *rationally* founded. But I think there is no doubt that we feel inclined to draw a conclusion which it seems natural to express in these terms—as though we find it easier to recognize what is irrational in morals than what is rational.

According to the rational or the perceptual notion of conscience, a deliverance of conscience is a belief, which must be either true or false. Our skeptical considerations may then be taken to show that conscience is unreliable, in the sense that the beliefs resulting from it are just as likely to be false as true.

According to the emotional conception of conscience, a deliverance of conscience is not a belief, and the question whether conscience is reliable does not arise in the same obvious way. Perhaps, however, a certain emotion might be a sign of a certain state of affairs. It may be that fear is sometimes a reliable index of danger. Similarly, perhaps a moral emotion might be a reliable index of the rightness or wrongness of some course of action. But it could not be if, as the arguments I have outlined suggest, there is great incompatibility between the objects to which different people's consciences attach the moral emotion: and if, as most moralists assume, an action right or wrong for one person would be right or wrong for anyone similarly placed.

2

I believe these skeptical considerations suggest their own antidote, though it may not be very potent. The findings of anthropologists and psychologists, if we interpret them in such a way as to discredit the notion of conscience, tell us how moral deliverances are produced in the individual by a process of which he is not himself conscious. But although he was not aware of these processes while they were going on, he may discover their existence and effects retrospectively, when he studies the findings of anthropologists and psychologists and applies them to his own case. He then has a new starting point for critical reflection upon his own standards of conduct. He finds (1) that some rule which he has hitherto accepted uncritically is at variance with other rules, on the same subject, which people at some other place and time have accepted uncritically: (2) that his own uncritical acceptance of his rule was very probably the result of the conditioning to which he was exposed by his home, his school, and so on, and would probably not have existed had he grown up under other conditions. And if he undergoes some form of psycho-analytical treatment he may also find, in the third place, that this last conclusion is not merely a deduction from generalizations; and that he can trace the history of the growth of his own moral preconceptions from stage to stage in his own life.

The mere act of viewing one's own assumptions as though one were a detached observer, and comparing them with those of others, is a big step towards the critical appraisal of them: and the discovery of their causes may be a further important step. How important exactly it is—that is a question I cannot answer without answering another to which I have already referred, and which is too difficult to be tackled now. That, of course, is the question what is meant by "good reasons" for a moral principle. In general, if we find that the causes of our forming a certain belief are not good reasons for it, we regard the belief as discredited: that is part of the normal process of discarding superstitions and old wives' tales. As I have said, we are strongly inclined to think that (for example) the training in hygiene which we received in infancy is not a good reason for any important moral principle: but our critical position is weakened here in proportion as we are in doubt as to what *would* be a good reason.

However that may be, we do in fact find that, after this cathartic treatment, we are in a position to reappraise the moral principles which we previously held uncritically. This does not necessarily result in moral nihilism, but in the adoption of modified principles which are held more consciously and reflectively.

When Butler spoke of a "reflex principle" or "principle of reflexion" the phrase was probably ambiguous. Part of what he meant was that, in the working of conscience, the mind turned inwards, reflexively, upon itself: and he also meant that conscience was a reflective or meditative faculty, that it acted by passing facts and possibilities in review, and reaching its verdict only after a train of thought; that it did not consist of a mere flash of impulse or intuition. As I have already shown, it did not occur to Butler that the findings of conscience might be highly variable from one man to another.

But if there is in fact the kind of variation in people's *naïf* moral findings which some anthropological and psychological teaching suggests, it is misleading to apply the name "conscience" without qualification to the power of producing those variable findings. It would be at least equally appropriate to give the name to the more critical kind of reflection which arises when we make allowance for the influences to which we have ourselves been subject, and by which our uncritical moral findings have—as may be held—been generated. Or perhaps we might speak of less and more enlightened stages of conscience.

At any rate, it seems clear that however fully the supposedly destructive consequences of modern research may be admitted, there is no reason whatever why moral reflection should stop. It may, on the contrary, be fertilized. One is tempted to say that the notion of conscience is destroyed, only to be reborn phoenix-like.

But I fear that whatever else I have to say must disappoint any who may be hoping for a rehabilitation of the idea of conscience. It seems to me that a good deal can be said about the mode of *reflection* on moral questions, but little that is satisfying upon the mode of decision. If a person is in a state of moral perplexity, there is a great variety of aids to reflection which he may use, any or all of which may contribute to clearing his mind and removing his perplexity. By "moral perplexity" I mean the state of someone who is uncertain how a given person should act in a given, or imagined, situation. Most commonly the given person is himself, and the situation is what he takes to be his actual situation: for then the perplexity is most urgent. But there is no formal reason why another person's plight, or an imagined situation, should not generate an exactly similar train of thought. (The notion of a special faculty, reserved for dealing with questions about *my* conduct, and not available when I consider questions about other people's, or conduct in general, seems to me superfluous; though I believe that is what "conscience" is sometimes taken to mean.)

I believe some of the classic theories of moral philosophers, whether they are well or ill founded in other respects, embody aids to reflection such as I have spoken of. For example, one of the most obvious aids is to ask oneself what the consequences would be of acting in a certain manner, or in another manner, or of not acting at all; and to compare those consequences: and, more specifically, to consider whether people in general, or people directly affected, are likely to be made more or less happy. Another such aid is to try to judge what someone whose character is taken as a pattern would do. Another is to contemplate the possibility that everyone might always act in such and such a way in situations of this type: should I welcome that state of things? Should I approve of a particular action of that kind by someone else? And if *I* acted in that way, what would other people think of me? These lines of thought might be elaborated almost indefinitely.

It seems to me that any of them may contribute to lessening moral perplexity, and that to think on such lines as these may properly be called an activity of conscience. When a course of action is resolved on without misgiving, that is a deliverance or as Butler would say "sentence" of conscience. But if there are many methods of reaching a decision, which do not necessarily produce the same result, does our attempted rehabilitation amount to much? Why should conscience be important if, even in this improved version, it is still capable of producing judgments which conflict among themselves?

3

Here, of course, we are touching on the basic problem of moral philosophy, which I have time only to mention without further discussion.

Is moral reflection an endeavor to find out a certain kind of truth—moral truth—which we sometimes succeed in finding out? If so, and if there are different modes of reflection, leading to conflicting results, it follows that there are correct and incorrect methods which we may use, and that I was mistaken a little time ago in saying that all the great variety of aids to reflection which I mentioned are equally serviceable. (I am presupposing that, if there *are* moral truths, they are to the effect that some way of acting would be right or wrong universally; that is, for anyone similarly situated.)

I cannot now review the arguments for holding or denying that there is a distinctive type of truth, consisting of truths of morality. But I should like to draw attention to a peculiar property which moral truths, if there are such things, must possess—the special relation between accepting a moral truth and acting on it. In any other matter, if I believe a true proposition for good reasons, I am so to speak doing all that can be demanded of me so far as that proposition is concerned. But if I accept a moral truth and fail to act on it, I am not: and my not doing so appears almost as a kind of logical absurdity— as though I accepted a proposition and denied its self-evident implications. I take this to have been part, though not perhaps the whole, of Butler's meaning when he spoke of the "authority" of conscience.

So I must conclude with an unsolved problem. I have argued that some supposed reasons for slighting the notion of conscience, though plausible, are not conclusive. Whatever we are taught by the sciences of human nature about the genesis of our uncritical moral promptings, while it must certainly lead us to scrutinize those uncritical promptings, will also help us to reflect on moral questions in a more critical and searching way. I maintain that if we think about our moral perplexities we shall sometimes solve them; that the effort is worth while, that a number of procedures have been described by moralists which help reflection; and that this kind of thinking may properly be called consultation of conscience.

But the important questions I leave open are whether, in every moral perplexity, there is just one right solution; whether, if so, it consists of the grasping of a moral truth; and what, if so, is the peculiar relation between a moral truth and the will, on account of which to believe and not to act accordingly is a kind of absurdity.

PART III

REASONS OF CONSCIENCE

INTRODUCTION

BOTH ordinary language and philosophical discussions indicate that the conscience is frequently construed as a *guide* in the moral life. Questions as to the manner of such guidance and the authority of the guide immediately suggest themselves. The difficult question of the infallibility of conscience will be postponed until Part IV. The former question—How does conscience function as a guide to conduct?—is our present concern. In "The Content and Function of Conscience," Bernard Wand approaches this question by examining the popular maxim that one ought always to obey one's conscience. Wand suggests that this maxim is to be analyzed as a hypothetical: "If anyone thinks he ought to do *x*, then he ought to do it." He then argues that the "ought" in the if-clause refers to the *content* of conscience, i.e., the ethical belief. However, the "ought" in the then-clause refers to nothing at all. It is an expression of the *function* of conscience, i.e., to insure behavior in accordance with the content of conscience. Wand argues that Broad's "intellectualist" analysis of "conscience" ignores its practical aspects: a man's conscience is not simply a collection of his ethical beliefs but consists, as well, in a disposition to act in accordance with those beliefs. He also argues that Ryle's "pragmatic" analysis of "conscience" ignores its cognitive aspect: being conscientious is not simply being regulated in one's conduct but involves behaving in such a way for reasons of moral conviction—reasons of conscience. Thus, conscience operates as a guide by co-ordinating ethical beliefs and regulated action.

In an article entitled "On Conscience," Martin McGuire argues that the conscience functions logically as a guide to moral action. Since the time of Hume it has been alleged that there is no justification for inferring statements about what one ought or ought not to do from statements of fact—statements about what is or is not the case. Recently, several philosophers and psychologists have asserted that a man's conscience consists of nothing more than his feelings about moral matters. On this conception of conscience there is no hope of discovering what one ought to do by consulting one's conscience, for mere psychological facts are neither reasons for nor against any course of action.

McGuire claims that the inference "My conscience tells me to do ..., therefore I ought to do ..." is thought to be invalid only because the locution "My conscience tells me ..." is thought to be analogous to "I feel ..." in the sense of, say, "I feel lonely." Actually, claims McGuire, the locution "My conscience tells me ..." should be considered analogous to "I feel ..." in the sense (which is quite a different sense of *feel*) of, say, "I feel his argument is inconsistent" or "I feel his equations are off." This latter sense of *feel*, which in the case of conscience might be illustrated by a statement such as "I feel it is wrong," *contextually* implies statements of the form "I think ...," such as "I think that his arguments are inconsistent" or "I think that his equations are off" or "I think that it is wrong." Thus, the feelings of conscience are not mere psychological facts, such as feelings of loneliness, for which no reasons can be given. They are rather feelings which suggest the existence of beliefs, for which, after due consideration, reasons could be found.

McGuire then considers a related question: How can a man's conscience be a reliable guide to what is right when it consists only of what a man thinks—albeit on the basis of reasons—is right? Surely, there is a difference between what a person believes to be right and what is right. McGuire's answer to this question depends on the logical privacy of conscience. McGuire agrees with Ryle's claim that a man's conscience applies solely to his *own* actions. Statements of conscience take the form "I feel (think) x is right; therefore, I ought to do x." McGuire argues that although there is a difference between what a man thinks to be right and what is right "in the first person, this distinction between subjective and objective vanishes ...." The conscience, then, is a guide to conduct.

John Donnelly's essay "Conscience and Religious Morality" traces the religious moralist's insistence on the role of conscience in ethical reasoning back to its source—the respective theories of Ockham and St. Thomas. It is instructive to note that for both Ockham and Aquinas, conscience is not simply an intuitive, authoritative censor of moral values, but instead a process of practical reasoning. Accordingly, conscience is not to be equated with any behavioristic account in terms of "acquired modes of reaction to stimuli," nor with "feelings of repugnance" (or conversely "feelings of approval"), nor with any occult voices of authority telling one wherein one's duty is to be found.

Taking as a paradigmatic case, the example of Abraham *qua* knight of faith, so ably described by Kierkegaard in *Fear and Trembling*, Donnelly anachronistically applies the respective theories of conscience of Ockham and Aquinas to such a moral dilemma (D): the puzzle being that Abraham *qua* father has a duty not to sacrifice his son, but Abraham *qua* knight of faith has a duty to sacrifice Isaac.

The Ockhamist would suggest that the resolution of (D) lies in the reasoning of conscience. However, Donnelly argues, the Ockhamist analysis is such that no solution is forthcoming. That is, the Ockhamist in defining conscience in terms of the will of God, as well as equating conscience with right reason (*recta ratio*), and moreover claiming that the two senses are intensionally equivalent, renders a verdict that Abraham both ought and ought not sacrifice Isaac! This analysis, Donnelly suggests, provides an "epistemic straight-jacket."

Turning to Aquinas' more sophisticated account of the reasoning of conscience, Donnelly argues for the novel thesis that St. Thomas had two distinct theories of conscience, one of which can at best provide a pyrrhic solution to the perplexity described in (D) (although it suggests interesting possibilities for a logic of moral forbearance); the other capable of providing a solution—albeit the infelicitous conclusion that Abraham ought to sacrifice Isaac. Donnelly maintains that Aquinas' basic triad of self-evident, moral propositions [The three propositions being: (1) "Evil should not be done"; (2) "The precepts of God's

will have to be obeyed"; and (3) "No injuries should be done
to anyone."] may be consistent (and indeed was intended to be
so by Aquinas), but, oddly enough, proves to be inconsistent on
the Thomistic analysis of the deliberations of conscience as applied to (D).

The Content and Function of Conscience

IT is scarcely possible that ethical theorists would have any subject matter with which to concern themselves unless ordinary men and women had consciences. Yet an analysis of the notion of conscience is not one which looms large in their writings. It is true that it has received passing mention in some textbooks [1] and even fair consideration in some rather recent general books on ethics.[2] In the main, however, the notion of conscience has been only a secondary or peripheral topic in writings on moral philosophy. Oddly enough, the two notable exceptions to this general observation have been written by philosophers whose primary interest is not in ethics.

The articles by Ryle [3] and Broad [4] on conscience are interesting not only because they interpret the nature of conscience in different and opposing ways but because they serve as pointed illustrations of two distinct philosophic approaches. This difference may be due not merely to a difference in philosophic approach and attitude; it may be due also to the selection for consideration of different features of conscience and conscientious action, so that each account, in its own way, is incomplete and abstract. Broad's intellectualist account focuses on the content of conscience, on the question of what a person ought to do.

---

1. Charles A. Baylis, *Ethics* (New York: Holt, 1958), pp. 80-90; Stephen C. Pepper, *Ethics* (New York: Appleton-Century-Crofts, 1960), pp. 178-181.
2. P.H. Nowell-Smith, *Ethics* (Baltimore: Penguin, 1954), pp. 260-269; Bernard Mayo, *Ethics and the Moral Life* (London: Macmillan, 1958), pp. 142-180.
3. Gilbert Ryle, "Conscience and Moral Convictions," pp. 25-34.
4. C.D. Broad, "Conscience and Conscientious Action," pp. 5-23.

Ryle's pragmatic account focuses on the function of conscience, the doing of that action which he ought to do.

I

The inadequacy of the intellectualist, Broad-type, analysis of conscience becomes explicit once the various senses of the words "right" or "ought" are considered. It is true that Broad himself does not explicitly make these distinctions in this particular article, but his analysis presupposes them, and he has made them elsewhere. Underlying the search for these distinctions is the assumption that matters of morals, like matters of fact, could be objects of belief and knowledge and that moral utterances were as capable of correction as factual ones. Given this assumption, at least three senses of "right" or "ought" are possible. If one had complete factual knowledge and unerring moral insight, then the morally appropriate act was called, using Broad's own terminology, "perfectly right." [5] If one had merely belief about the facts but one's moral appraisal was still unerring, then the morally appropriate act was called, again using Broad's terminology, "formally right." [6] Finally, if one might be mistaken both with respect to the facts and with respect to morality, the morally appropriate act in this situation was termed by Broad the "subjectively right" act. [7]

On Broad's view, if we consider the way in which the term "conscience" is used in a sense that can sustain analysis, to say that a person has a conscience is at least to say that he is capable of moral cognition but that such cognition can only be of the subjective rightness of an action. Thus by implication and also explicitly, he rules out the attribution of infallibility to conscience. [8] Which particular moral act is appropriate to a given set of circumstances can only be a matter of belief, al-

5. "Some of the Main Problems of Ethics" in *Readings in Philosophical Analysis*, ed. by H. Feigl and W. Sellars, (New York: Appleton-Century-Crofts, 1949), p. 557.

6. *Ibid.*

7. *Ibid.*

8. Broad, op. *cit.*, p. 16.

though, with luck, it may accord with either perfect or formal rightness.[9] But, of course, conscience is not a purely intellectual concern. Accordingly, part from his ability to reflect on the morality of his own actions, a person with a conscience is also capable of experiencing specifically moral emotions and of being moved to perform those actions which he believes to be moral. Moreover, the agent's moral belief, in serving as a motive, has the status of a cause capable of leading to the subjectively right action.[10]

Toward the close of his article Broad makes a remark which reveals that there is some sense of "ought" that cannot be explicated in terms of a person's factual or moral beliefs. Broad himself declares it to be a "very important sense of 'ought'" but provides no analysis of it. The sense of "ought" involved here is that in which, as he puts it, "it is true to say that a person ought always to do the alternative which he believes, at the time when he has to act, to be the most right or the least wrong of all those that are open to him."[11] It is the same sense of "ought" which is expressed by the sentence, "A person ought always to obey his conscience."

Although this sense of "ought" is readily recognized by those who adopt the intellectualist analysis of conscience, it is, nevertheless, totally incapable of this type of analysis. For whatever meaning is to be attached to it, it cannot be established by reference to a person's factual or moral beliefs.[12] It is readily conceded by Broad that this sense of ought is *always* applicable no matter how erroneous the agent's information, how incompetent his inferences, or how deluded or perverted his moral appraisals may be.[13] It is of course true, as Broad himself insists, that others may for conscientious reasons oppose him. If so, they ought, in the same sense, to obey their consciences by

---

9. "Some of the Main Problems of Ethics," p. 557.
10. Broad, *op. cit.*, pp. 7, 10.
11. *Ibid.*, p. 21.
12. *Ibid.*
13. *Ibid.*

restraining him from doing what he thinks he ought to do.[14] But this still leaves this sense of "ought" unanalyzed and independent of factual or moral beliefs.

The extreme to which the intellectualist may be put in his attempt to analyze this sense of "ought" is, perhaps, best exemplified by Ewing in his claim that moral utterances in which it appears are synthetic *a priori* propositions.[15] One could engage in a frontal attack on this view by bluntly insisting that the sentence "One ought always to do what one believes one ought" does not express a proposition at all but merely a command or a prescription. Or one could simply claim that whatever else it may express, such a sentence cannot express a proposition of any kind and, hence, certainly not a synthetic *a priori* one. But to adopt this type of approach would be to prejudice the issue. It would merely set one basic view of the status of moral utterances against another without engaging in an explication of the nature of *this* particular moral utterance. Nor, again, is there any *a priori* reason for rejecting synthetic *a priori* propositions out of hand. At the same time, however, it should be recognized that they ought not to be multiplied beyond necessity. Whether or not this particular sentence expresses a proposition may be left an open question, but, assuming that it does, as synthetic it should yield new information. But this it fails to do, and whatever necessity may be attributed to it is due to its being, in a propositional sense, analytic.

That one ought to obey one's conscience is normally considered a categorical proposition. Viewed in this way it is natural, perhaps inevitable, to consider the proposition as significantly connecting two distinct senses of "ought." However, it is really a hypothetical proposition which can be better expressed by the sentence, "If anyone thinks he ought to do *x*, then he ought to do it." The "ought" that appears in the if-clause refers to the content of one's conscience; but the "ought" that appears in the then-clause refers to nothing at all. It has a quite different

---

14. *Ibid.*
15. A. C. Ewing, *The Definition of Good* (New York: Macmillan 1947), p. 120.

function: it makes explicit the practical or regulative force of conscience. In short, it focuses attention on the function of conscience as a director of human conduct, and it does so by reminding the agent that to think oneself obliged to perform an act provides a sufficient reason for doing it. What is missing in the intellectualist account of conscience is its voice. The practical function of conscience as committing a person to action is really common to all three senses of "ought" and is not to be isolated as a distinct, unanalyzable sense. To point this out is not to provide additional information nor to fill in the content of one of our duties in the form of a distinct moral principle, but merely to make explicit that to believe one has a duty entails being morally bound to do it.

II

The inadequacy of the pragmatic account of conscience becomes explicit once one presses for reasons for conscientious actions. For Broad the belief that an action is right depends on the ability to cognize certain moral characteristics. For Ryle not only is it not a matter of cognizing peculiar moral characteristics, but it is not a matter of cognition in this sense at all. What is "known" is a rule of conduct, and "to know" a rule of conduct *is* to be regulated in one's conduct,[16] i.e., to be disposed to act, in the appropriate circumstances, in a certain way. Again, for Broad, moral cognition engenders the disposition to act. For Ryle, the distinction between moral cognition and moral action is an unwarranted one. According to him, "in one sense, and a very important sense of the word, my being 'convinced' of something or my 'knowing' it do not *cause* but *consist* in my tending to feel certain feelings and to enact certain actions,"[17] and what makes conscience authoritative and, in part, distinguishes it from mere moral conviction is its operativeness, its issuing in actions.[18]

On Ryle's view, conscience and conscientious action are

16. Gilbert Ryle, *op. cit.*, p. 28.
17. *Ibid.*, p. 33.
18. *Ibid.*, p. 29.

identical, but a conscious *appeal* to conscience occurs only when the disposition to act conscientiously is challenged by a disposition to behave in another way.[19] For the conscientious person now no longer knows how to behave. Furthermore, in so far as he is conscientious, a person can never be taken as issuing prescriptions or rules to himself. For rules are merely abstract descriptions or formulas of such behavior. Again, it is only when such behavior is interfered with that these prescriptions would be uttered by the agent to himself.[20]

This identification of conscience with a certain mode of behavior is open to a basic objection from which the intellectualist account is immune. Consider Ryle's own comparison between a skillful chef and an honest man. There are all sorts of reasons for becoming a skillful chef: love of cooking, love of eating, desire for reputation, love of money. Equally, there are all sorts of reasons for behaving honestly: desire for reputation, self-interest, the recognition that it is the right kind of behavior. In the case of honest behavior, only the last is a moral reason. It is only in so far as a person behaves honestly for moral reasons that his actions can be truly called conscientious. But the pragmatic interpretation of conscience does not enable us to decide what reason or reasons a person may have for acting in a certain way, particularly whether or not they are moral. To indicate that an act is an act of a certain sort, namely honest, is not to give a reason for it nor to indicate the agent's reasons for doing it.

Other, perhaps, more telling, criticisms arise with respect to Ryle's interpretations of the appeal to conscience in cases of temptation or perplexity. For Ryle to consult one's conscience "entails attending introspectively to (one's) conflicting dispositions to act," [21] one of which is an operative moral principle. Conscience, then, is merely a competitor in the conflict: neither a judge nor a referee. Elsewhere, Ryle depicts the morally perplexed person as one who does not know how to behave and

19. *Ibid.*, p. 29.
20. "Knowing How and Knowing That," *Analysis* 5 (1945-46), p. 14.
21. Gilbert Ryle, *op. cit.*, p. 30.

who bridges the gap of "know-how" by issuing prescriptions to himself.[22]

These descriptions of what is involved in cases of moral crises are, to say the least, perplexing. Surely the man who has been honest, who has been conscientious, knows perfectly well how to be an honest man. There is no point to filling up the gap in his knowing-how; he has lost neither his memory nor his skill. What such a person wants to know is *not* how to behave honestly but whether or not he ought to be honest. In cases of moral perplexity, he does not know what to do, and no amount of "knowing-how" will aid him. Normally, in appealing to our conscience, we presuppose that we will be able to act in the way it may recommend, but we would not expect to learn new skills from it.

Furthermore, to look at conscience as merely an internal competitor in cases of moral conflict is to deprive it of its authority. For the fact that conscience is operative is a test not of the authority of one's moral convictions but merely of their sincerity. What makes conscience authoritative is not, as Ryle contends, its operativeness, but rather that it constitutes the final or conclusive reason a person can give for performing an action. In short, a reference to conscience serves once again as a reason for acting, although this time not in a general way, as above, but rather in a particular moral crisis.

It is precisely the strength of the intellectualist account of conscience that it not only allows for, but insists upon, conscience's serving as a possible motive, or reason, for action.[23] For it does not matter, in this particular context, whether it is a belief or a rule that is taken as appropriate to the given situation. In appealing to conscience, a person is concerned with which rule he shall adopt, and this involves "knowing that," or, more accurately, believing that, a particular action is subjectively right. For this reason Ryle's analogy between skill in the rules of arithmetic and conscientious action breaks

---

22. "Knowing How and Knowing That," p. 14.
23. Broad, *op. cit.*, pp. 17ff.

down.[24] Although it may be true that skillful computation is roughly comparable to conscientiousness, it is not true that a breakdown in each is the same. The computer who through heedlessness makes a mistake simply attends to the rule that, when heeded, will remedy it. The conscientious person is not quite sure, indeed he is rather uncertain, which rule should be applied, and no amount of mere rechecking of the rules of conduct will aid him out of his perplexity.

It is probably correct to claim, as Ryle does, that "moral imperatives and ought statements have no place in the lives of saints or complete sinners." [25] But no human being is an angel, and, it is hoped, very few are complete sinners. Most of us, in times of moral crisis, particularly those crises which emanate from moral perplexity, must decide *what* we ought to do, not merely how to do it, and the appeal to conscience is one way of expressing the need for moral decision between different rules of conduct.

III

In any description and account of conscience two precautions are advisable: (1) an essentialist bias must be avoided, namely, that conscience must be one and only one thing and cannot be another; (2) an appeal to common sense must not be taken as the ultimate authority on the matter. For although it is quite true that an account of conscience cannot begin without such an appeal, it need not end there. There is no reason to hold that the variety of common-sense beliefs on the subject are necessarily compatible or that all are equally justifiable.

It has been said of conscience that it is fallible (Broad), that it is infallible (Butler); that its ultimate basis is emotional (Mill), that its ultimate source is rational (Rashdall); that it is the voice of God (Hartmann), or the voice of custom (Paulsen); that it is merely advisory (Nowell-Smith), that it is a command

---

24. Gilbert Ryle, *op. cit.*, pp. 31ff.
25. "Knowing How and Knowing That," p. 14.

internally imposed (Mayo); that it is conscious (Butler), that it is unconscious (Freud); that it is a faculty (Butler), that it is not (any contemporary moral philosopher); that it is the disposition to have certain beliefs, emotions, and conations which, when operative, issue in conscientious actions (Broad), and that it *is* conscientious action (Ryle).

It is fairly obvious that the truth of one of the members of each of these pairs of opposites entails the falsehood of the other, although, since they may be contraries, the falsehood of one need not entail the truth of the other. Moreover, it must be granted that all these positions have at some time or other found their justification in common-sense beliefs.

Although subjective conviction may often be confused with objective rightness and consequently lead to the view that one's conscience is necessarily infallible, it is clear that the conscience of each of us must be taken as always open to possible error. Otherwise we should, without further argument, have to concede the impossibility of holding to objective rightness even as a goal and admit that no conscience could ever be mistaken or capable of enlightenment. Although conscience has been interpreted as an external voice or command, it must be recognized that it is not always to be identified with such commands. If it were, a reference to conscience as a reason for action would preclude the possibility of personal, moral decision. For acting conscientiously would merely be doing what one has been told to do—whether by the voice of God or the voice of custom is irrelevant—rather than doing what one has decided was right.[26] However, if the context of the various moral utterances in which the word "conscience" occurs is examined, it can readily be seen that conscience does not always appear in this form. The utterance, "Let your conscience be your guide," provides evidence for such an interpretation; but the utterances, "Consult your conscience," and "It is a matter of conscience," do not. In this latter case, reference to conscience implies that the agent him-

---

26. P. H. Nowell-Smith, *op. cit.*, p. 263.

self must decide what the right act is, that in fact either no one can tell him or no one ought to tell him what to do. In depriving conscience of its externality but still insisting on its practical function, the claim has been made that conscience is a command issued by oneself to oneself.[27] But this is to strain the notion of command beyond its legitimate bounds, and requires a far too elaborate theory to explain the authority of conscience. To speak of the "voice of conscience" in a fashion that conveys the intent of the phrase without straining the way in which language is normally used, the notion of command must be abandoned. To speak of conscience as having a voice is to emphasize its practical function. This practical function can be preserved even though the content of conscience is identified with a particular belief about the morally appropriate act to perform in a given situation.

The assumption that there must be a gap between our moral beliefs (or reason) and our moral practice (or volition), which conscience, sharing the characteristics of each, bridges, has led to the traditional view of conscience as a faculty. It is doubtless for this reason that Ryle identifies conscientious action with knowing how. For, if they are identical, no gap requires to be closed. But this identification, as has been seen, has its own difficulties. At the same time, however, the intellectualist position is not immune from criticism, particularly with respect to the causal connection between moral belief and moral practice.

The two opposing types of difficulty are avoided once it is recognized that, in appealing to conscience, a person *by that very appeal*, is committing himself to act morally. Had he not already decided that he ought to do something, the appeal would never have been made. The attribution of moral responsibility to a conscientious person is warranted only on such grounds. The connection between the content and function of conscience, between moral belief and moral practice, is not causal, because, although distinct, these factors are not separable. They would

27. Bernard Mayo, *op. cit.*, pp. 170-72.

be separable only if what a man ought to do were externally dictated to him. But on the above interpretation an appeal to conscience is preeminently the attempt to determine for oneself what one ought to do in a given situation.

VIII

On Conscience

MARTIN C. MCGUIRE

I

It used to be that we were told that a man's conscience was an infallible guide to conduct. That is, it was held that one could gain certain knowledge of the moral value of an act from consulting one's conscience alone. It was as if the conscience had direct access to moral facts, facts of such a nature that only through his conscience could a man be apprised of them. The conscience then was characterized as a sort of magistrate, pronouncing verdicts that such an act was good or bad; but further, as a magistrate, it was thought of as issuing commands to do what it declared to be right and adjudging rewards for obedience and punishments for disobedience.[1]

More recently we have been told, in direct contrast to this picture of conscience, that statements about a person's conscience are nothing more nor less than statements of psychological fact, that is, statements that one has certain feelings—feelings, in this case, of obligation.[2] From this it follows, we are told, that no knowledge of what one ought to do is to be had from consulting one's conscience, for no judgment of value can be entailed by a statement of fact alone nor by any number of such statements. The conscience here is characterized as a feeling, and, although directed toward moral questions, it remains a psychological fact and nothing more. As such, the conscience is given a position close to feelings of loneliness or self-pity or grief, and perhaps also akin to hunger and pain.

---

1. Bishop Butler, *Sermons,* I, II, III.
2. R. M. Hare, *The Language of Morals* (Oxford: Clarendon Press, 1952), pp. 43, 170.

I wish to question those accounts of ethics in which the conscience is construed as consisting solely in certain psychological facts. The obvious fact that different men, each in consulting his own conscience, can and do arrive at exactly opposite conclusions about what they ought to do counts decisively against the earlier notion of conscience as an infallible judge of objective (i.e., public and communicable) right and wrong. Such theories now are held largely in discredit. The force of this fact, that men's consciences differ so widely, accounts perhaps for the extreme views now being offered. But to thrust the conscience into the realm of "mere" psychological fact, without further ado, is to ignore the important position that this conscience does as a clear matter of fact hold in the moral lives of ordinary people. Moreover, treating conscience in this way has obscured certain questions of importance in ethics, namely questions of the sort: "I know that this is the right thing to do, but shall I do it?"

If we are to speak of a man's conscience and of certain psychological facts in the same context, let us be specific about the facts to which we refer. The notion of conscience regarded as consisting in feelings is open to two interpretations. Such feelings might, on the one hand, be thought of as comprising remorse, guilt, and shame, or serenity and contentment. On the other hand, "feelings of conscience" might be construed to mean feelings of moral revulsion or attraction such as are evoked in their extremes by a brutal crime or an act of heroism. The differences between feelings of these two sorts are important. For we have been told that to say (1) "My conscience tells me to do ..." is really only to make a statement of fact, i.e., (2) "I have these feelings ...," and that consequently the inference, $(I^{(1)})$ "My conscience tells me to do ... and therefore, I ought to do ...," is invalid. This inference, $(I^{(1)})$ is invalid, because if, for (1) "My conscience tells me to do ...," we substitute (2) "I have these feelings ...," its equivalent, we arrive at $(I^{(2)})$, " I have these feelings ..., therefore, I ought to do ...," which is obviously not a valid inference, since from a statement of fact, such as (2), no judgment of value can follow. But is this reasoning valid? I propose to show that it is not. I propose to show this: there is an ambiguity in the meaning of "feelings" as contained in (2) "I have these feelings..." such that, if this expression is taken to be equivalent to (1) "My conscience tells me...," then the inference ($I^{(2)}$) is by no means obviously invalid. And if the sense of "feelings" is such that ($I^{(2)}$) is invalid, then it is not true that (2) "I have these feelings..." is equivalent to (1) "My conscience tells me...."

If the feelings referred to are those of guilt and shame, it is clear that such feelings arise only after a conclusion about the moral worth of the act in question has been reached. Therefore, it can scarcely be supposed that, in saying ($I^{(1)}$) "My conscience tells me..., therefore, I ought to...," I am wrongly basing the conclusion "I ought..." upon statements of fact, viz., "I have a feeling..."; for these feelings cannot have yet arisen. At most, one might try to imagine what feelings one would have if such and such a conclusion were arrived at. But the point is that, in this sense of "feelings" in which ($I^{(2)}$) is not a valid inference, to consult one's conscience is not to note one's feelings

It might be protested that, in the sense of "feelings" in which it is said that to consult one's conscience is to note one's feelings, the feelings in question are in no way to be taken as those of guilt and shame. What was meant by "feelings" in this case, one might object, was precisely the feeling that this was good or bad; what might be expressed after a thoughtful pause by "No, I don't feel that that would be right." There is a very good reason why we should refuse to call feelings of this sort "feelings of conscience" and why we should question any theory that claims that feelings of the two sorts are, in logic, equivalent. For the moment, however, I wish to question only the claim that feelings that such and such is good or bad, right or wrong, are nothing more than psychological facts, in the sense in which feelings of loneliness, for example, are psychological facts and nothing more. More precisely, I am interested in comparing statements of the form "I feel that that is wrong" with statements of the form "I feel lonely (sad, sorry for myself, etc.)", with a view toward deciding whether both ought to be placed in the same category and labeled "statements of psychological fact."

II

Clearly, in no ordinary sense do I have reasons to support the statement "I feel lonely." To say this is to say there are no reasons that *I have* for my feeling. To ask a man to justify a statement of this sort is inappropriate. And what of statements of the form "I feel that that is wrong"? Statements of this second kind are, in respect of their justification, different from statements of the first kind. The difference is important, but it is complex. To help clarify the difference I wish to introduce a type-statement of feelings of yet another sort, a statement which will be of value to us because of its relationship to "I feel that that is wrong." Sometimes, for example, we say "I have a feeling his argument is fallacious, but I cannot see where he has gone wrong"; or we say "I have a feeling his equations are off, but I can't find his error." The implication accompanying such statements is that, with further study or instruction one could find the error in logic or mathematics. I suggest that our moral sentiments are expressed in ways that resemble statements such as "I feel his argument is inconsistent" more than statements such as "I feel lonely." For to say "I feel that that is wrong" does seem to imply that reasons exist to show that it is wrong in just the way in which saying "I feel that that is inconsistent" implies the existence of reasons to demonstrate that it is inconsistent.

But what then is the difference between statements such as "I feel that is inconsistent" and "I feel lonely" on the one hand and "I feel that that is wrong"? Is it not this? To say "I feel lonely" is primarily to report a feeling, as saying "I feel a pain" is to report a feeling. Sometimes we make such reports of our feelings, evoked by moral issues, as in "I was shocked at the inhumanity of the thing." When we say "I feel that that is wrong," we do make such a report of a feeling, viz., the feeling "that that is wrong." But we do more than this. We mean also to make something like a claim; that is, we mean also to say something similar to, though not exactly like, "I think that that is wrong." In the case of statements such as "I have a feeling that his equations are off," the connection with making a claim is perhaps more clearly seen. Here, the feeling, the psychological fact that corresponds to the feeling of loneliness in the first case, is especially elusive. The point, however, is that these two elements, the one of statements such as "I feel lonely" (the psychological fact) and the other of statements such as "I feel his argument is inconsistent" (the claim), are both present in statements of moral feelings such as "I feel that that is wrong."

When a man says "I think that such and such is wrong," he must be prepared to support the claim with reasons. That is, he "contextually implies" that he can, if questioned, give reasons to support the proposition, "such and such is wrong." But when a man says "I *feel* that that is wrong," we cannot properly feel tricked when we find that he can give no such reasons (as we would properly feel if the person saying "I think..." could give none). A person who says "I feel..." (to repeat) does, however, imply that such reasons do exist or could be found, with further thought or study, and we should properly be surprised to find a man saying "I feel that that is wrong" who yet professed to believe that no argument could ever be found to support "That is wrong." The mistake implicit in the modern accounts is the assumption that, because I may not be in a position to say "I think that..." when I say "I feel that...," I therefore cannot be doing more than reporting a psychological fact, viz., my feelings. The line between thinking and feeling is not so unambiguously clear as presupposed. But why is it, then, if we cannot give reasons to support "it is wrong" or "there is an inconsistency," that we come to have the idea that there are such reasons? The answer to this lies along the following lines. When we make such statements as "I feel that his argument does not fit together," we refer to a structure that we accept as a means of explanation, a structure in logic or mathematics. Then there appears to be a way in which this argument or those equations do not fall into place within the accepted structure. This applies with equal truth to statements of the sort "I feel that such and such is wrong"; they are grounded upon the notion that to do such and such does not fit in with the structure of moral rules already accepted by the person making the statement. It might be thought that moral feelings, therefore, are of a special kind—that, unlike feelings of grief or pity or loneliness, they are in need of justification. But to think that would be to make a mistake. It is not that the moral feelings are of a mysteriously different kind; there are instances, indeed, when we do no more than report a moral feeling, e.g., "I was shocked." The distinctions rather lay in this: to say "I feel that such and such is wrong" is not only to report a feeling; it is also to do something quite different from reporting a feeling, something closely related to making the claim, "I *think* that such and such is wrong."

Now let us return to the argument that the inference $(I^{(1)})$ "My conscience tells me to do ..., therefore I ought to ..." is invalid since, if for (1) "My conscience tells me ..." we substitute (2) "I have these feelings ...," its equivalent, we arrive at $(I^{(2)})$ "I have these feelings ..., therefore I ought to ...," which is obviously invalid, since no judgment of value follows from a statement of fact. When we think of feelings in connection with our conscience, we may think of feelings of two sorts. We may think of feelings of guilt or shame, or we may think of the feeling "that such and such is wrong." The former case has been covered. Feelings of guilt and shame are indeed psychological facts, such that, if they were the feelings referred to in $(I^{(2)})$, this inference would clearly not be valid. But again, we are speaking in a context in which what my conscience tells me is presumed to precede my conclusion about what I ought to do, and, in this context, guilt and shame do not arise. Statements concerning these feelings, therefore, cannot be the equivalent of (1). If by "feelings" is meant the second possibility, the "feeling that such and such is wrong," it may seem plausible that to say "My conscience tells me ..." is equivalent to saying "I have the feeling that such and such is wrong." But if this is true, then the force of $(I^{(2)})$ is lost. For if to say "I have the feeling that such and such is wrong" is not only to report a fact but also to make a claim related to "I think that such and such is wrong," then the formula $(I^{(2)})$ begins to take on the appearance of "I think that such and such is wrong ..., therefore I ought to avoid doing it." Now, although questions of logic arise here also, it is by no means *obvious* that this latter inference is invalid. That is, although I might plausibly claim that (1) "My conscience tells me ..." and (2) "I have these feelings ..." are equivalent and although I might certainly deny that "I have these feelings ..., therefore I ought to ..." exemplifies a valid inference, I cannot *therefore* hold with reason that the inference "My conscience tells me ..., therefore I ought to ..." is invalid.

III

The first conclusion of the argument to this point was that, if there is any sense of "feelings" in which statements such as "My conscience tells me ..." can be translated into statements such as "I have the feeling that ...," this must be that of "feelings" as consisting of moral disgust or something similar. Now if it is true that there is this sense of "conscience," then the argument to this point may be taken as evidence *against* the view which holds that to pass from "My conscience tells me ..." to "I ought ..." is to attempt to derive a judgment of value from a statement of fact and therefore fallacious.[3] But is it not a mistake to associate a man's conscience with feelings of this sort, that is, with feelings of moral disgust, etc.? For to the extent to which such feelings are relevant to my judging whether *I* should or should not do a thing, they are equally relevant to my judging whether *you* should do it or not. But I wish to maintain that it is essential to our notion of conscience that a man's conscience has to do exclusively with his own acts.[4] We judge only ourselves by our own consciences. How then could those moral feelings to which we sometimes refer in making judgments, not only of ourselves but of others as well, be supposed to make up a man's conscience? Further, if one's con-

---

3. Webster's International Dictionary defines "conscience" as follows: "1. Sense or consciousness of right or wrong; sense or consciousness of the moral goodness or blameworthiness of one's own conduct, intentions, or character, together with a feeling of obligation to do or be that which is recognized as good;—often with special reference to feelings of guilt or remorse for ill-doing. Hence, a faculty, power, or principle, conceived to decide as to the moral quality of one's own thoughts or acts, enjoining what is good ...."

4. See G. Ryle, "Conscience and Moral Convictions," pp. 25-34.

science is concerned solely with one's own conduct, how could this conscience possibly pronounce on the *morality* (which is public) of an act? Given that I conceive of my conscience as concerned solely with my own acts, can I, without inconsistency, hold that my conscience informs me of the rightness or wrongness of an act? The judgment, "That is wrong" or "To do that would be wrong," surely carries the implication that for anyone in similar circumstances it would be wrong—the implication, in current terminology, of "universalizibility." Because we have at the center of our notion of conscience the idea that the conscience applies solely to the acts of the owner of that conscience, a man's conscience cannot tell him with authority, "That *is* right (wrong)." A man's conscience, in virtue of its peculiar relation to that man, cannot be thought of as a judge of objective right or wrong. Neither, then, is the conscience a magistrate over moral issues, nor is it the sort of feeling from which judgments of good and evil might be thought to follow. (From this point on the meaning of "conscience" will be restricted so as to have to do only with one's own acts. Further mention of the conscience, therefore, should *not* be taken as referring to the "feeling that such and such is right [wrong]," as has hitherto been possible.)

The broad outlines of our concept of conscience remain to be drawn. We have seen that the conscience is not a special unerring faculty for making ethical judgments. We have not excluded the possibility that statements making reference to the conscience are reports of psychological fact. We have excluded only the case where a person *both* does nothing more than refer to such facts *and* claims to have knowledge of the rightness or wrongness of an act on the basis of those facts alone. In the central case, I believe, we can say that one's conscience is a sanction against doing what *one believes to be wrong*, under the threat of feelings of guilt. That is, the conscience directs, "Do what you believe to be right." Or, more generally, a man's conscience tells him, "Do good, avoid evil." The province of conscience in the Moral Life may be clarified in the argument which follows.

I take it as an analytic truth that all cases in which questions of feelings of guilt arise are cases in which there is a question of acting contrary to one's conscience and that all cases of the latter are cases of the former. Further, it is, as a matter of fact *and* of logic, true that questions of guilt or shame arise only in cases in which the agent believes the act to be wrong. That is, the moral worth that I judge a thing or an act to have is logically prior to any feelings in the nature of guilt or shame. It remains to be shown how, in the individual case, it comes about that a person's regard for the moral worth of an act is prior to any feelings of guilt or shame that might be associated with the act. Let us first note, however, that from the above account of the matter it follows (1) that all the cases in which there is a question of acting contrary to one's conscience are cases in which the agent believes the act to be wrong, and (2) that some of the cases in which a person believes a thing to be wrong or holds a thing in disapproval are cases in which the question of acting contrary to one's conscience arises. To account for the conscience in this way allows for the possibility that a man's actions are frequently in conflict with his beliefs, when he yet claims sincerely to believe that what he does is wrong. The above argument is stated also so as to allow for feelings of "guilt anticipated," so to speak, which might occur before a decision is made about what to do, feelings which, for example, one might have in considering a dishonest act and which might lead one to say, "No, I can't do that." What exactly the status of feelings of this sort may be need not detain us. The point here is that such feelings of guilt cannot arise until after a judgment of moral worth has been made. Whether it is decided to accord those feelings which might occur before a decision to act after the corresponding judgment of value the same status as those feelings which might occur after both the judgment and the decision have been made, will not affect the validity of the account of conscience given to this point.

Let us now consider, in general terms, the way in which we acquire dispositions to have feelings of guilt and the way in which we learn the concept of "guilt." Clearly, we do not learn to have feelings of guilt in the way in which we learn so many other things, namely, by imitating our elders. We do of course learn to call this particular sort of feeling by the name "guilt"; that is, we are taught the concept of "guilt." But the feeling itself is what one might call an unlearned or natural or spontaneous reaction. As children we did not observe our parents feeling guilty and try to copy them; being ashamed, feeling guilty, etc., were natural, unlearned responses to certain situations. The notion, once widely held, that the conscience is "inborn" was not entirely without point; for it is true that the feeling of guilt is not a feeling that we learn to have (this is true as a matter of fact). It is, however, equally clear that we are instructed about when to be ashamed, that, in general, we are taught to be ashamed only of those things of which our parents disapprove, and that we learn to disapprove of or label "bad" or "wrong" only those things of which we are taught to be ashamed. This is not by accident. Part of learning that such and such a thing is bad or wrong is to learn that I am to be ashamed of doing it (This is a matter of logic). We do not learn that we are to be ashamed solely on the basis that our elders disapprove, but on the bases that they disapprove *and* that such and such a thing is bad, naughty, etc. That is, an integral part of our learning to be ashamed here and now is that we learn to disapprove (This is a matter of imitation). Because of the way in which we come to have, on the one hand, dispositions toward having feelings of guilt and, on the other, attitudes of disapproval and the concepts of "right" and "wrong," we do not experience feelings of guilt except in those cases in which the action in question is one of which we disapprove or which we believe to be wrong. One cannot claim, therefore, both that a thing is or would be the right thing to do and that one's conscience tells one to refrain from doing it (This conclusion is true as a matter of fact and of logic). For as we learn under what circumstances to feel guilt or shame, we learn corresponding values. If one concludes that a thing is bad or wrong, one's conscience advises one against doing it. To say this is to say that the conscience, rather than an innate faculty for perceiving objective right and wrong, is a guide to conduct, exhorting its owner to do what he believes to be right, under the threat of a guilty conscience. Although it was a mistake to think of a man's conscience as an innate faculty, to fail to recognize the fundamental place it occupies in a man's life is to make a mistake of equal proportions. Indeed my conscience does in a way tell me, "Do X because it is right" (the emphasis being on "right" rather than on "is"), but this is not to say that my conscience gives me independent information about the moral worth of an act or thing. (The grammar of "Avoid X because it is wrong" may be misleading; the logic of such expressions has been elucidated.[5] The core of the argument is this: there is a difference, of course, between what *is* right and what a person *believes* to be right, but, in the case of statements made in the first person, this distinction between objective and subjective vanishes, for the person making the statement.) When a man's conscience exhorts "Do X because it is right," that is, for him, equivalent to the exhortation "Do X because it is what you believe to be right." In general terms, the conscience tells a man "Do what you believe you ought to do." When the conscience does speak, therefore, it cannot (logically) contradict the judgment; the force and function of a man's conscience is to encourage him to *follow* his judgment. This fact arises from the way in which we, as children, meet the concepts of "right" and of "wrong" and the way in which we come to have the appropriate feelings.

IV

There is one further objection to be met. What of the person who says "I believe I ought to do X, but I will have a guilty conscience if I do" or "... but my conscience tells me not to"? How, for example, is the ex-Nazi to fit into this account of the conscience? In these cases it is supposed that a person's judgment leads him to recognize that a thing, X, is wrong and yet that his background accounts for his having feelings of guilt if he avoids X. In truth, the case of the ex-Nazi[6] does not

---

5. See Baier, "Doing My Duty," *Philosophy*, Vol. 26, 1951.
6. Hare, *loc. cit.*, p. 166.

constitute a genuine exception to the general rule that the conscience always in fact exhorts "Do what you believe to be right." The proof of this is to be found in the most general features of moral life. In the case of the ex-Nazi, it was assumed that, at one instant, he could say "I believe X is right, and my conscience tells me to do X," and, at the next instant, he could say, "I believe X is wrong; yet my conscience tells me to do X." But a change in a man's moral principles or opinions is in no way so simple a thing as this example implies. If the change concerns a principle of any importance it will surely take time. During this time there will occur much introspection, e.g., "Do I really believe that?" as well as thought on the problem itself, e.g., "But is it really wrong?" The change from accepting one principle to accepting another contrary to the first, we should expect, would require periods of thought and hesitation. Moreover, the change is not entirely a matter of rational thought. Not only must one change one's rational convictions, but also one's dispositions to act, attitudes of approval and disapproval, *and* one's dispositions to feel guilty. That is, as the change is more or less severe, a more or less total reorientation of the individual is involved. To change from a Nazi to a Christian is no small thing. To say of a man that he accepts a certain principle is to say all those things of him (dispositions, attitudes, feelings) and not simply that he assents to the proposition, "X is good." The case, then, in which it might appear that a man's conscience tells him to do (avoid) a thing he judges to be wrong (right) will prove to be a case where in fact we should be inclined to say of the man neither that he really does nor that he really does not believe such and such to be wrong, nor again that his conscience provides an unequivocal sanction in either direction. The patterns of our feelings of conscience and our judgments of value are so closely interwoven that it is only in a context in which a man's beliefs are for him at the time established that it is appropriate to speak of his conscience advising him. A person may well *say* "I know my conscience tells me to do it, but really ought I?" but if the question is serious it is only the first in a series of moves leading to the further questions: "Would I really feel guilty?" and "Do I really believe that?" In this context, my conscience does not advise me at all. When the doubt is resolved, if it is, then the conscience will speak again on the matter, and in such a way that what I believe to be right and what my conscience tells me to do will coincide.

IX

Conscience and Religious Morality

JOHN DONNELLY

ONE would be hard pressed to deny the ordinary man's trust in the moral deliverances of his conscience. Joseph Butler put the case for the infallibility of conscience, when he remarked: "Had it strength, as it had right; had it power, as it had manifest authority; it would absolutely govern the world" (*Fifteen Sermons*, ii, 13, 14). I think it obvious, in retrospect, that Butler underestimated its "strength" and "power," while overextending its "right" and "authority." Perhaps it is too rash a claim to maintain that conscience serves as an inadequate guide in our moral deliberations, but, to be sure, it can hardly be defended as a sufficient guide to moral conduct.[1]

I wish to trace the religious moralist's insistence on the role of conscience in ethical reasoning back to its sources—the respective theories of Ockham and Aquinas. It is instructive to note that for both Ockham and Aquinas, conscience is not simply an intuitive, authoritative censor of moral values, but instead a process of practical reasoning. Accordingly, conscience is not to be equated with any behavioristic account in terms of "acquired modes of reaction to stimuli," nor with "feelings of repugnance" (or conversely, "feelings of approval"), nor with any occult voices of authority telling one where one's duty is to be found. I intend to argue that conscience, conceived by Ockham and Aquinas as a piece of mental equipment (what

---

1. For instance, how does one ascertain when conscience is operative and not just my desires, fears, anxieties, moods, etc.? To be sure, I am not suggesting that there does not exist such a recondite agency that causes certain conscious manifestations of a moral sort (i.e., the moral explanatory entity called "conscience"), but I would suggest that the epistemological ramifications of how one exactly determines when the voice of conscience speaks is as yet undetermined.

Ryle terms "a private monitor") fails to authoritatively pronounce for us what is right or wrong, and hence proves an inadequate means of ethical reasoning.

Taking as a paradigmatic case, the example of Abraham *qua* knight of faith, so ably described by Kierkegaard in *Fear and Trembling*, I wish to anachronistically apply the respective views of conscience of Ockham and Aquinas to such a moral dilemma (D): the puzzle being that Abraham *qua* father has a duty not to sacrifice his son, but Abraham *qua* knight of faith has a duty to sacrifice Isaac. If I am not mistaken, both the Ockhamist and Thomistic theories will prove internally inconsistent, and hence most inadequate guides in our moral deliberations.[2]

I

William of Ockham equates conscience with the voice of God that speaks within, anticipating the work of H. D. Lewis, who argues that conscience is the medium of divine disclosure to us: "the voice of God is above all the voice of conscience, but not in the sense that it is nothing but one's conscience; it is a divine refinement of the working of conscience."[3] For the Ockhamist, God is not subject to judgments of moral obligation, inasmuch as the divine will is the ultimate norm of what is right and wrong (*potentia absoluta*), and man as moral agent is obliged to do what the will of God prescribes (*potentia ordinata*). Hence the Ockhamist as a potential sympathizer of Abraham would exonerate the knight of faith in (D) by offering the following justification[4]: (1) If God wills x (where "x" = the

2. Conscience theorists speak of "judicial conscience" which pronounces a moral judgment on some past performance, and "legislative conscience" which enables one to decide what one ought to do confronted by a situation demanding moral choice. My use of conscience is quite obviously to be confined to "legislative conscience."

3. *Philosophy of Religion* (London: The English Universities Press, 1965), p. 265.

4. Cf. 4 *Super Quattuor Libros Sententiarum Subtilissimae Quaestiones* 9, E-F.

act of sacrificing one's son), then it is right for the knight of faith to do x; (2) God wills x; (3) therefore, it is right for the knight of faith to do x. (To be sure, the above argument would stand in stark contrast to the Kierkegaardian account which stresses the moral individuality of the knight of faith.) Ockham proceeds to introduce complications into this neat solution by suggesting that conscience is not just having onself attuned to the will of God, for indeed right reason (*recta ratio*) is the norm of morality, so that "no act is perfectly virtuous unless in that act the will wills that which is prescribed by right reason because it is prescribed by right reason." [5] Given this further interpretation, conscience is now to be equated with *recta ratio,* so that a moral agent is duty-bound to follow his conscience *qua recta ratio.*

It needs to be pointed out that Ockham's employment of the fuzzy concept *recta ratio* is not clearly delineated, and seems to admit of a dual interpretation. That is, the Ockhamist may be using *recta ratio* in either of the following two senses: (4) the *Humean view,* wherein a moral agent employs *recta ratio* to decide if x is his duty, if and only if he is free, impartial, fully informed about the relevant factual nature of the case, conceptually clear, willing to universalize, etc. Ockham was a precursor of Hume in a number of historically-interesting ways, and this view suggests, somewhat analogous to C. S. Pierce's epistemic quest for absolute truth, that an ideal consensus in our moral deliberations will eventually be reached upon successful application of (4). However, the Ockhamist may be using *recta ratio* in the (5) distinctly medieval sense of indicating the intellectual process of reflecting on human nature to decide wherein one's duties lie.

It should be noted that (4) and (5) are not identical in their substantive verdicts, for presumably application of (4) will decide that abortion has right-making characteristics, while employment of (5) will decide it has distinctly wrong-making characteristics. Ockham is then clearly mistaken in thinking

---

5. *Ibid.,* 3, 12, c.

that (4) and (5) are intensionally equivalent. Nonetheless, let us bypass this equivocation on *recta ratio*, and grant Ockham the identity of (4) and (5). Now, in a move far more damaging, Ockham proceeds to claim that his two senses of conscience are complementary notions, and that moreover, an act contrary to the dictates of conscience *qua recta ratio* is always contrary as well to the dictates of conscience *qua* will of God, because: "the divine will wills that an act should be elicited in conformity with right reason."[6] By no means is Ockham saying that an action is not only right because it is commanded by God, but also that it is commanded by God because it is right, for he clearly disavows the latter claim. That is, God does not command us to be just because justice has right-making characteristics; rather Ockham holds, justice has these moral qualities precisely because of God's will. Had God decided to will that injustice have right-making characteristics, then acts of injustice would be morally appropriate. Leaving aside this obvious retreat to theological voluntarism, it can still be shown that the Ockhamist view offers only an impasse to (D). Consider the following maneuver to attempt to offer a "way out" for Abraham (so that he need not sacrifice Isaac), applying the Ockhamist mode of ratiocination: (6) Abraham, applying *recta ratio* (i.e., we are assuming contrary to fact, that the two senses are intensionally equivalent) elicits the dictate of conscience that he has a duty not to do x. But (7) God *via* divine revelation lets it be known that he wills that Abraham be duty-bound to do x.

Quite clearly (6) and (7) offer opposing edicts, so it seems implausible to suggest that Ockham's principle of God's willing that we follow conscience's dictates is a sufficient condition of moral conduct. Rather, given Ockham's line of argument, *mutatis mutandis*, Abraham both ought and ought not to sacrifice Isaac. Were the Ockhamist, somewhat inconsistently, to claim that (7) takes precedence over (6), so that (7) describes the actual duty, we would be left with a decision procedure that is (perhaps) theologically justifiable, but morally most unenlightened. The

---

6. *Ibid.,* 3, 13, c.

Ockhamist theory of conscience has led us to an impasse with
(D). Conscience as a recondite agency that causes certain
conscious manifestations of a moral sort has led us, at least
on the Ockhamist account, into an epistemic straight-jacket.

II

Hopefully having shown some intrinsic flaws in the Ockhamist
account of conscience, I now wish to consider St. Thomas'
more sophisticated account. Aquinas considered the following
three assertions to be examples of self-evident moral principles:

(8) "Evil should not be done" (*per se nota secundum se*)
(9) "The precepts of God's will have to be obeyed (*per se
nota quoad nos*).[7]
(10) "No injuries should be done to anyone"[8]

Historically speaking, it seems quite clear that St. Thomas
regarded the above three moral propositions as analytic assertions.[9] From our Kantian vantage-point, we can *at best* grant
them the status of synthetic *a priori* assertions, overlooking the
perplexing epistemological question as to whether there are any
synthetic *a priori* propositions, moral or otherwise. To be sure,
Aquinas' claim that (8), (9), and (10) are analytic assertions
is clearly mistaken, for there is no logical contradiction involved
in denying any of the three assertions, and if *per impossibile*,
the above three assertions were tautologous, one wonders how

---

7. (8) and (9) are called such in *Scripta Super IV Libros Sententiarum
Petri Lombardi* II, 24, 2, 3, c.
8. *Quaestiones Quodlibetales* III, q. 12, a. 26, c., although the principle
in question is not specified as being *per se nota secundum se* or *per se
nota quoad nos.*
9. "...the precepts of the natural law...are self-evident principles.
Now a thing is said to be self-evident in two ways: first, in itself; secondly,
in relation to us. Any proposition is said to be self-evident in itself, if its
predicate is contained in the notion of the subject.... But some propositions
are self-evident only to the wise, who understand the meanings of the
terms of such propositions..." *Summa Theologica* I-II, q. 94, a. 2, c.

they would aid one in his practical-decision making. Also, for Aquinas, some self-evident moral propositions are self-evident only to the wise, as in (9) and possibly (10), but clearly this move proves circular, in that "the wise" are just those agents who accept such moral principles. That is, the criterion of a wise man, on Aquinas' account, is not independent of the specific principles, said to be self-evident.

I suggest we leave aside such questions as to whether moral propositions are analytic, synthetic *a priori*, etc., and instead analyze Aquinas' theory of conscience, with a view to providing a "way out" for Abraham in (D), so that he needn't sacrifice Isaac. It is instructive that for St. Thomas conscience was the practical judgment of reason upon an individual act that determined whether that act is obligatory, permitted or forbidden. Accordingly, conscience was equated with "a kind of practical syllogism," what Aquinas termed *syllogismus operativus*. To see the operative syllogism in force consider the following Thomistic illustration:[10]

(11) I must not do anything which is forbidden by the law of God. (This premise is derived by *synderesis*, which is the disposition by virtue of which one grasps the most general principles of morality. It is accordingly an infallible and innate disposition that enables us to grasp certain basic moral principles.)

(12) Sexual intercourse with w is forbidden by the law of God. (This premise is derived from reason.)

(13) I must abstain from intercourse with w. (This is a dictate of conscience.)

Now, according to St. Thomas, error in the deliberations of conscience takes place if and only if (i) there is a mistake in the minor premise (12), and/or (ii) the application of the syllogistic form is itself erroneous. Furthermore, recall that Aquinas claims that (8), (9), and (10) are self-evident moral truths, so that conscience can never err "when the particular act

---

10. *Quaestiones Disputatae De Veritate*, q. 17, a. 2, c.

to which conscience is applied has a universal judgment about it in *synderesis*." [11] But this raises the following two puzzles: (a) Aquinas agrees that (8) and (9) hold, yet for Abraham to obey (9) and intend to sacrifice Isaac is clearly to violate (8) by committing an act of homicide; and, on the other hand, by ascribing to (8), and so refusing to sacrifice his son, Abraham will commit an offense against (9) by violating God's command; (b) likewise, Aquinas wants to maintain that (9) ought to be the case and (10) as well, yet for Abraham to obey (9) is clearly to violate (10), and to obey (10) is to disobey (9). Accordingly (contrary to Aquinas' belief), the conjunction of (8), (9), and (10), seems to be an inconsistent triad when applied to (D).

The situations described in (a) and (b) do appear paradoxical, and Aquinas offers two means of dissolving such puzzles. On solution [1], Aquinas would seem to argue that Abraham should refrain from acting on the issue of the application of (8) versus (9), and/or (9) versus (10), because:

"... no one is bound by a precept except through his knowledge of the precept. Therefore, one who is not capable of the knowledge of a precept is not bound by the precept. Nor is one who is ignorant of a precept bound to carry out that precept except insofar as he is required to know it ... since the knowledge binds only through the power of the precept, and the precept only through the knowledge." [12]

However, Aquinas appears to decide against this solution [1] of dissolving the puzzles in favor of solution [2]. On solution [2] it follows that Abraham ought to sacrifice Isaac.

"... it does not seem possible for a man to avoid sin if his conscience, no matter how mistaken, declares that something which is indifferent or intrinsically evil is a command of God, and with such a conscience, he decides to do the opposite. For as far as he can, he has by this very fact decided not to observe the law of God. Consequently, he sins mortally ... such a false conscience in as long as it remains is binding...." [13]

---

11. *Ibid.*
12. *Ibid.*, q. 17, a. 3, c.
13. *Ibid.*, q. 17, a. 4, c.

From solution [1] we can develop the following puzzle, which I term the "Johannine puzzle," for John 16:2 relates "the hour cometh when whosoever killeth you, will think that he doth a service to God":

(14) God commands only that good be done and evil avoided.
(15) But God commands that x be done, and x is an evil act. (e.g., "x" = the slaying of Isaac by Abraham)
(16) Therefore, God commands that evil be done.
(17) *But,* God cannot command that evil be done.
(18) Thus, *either* (i) x is indeed an evil act, but God didn't command x, *or* (ii) God did command x, but x isn't an evil act.

Now, adopting St. Thomas' use of the operative syllogism, it follows that: (14) is true by application of *synderesis;* (15) is an application of reason, and error can set in here, but suppose it is the case that Abraham received a legitimate mandate from God; so that (16) follows by operative syllogism, and so is a decision of conscience; (17) seems true, as an application of *synderesis* in (14); so we are left with a dilemma (18), and since the reasoning process is correct, this conclusion becomes our decision of conscience.

Given the state of affairs, described by the "Johannine puzzle," it follows that our solution [1] takes two forms: (a) an ethical solution, wherein we recognize a moral dilemma, so that Abraham must simply refrain from acting, for on either alternative he commits a morally forbidden action; and (b) an epistemic solution, in that such a moral puzzlement vanishes under solution [1], for St. Thomas says "one who is not capable of the knowledge of a precept is not bound by the precept." Now, substituting "state of affairs" for "precept," it seems Abraham is presented with a contradictory state of affairs in the "Johannine puzzle," and since the problem is absurd, he needn't consider it any longer. What I wish to assert here as regard to the epistemic difficulty is not that the knight of faith cannot understand the situation in which he finds himself, but rather that he cannot act or pursue the line of conduct enjoined by such contradictory assertions. That is, Abraham can understand his plight in the "Johannine puzzle," but what he cannot understand is how to morally act on it. It thus seems clear that one simply cannot act on the absurd, although Kierkegaard, at times, felt one could: "This is his comfort (Abraham's) for he says: 'but yet this will not come to pass, or if it does come to pass, then the Lord will give me a new Isaac, by virtue of the absurd.' " [14] However, a more enlightened Kierkegaard, seems to give way to the datum of the "Johannine puzzle," so that recognizing solution[1], Abraham needn't sacrifice Isaac:

"Isaac asks Abraham where the lamb is for the burnt offering. And Abraham said 'God will provide himself the lamb for the burnt offering, my son . . . . , If there were not this word, the whole event would have lacked something; if it were to another effect, everything perhaps would be resolved into confusion." [15]

Accordingly, on solution [1], we have a genuine "way out" for Abraham qua knight of faith, for the triad of (8), (9), and (10) is indeed inconsistent, so that given the datum of the "Johannine puzzle" which is engendered from the Thomistic account of conscience, it follows that Abraham ought to refrain from sacrificing Isaac.

Nonetheless, while solution [1] seems to affirm the ability of conscience to reach a moral decision in regard to (D), the decision procedure is somewhat pyrrhic, for to effect such a result, the initial triad of (8), (9), and (10) must be rejected as inconsistent. This ought to prove disturbing to the religious moralist as indeed it did to St. Thomas. In his Summa Theologica II-II, q. 64, a. 6, obj. 1, St. Thomas would seem to affirm the sacrifice of Isaac, in saying "God is Lord of death and life, for by His decree both the sinful and the righteous die. Hence he who at God's command kills an innocent man does not sin, as neither does God whose behest he executes; indeed his obedience

14. Soren Kierkegaard, *Fear and Trembling*. Trans. Walter Lowrie (New York: Doubleday and Co., Inc., 1954), p. 124.
15. *Ibid.*, pp. 124-25.

to God's command is a proof that he fears Him." Yet this is inconsistent with Luke 10:16, which passage Aquinas in q. 64 approvingly quotes: "He that despiseth you despiseth me." The point is to affirm the consistency of the initial triad and thereby preserve the prescription of I John 4:20: "If a man says I love God and hated his brother, he is a liar," but St. Thomas' solution (1) will not allow him this luxury.

Unfortunately, Aquinas appears to favor the explanation of solution (2). Aquinas hints at the possibility of developing what I term "solution (1)" in his *Quaestiones Disputatae de Veritate,* q. 17, a. 3, but he quickly decides in favor of what I term "solution (2)." He draws a distinction between: (19) "a correct conscience," that one is required to follow unconditionally in all circumstances due to its intrinsic worth; and (20) a "false conscience," which one is required to follow in a conditional manner in that it binds only for extrinsic reasons. It is interesting to note that for Ockham, Newman, and Butler, the slogan "always let your conscience be your guide" implies "always be guided by what is right;" whereas for Aquinas it has the implication at least on solution (2) of "always be guided by what you believe is right," leaving it a moot issue as to whether the voice of conscience in question is morally appropriate.

"A false conscience which is mistaken in things which are intrinsically evil commands something which is contrary to the law of God. Nevertheless it says that what it commands is the law of God. Accordingly, one who acts against such a conscience becomes a kind of transgressor of the law of God, although one who follows such a conscience and acts according to it acts against the law of God and sins mortally." [16]

Given such a distinction, it now appears that a less enlightened Abraham, can avoid the inconsistency in the triad of (8), (9), and (10). Consider the following situation: (a) x is a contemplated action of Abraham, and x is against the law of God, and hence morally wrong (Aquinas obviously falls back on theological ethics and commits the supernaturalistic fallacy

---

16. *De Veritate, op. cit.,* q. 17, a. 4, c.

here, but suppose it is the case that there is a contingent connection between God's law and morality, such that whatever
is morally wrong is *ex hypothesi* against the law of God as well),
yet Abraham's conscience tells Abraham that x is a morally
right action to perform; (b) $\bar{x}$ is a contemplated action, and $\bar{x}$
is in accord with divine law, hence morally right, yet Abraham's
conscience tells him he should abstain from performing $\bar{x}$. In
our case, Abraham's conscience tells him he should abstain from
not sacrificing Isaac. Now, in case (a), Abraham is morally
right in obeying his false conscience and doing act x (i.e.,
sacrificing Isaac), although in case (b) Abraham is morally
wrong in doing action $\bar{x}$ due to the testimony of his conscience
to the contrary. For, as St. Thomas says: "Conscience is said
to bind insofar as one sins if he does not follow his conscience,
but not in the sense that he acts correctly if he does follow it." [17]
Accordingly, we can bypass the stalemate of the "Johannine puzzle," in that Abraham ought to sacrifice Isaac in solution[(2)] out of
obedience to his false conscience.

Quite obviously, this solution proves somewhat unsatisfactory
to Aquinas, since he has to fall back on the traditional ploy
that what Abraham did would have been subjectively right,
although objectively wrong. Presumably, given such a ruse
as the concept of "false conscience," and the permissibility of
acting conditionally on it, it was subjectively right for an
Eichmann to murder millions of Jews, although his action was
judged objectively wrong! I suspect that "wrong" functions in
such ascriptions of false conscience as an evaluative term, but
the phrase "subjectively right" is used descriptively, so that
judged from a moral point of view, the action nonetheless remains objectively (i.e., morally) wrong. This Aquinas, at least
on solution [(2)], failed to realize.

Recall, it was previously mentioned, how error in conscience
for Aquinas takes place if and only if there is a mistake in the
minor premise of the operative syllogism, and/or the application

---

17. *Ibid.*

of the syllogistic form is itself erroneous.[18] Now consider the
following operative syllogism: (21) Abraham out of obedience
to a divine command, ought to sacrifice his son; (22) Isaac is
Abraham's son; (23) therefore, Abraham ought to sacrifice Isaac.
Surely, we can agree that the above illustration of an operative
syllogism fails to violate Aquinas' two rules, so that (23)
presents Abraham with his decision of conscience. Although,
Aquinas feels this is not a correct decision of conscience, yet his
two rules are not violated, so that his two conditions can hardly
be construed as sufficient and necessary conditions of a false
conscience. Presumably, Aquinas would argue that one ought
always to obey a correct conscience, a moral judgment that one is
psychologically, epistemologically, and logically certain of; but
that one ought only to conditionally obey a false conscience,
a moral judgment that one is but psychologically certain of, and
that (23) is but a judgment of false conscience. One is not
logically certain of (23), for Aquinas, since it is not analytic (or
synthetic a priori), nor is one epistemologically certain of (23)
either, for it is questionable whether the divine command was
to be acted on. I argued above that our syllogism in question
doesn't appear to have violated Aquinas' two conditions for
error in the deliberations of conscience. However, to allow some
consistency to Aquinas' claim, we might regard his vague talk
of "the application of the syllogistic form being erroneous" as
applicable to mistakes such as those just cited. But, this leaves
Aquinas with the claim that: (24) if Abraham were not required
to follow a false conscience, Abraham would not be required
to follow a correct conscience, inasmuch as psychological certitude is often a sufficient condition for moral action; (25) but,
Abraham is required to follow a correct conscience; so that
(26) Abraham is required to follow a false conscience, as well.[19]

---

18. *Ibid.*, q. 17, a. 2, c.
19. This Thomistic distinction has rather close affinities with the
Kierkegaard of *Concluding Unscientific Postscript*, who speaks of the
"subjective certainty" of Socrates (i.e., in his immortality) and his "objective uncertainty" as well (i.e., the openness of the scientific evidence in
the dispute on immortality). I suggest that this is similar in detail to St.

"Thus one who loves wine because of its sweetness loves sweetness for an intrinsic reason, and wine for an extrinsic reason. But one who has a false conscience and believes that it is correct, clings to his false conscience because of the correctness he believes is there, and strictly speaking, clings to a correct conscience, but one which is false accidentally, insofar as this conscience which he believes to be correct, happens to be false . . . strictly speaking, he is bound by a correct conscience, but accidentally by a false conscience." [20]

Thus, in accord with solution [2], Abraham ought to sacrifice Isaac out of obedience to his false conscience. But obviously there are difficulties with the concept of a "false conscience." Aquinas might here reply that suppose we were to revert to solution[1], and the Johannine puzzle; we still can derive a normative solution [2] from such a dilemma. Recall that in the Johannine puzzle, we were presented with Abraham's doubtful conscience (he being neither psychologically, epistemologically, or logically certain wherein his duty lied), and it was suggested that one ought not to act with a doubtful conscience. Aquinas might agree with the analysis presented therein, but claim that such doubt can be removed by seeking to answer the following two questions: (Q.1) What is the actual moral status of the proposed course of action? and (Q.2) What is Abraham obliged to do? Now, since (Q.1) generally can be ascertained (it is theoretically invincible in Thomistic terminology), the practical doubt of (Q.2) can be resolved by "forming one's conscience." Such a normative state of affairs takes place by deciding to choose the

---

Thomas' concept of "false conscience," where the agent is subjectively certain (i.e., psychologically certain), but also objectively uncertain (i.e., as regard to the epistemic logic of the case). If there is a legitimacy then to the Thomistic distinction, and if furthermore it runs parallel to the above-mentioned Kierkegaardian distinction, then Robert Herbert is surely mistaken in seeing a real paradox in the case of Abraham in this regard: "The facts which would justify our saying that a person is objectively uncertain are the very facts which would justify our saying that he is not subjectively certain, and vice versa." "Two of Kierkegaard's Uses of 'Paradox,'" *Philosophical Review*, vol. 70, 1961, p. 45.

20. *De Veritate, op. cit.*, q. 17, a. 4, c.

morally safer-course, and by recalling that a doubtful conscience does not bind.

Now, consider the former method of resolution of the practical doubt. Suppose, it is the case that S is not obliged to do Y, but he doubts whether he is obliged to do Y or obliged not to do Y. And, suppose furthermore, that the second alternative is the morally more hazardous action. But, whereas St. Thomas claims S is now obligated to do Y, this has the effect of making a *de facto* morally neutral act for S into a requirement for S. For example, Thomas Watson may wonder whether to give one million dollars to the Harlem Improvement Association, and surely in wondering whether he is obliged to or obliged not to give n-sum of money, the morally safer course is to give the money; but this has the result of making a philanthropic act into a duty. In regard to the latter option, and the question of the doubtful conscience, it seems the overly scrupulous person may take advantage of a doubt, and turn a forbidden act, or an obligatory act, into a morally indifferent one.

Actually, Aquinas felt he had a "way out" of the state of affairs, described in the Johannine puzzle, so that he would opt for (18), (ii). He cites the case of the monk (cf. *Quaestiones Quodlibetales*, III, q. 12, a. 27, ad. 2 m) who has the duty to chant vespers, yet who because of his sinful state would do wrong in so performing his vespers. The monk finds himself in the following quandary: if he performs his duty of chanting vespers, he commits a wrongful act, inasmuch as he is in a state of sin; but if he doesn't perform his duty of chanting vespers, he also does a wrongful act, inasmuch as the opposite of a required act is a forbidden act.

St. Thomas avoids such a predicament by suggesting that the monk first do penance, then "sing without sin." Somewhat analogously, he might argue that Abraham could first do penance, then obey the command of God to sacrifice Isaac. There is strong textual evidence to suggest that, for Aquinas, conscience never fails, as I claim it did in the Johannine puzzle. Aquinas maintained: "speaking absolutely and without qualification, no one is perplexed."[21] Yet, if we accept the Aquinas who said in solution [1] "no one is bound by any precept unless he understands that precept," then conscience offers us only an impasse in the Johannine puzzle, unless this perplexity is itself a judgment of conscience. If so, then one might argue: no one is bound by any precept unless he knows the precept; Abraham knows of no precept applicable to this case; therefore, Abraham is not bound by any precept in this case. But this is not to remove the perplexity, so much as it is to recognize it.

Enough, I believe, has been said to question the religious moralist's insistence on the role of conscience in ethical reasoning. It would appear that Aquinas is himself confused on the issue of solution [1] and solution [2], apparently deciding he has drawn a distinction without a difference, and opting for solution [2] as the "real" interpretation of his views of conscience. If I am not mistaken, there remains a distinction *with* a difference. The Thomistic solution [1] suggests interesting possibilities for a logic of moral forbearance, but fails to remove the perplexity of (D). Solution [2] offers a normative verdict, but the infelicitous one that Abraham ought to sacrifice Isaac, a solution [2] that renders inconsistent the basic triad of self-evident moral propositions, (8), (9), and (10), so essential to the religious moralist's theory of conscience.

---

21. *Scripta Super IV Libros Sententiarum Petri Lombardi* II, d. 39, q. 3, a. 3, ad. 5 m.

PART IV

THE AUTHORITY OF CONSCIENCE

INTRODUCTION

THERE appear to be occasions on which a man performs a particular action for reasons of conscience. On such occasions does a man always do what he ought to do? Suppose a political fanatic assassinates a ruler and claims that reflection and deliberation led him to this course of action. Surely, this assassin has followed his conscience. But has he done what he ought to do? Is it not possible for a man to do as his conscience directs and yet do what he ought not to do?

Philosophers and laymen alike often appear to believe that the authority of conscience is ultimate and that we ought to do what we believe (in conscience) that we ought to do. In "Obedience to Conscience," D. O. Thomas attempts to qualify the sense in which it is true that we ought to do what we think we ought to do. He distinguishes between "what I *privately* think I ought to do" and "what I *ultimately* think I ought to do." This distinction is based upon the existence of a legitimate moral authority or a competent moral adviser. What I privately think I ought to do refers to what I think I ought to do after reflecting on my contemplated action. What I ultimately think I ought to do refers to what I think I ought to do after such reflection *and* after consultation (when the situation permits) with authorities and advisers. Thomas claims the view *that we do what we ought to do when we do what we think we ought to do* does not entail that we do not act conscientiously unless we follow our own *private* judgment. We may in certain circumstances (when our adviser can be impartial and we cannot, for example), defer to the judgment of another (an adviser or authority). To say that we act conscientiously is to say that we do what we *ultimately* think we ought to do. Thomas later suggests a sense of "ought" in which it is true that an agent *ought* to do what he does not, even ultimately, think he ought to do. This sense of "ought" applies to an agent whose "construction of duties" is in error.

In "The Value of Conscientiousness," P. H. Nowell-Smith examines a view held by Sir David Ross, among others, that if a man performs an action he believes (in conscience) to be right, then the man is doing what he ought to do. He argues that the conscientious act is not always the right act and that the proposition: "You think that you ought to do A, but you would be a better man if you did B," is not contradictory or even logically odd. He also disputes the "supreme value of conscientiousness." *Conscientiousness,* he contends, is simply the disposition to obey certain rules. However, one acts as he ought to act only by conforming to rules which are *right*.

In "Conscience and Conscientiousness," A. Campbell Garnett argues against Nowell-Smith's critique of conscience. Arguing for a logic of "critical conscience," Garnett elucidates the cognitive and motivational components of conscience, noting "moral approval and disapproval are moved by the thought of the effect of our actions upon the weal or woe of human beings." The critical conscience is grounded in the universally accepted principle of *beneficence*—that the welfare of persons is a good reason for approving x and the resultant harm to persons a good reason for disapproving y. Garnett, like psychologists Fromm and Allport, argues for the psycho-therapeutic usefulness of conscience as providing the integrity necessary for mental health. Conscientiousness, the firm resolve to seek to do what is right, if properly critical, is an unqualified good. It would be self-contradictory for a man to assert in a particular case that he ought not to do that which he believes he ought to do. Hence, Garnett, like Butler, upholds the magisterial authority of (critical) conscience.

John T. Granrose argues in "The Authority of Conscience" that there is an important sense in which it is true that one always ought to follow his conscience. Drawing an often unnoticed distinction between (i) the authority of conscience and

(ii) the infallibility of conscience, Granrose argues that (ii), but not (i), is philosophically bankrupt.

Should one then *always* follow his critical *conscience?* To be sure, conscience often proves fallible, and conscientious action often produces ill effects. But could one be a better man by refusing to do what one believes it is his duty to do? Granrose asserts "it is not that following one's critical conscience is superior to being right, but that the way in which one tries to be right is by following one's critical conscience."

Granrose argues (*via* a "prudential argument") that following the dictates of one's conscience is necessary for a meaningful and satisfying life (cf. Allport's sense of "personality-integration"). He concludes that "consulting one's conscience" is doing that action which, after "due rational deliberation," one sincerely believes to be right. This suggests a sense of the authority of conscience which is philosophically acceptable. Granrose qualifies his view by adding that it may also be right for society to restrain an individual's conscientious action.

William Earle's phenomenological essay, entitled "Some Paradoxes of Private Conscience as a Political Guide," explores the conflicts arising from the injunctions of private conscience and the edicts of public law. Paradox results when one's private conscience becomes tyrannical and the public conscience becomes an irrational power responsive to itself alone. Earle foresees no theoretical solution to this problem. However, he claims that the realization that such conflicts are "theoretically insoluble" is itself of great value. Such a realization emphasizes the "essential moral risk of existence," deters the fanatic and the absolutist, and suggests a "dialectic of listening" as crucial to the practical life.

X

Obedience to Conscience

D. O. THOMAS

WHEN we say of a person that he does what he ought to do we may mean simply that he does what the situation requires; but we may mean something more, we may mean that when he does what the situation requires he intends to fulfill his obligations. In this latter sense we assert that the performance is dutiful. Although all actions which are instances of doing what one ought to do in the latter sense are instances of doing what one ought to do in the former sense, the converse is not true. Not all our compliances with the requirements of duty are dutiful compliances.

Doing what we ought to do in the latter sense entails doing what we think we ought do to; the person who is intent upon fulfilling his obligations and discharging his duties has no alternative to doing what he takes his obligations and duties to be. But this is not true of doing what we ought to do in the former sense. Meeting the demands of the situation does not entail intending to do what one ought to do, neither does it entail that we think that what we do is what we ought to do. It is not self-contradictory to suppose that a person might do the action which the situation requires without thinking or believing that it is the action which the situation requires. In brief, we can distinguish one sense of "doing what one ought to do" (that embodying dutiful action) in which it is true, and one sense (that embodying compliance with the requirements of duty) in which it is false, that doing what one ought to do entails doing what one thinks one ought to do.

Now for neither of these senses of "doing what one ought to do" is it true that doing what one ought to do is entailed by doing what one thinks one ought to do. It is not self-contradictory to suppose that a person may fail to do what he ought to do if he does what he thinks or believes he ought to do. His action may fail to comply with the demands of the situation and, even if he intends to do what he thinks he ought to do, his action may fail to be a dutiful compliance. That doing what one ought to do is not entailed by doing what one thinks one ought to do is shown by the fact that an agent who intends to do what he thinks or believes he ought to do may wonder whether he will succeed in meeting the demands of the situation.

Some philosophers have maintained, however, that although doing what one ought to do is not *entailed* by doing what one thinks one ought to do, it is nevertheless true, for the sense of "ought" which is of greatest importance in ethics, that we do what we ought to do when we do what we think we ought to do. It is claimed that he who, after informing his mind to the best of his ability, does what he thinks or believes he ought to do discharges his main moral responsibility. To follow one's conscience in this sense is the essential condition of moral praiseworthiness. If we accept this view, however, we shall need to distinguish other senses of "doing what one ought to do" which allows us to say that a person may fail to fulfill his obligations if he does what he thinks or believes he ought to do. The conscientious person may fail either because he misconstrues the situation or because he misjudges what is morally required in the situation as he construes it. The conscientious person may fail either because his information is inadequate or because his judgment is erroneous. In one, and the most important, respect, he does what he ought to do, but in other respects he may fail. It is important to discriminate these different ways in which we may fail to do what we ought to do if we are to avoid the fallacy of assuming that conscientiousness exhausts morality.

In what follows I wish to explore a further ambiguity in the claim that an agent ought to do what he thinks he ought to do. This claim might be taken to exclude the permissibility of deferring to the moral judgment of another or of relying upon the moral authority of another. To be moral or conscientious, it may be alleged, requires that we rely upon our own judgment and that we cling to our own interpretation of the situation when we find ourselves opposed. To defer to the judgment of another is to fail to accept moral responsibility; it is to renounce an essential conditon of moral personality. Certainly, it may be conceded, where a person defers to the judgment of another and in doing so violates his own sense of what is required without pausing to consider whether such deference is justified, he forfeits all claim to moral worth. But what are we to say of those cases in which a man seeks the advice of one whose judgment he respects and comes to believe that he ought to defer to his judgment? Does conscientiousness always require that we follow our own private judgment or is it sometimes morally permissible or morally enjoined to adopt the judgment of another?

Moral perplexities may sometimes be resolved by reflection and sometimes in the course of discussion. Consideration of the circumstances in which we find ourselves, consideration of the probable consequences of action, consideration of the relevant principles, consideration of the interests or expectations of others will often bring us to a point where we see clearly what we ought to do, what policy or programme we ought to adopt. And where we come to share the point of view of those who advise us, there is no conflict between what we think we ought to do and respect for authority. But discussion may not always be so successful; my adviser may fail to convince me that his point of view is correct. In such a case I shall find myself having to decide whether to rely upon my own judgment or defer to his. Let us suppose that, when I have informed my judgment to the best of my ability, I judge that I ought to do action x, that B advises me that I ought to do action y, that my doing action x is incompatible with my doing action y, and that my respect for B's judgment is such that, although I do not agree with his judgment in this case, I nevertheless believe that I ought to do what he advises me to do. And let us suppose further that my belief that I ought to do what B advises me to do, when weighed against my own belief that I ought to do action x, brings me to the point where I come to think that I ought to do what *B* advises me to do. In such cases what are we to say that conscience requires?

For ease of reference I shall use the phrase *what I privately think I ought to do* to refer to what I think I ought to do when I have considered all the relevant data and reasons that may be presented for and against acting as I propose to act, but when I have not taken into account the fact that my adviser is of a different opinion and the possibility that I ought to defer to his judgment; and I shall use the phrase *what I ultimately think I ought to do* to refer to what I think I ought to do when I have taken these further factors into account. Now, we may ask, does conscience require that I do what I privately think I ought to do or what I ultimately think I ought to do?

The former view entails that a person who does what he believes he ought to do will fail to act conscientiously if he does not follow his own private judgment. The latter view entails that a person may be acting conscientiously even if he fails to follow his own private judgment, provided that he believes that he ought to defer to the judgment of another. The former view insists that to accept and act upon the judgments of another without agreeing with those judgments is inconsistent with conscientious action, while the latter view allows that a person may be acting conscientiously when he accepts the moral authority of another without agreeing with the judgment of that authority on a given occasion.

However this issue is to be decided, if it is admitted that there are genuine moral perplexities and that men may come to believe that they ought to accept the authority of those whose judgment they respect, it is important to be clear that doing what one ultimately believes one ought to do is not identical with and is not necessarily compatible with doing what one privately thinks one ought to do. The claim that the individual must believe that his conduct is justified must not be confused with the claim that the individual can always determine what conscience requires by the exercise of his own private judgment. That conscience has been thought of as a private mentor can be seen from the connotation of the term, especially in its early uses. Originally, the connotation of "conscience" was not restricted to moral knowledge but included all inward knowledge or conviction. It is significant that, according to the O.E.D., the term "conscience" succeeded to the term "inwit." In the first half of the eighteenth century the connotation of "conscience" becomes restricted to moral knowledge or conviction, but the emphasis upon privacy and immediacy remains. Butler, for example, stresses the immediate non-discursive nature of conscience and, in consequence, pays little attention to the problems of moral perplexity:

"But there is a superior principle of reflection or conscience in every man, which distinguishes between the internal principles of his heart, as well as his external actions: which passes judgment upon himself and them; pronounces determinately some actions to be in themselves just, right, good; others to be in themselves evil, wrong, unjust; which, without being consulted, without being advised with, magisterially exerts itself, and approves or condemns him, the doer of them, accordingly; and which, if not forcibly stopped, naturally and always of course goes on to anticipate a higher and more effectual sentence, which shall hereafter second and affirm its own." [1]

Butler suggests that "in all common ordinary cases" to argue with or question the immediate deliverances of conscience is to invite corruption.[2] On this basis there is little room for the notion that man may need to consult another or take into account the fact that others differ from him as to what ought to be done. This distinction has also been obscured by those, like Kant and his followers, who have maintained that the individual by his own unaided reason, can determine for himself the nature of his obligations and duties. The interpretation of conscientious action as autonomy, understood both as individual self-legislation and as compliance with the universal laws of practical reason, obviates the need for inter-personal consultation and advice. As far as moral judgment is concerned all rational men are

---

1. *Fifteen Sermons*, ed. W. R. Matthews (London: G. Bell, 1914), p. 55. Cf. p. 63. "He hath the rule of right within: what is wanting is only that he honestly attend to it."

2. *Ibid.*, p. 117.

equal in capacity. There is no place for the expert, the *phronimos;* no one can lay claim to moral authority.

If, however, we bear in mind that a man may sincerely believe or come to believe that he ought to follow the judgment of another, even though he does not on a particular occasion agree with that judgment, we can see that doing what one ultimately believes one ought to do is not necessarily identical with or compatible with following's one's own private judgment. The distinction between what we privately think we ought to do and what we ultimately think we ought to do is forced upon us, and we have to decide what it is that conscience requires.

I wish to argue that conscience requires that we do what we ultimately think we ought to do, and that is may be consistent with conscience to defer to the judgment of another. If the thesis that conscience always requires that a person should follow his own private judgment were true, it would be the case that a man who believed that he ought to defer to the judgment of another, and who did so for the sake of doing what he ought to do, would not be acting conscientiously. His action would not have the peculiar merit or moral worth which we ascribe to conscientious action. It seems to me, however, that we regard as morally worthy those who do what they believe they ought to do even if this involves deferring to the judgment of another. If moral praiseworthiness and moral blameworthiness attach to doing and failing to do what we believe we ought to do, conscience does not require that we always follow our private judgment. Furthermore, as was pointed out earlier, if it were the case that conscience requires that one follows one's own private judgment, then where a person follows his own private judgment even though he believes that he ought to defer to the judgment of another, he would be acting conscientiously. But it seems to be absurd to say that a person can act conscientiously and yet not do the action which he believes he ought to do. These considerations seem to me to support the view that conscience requires that, where they conflict, we do what we ultimately think we ought to do and not what we privately think we ought to do.

A supporter of the view that we ought always to follow our own private judgments might concede that one who in good faith defers to the judgment of another acts conscientiously, and base his case on the claim that a person who defers to the judgment of another in moral matters always acts mistakenly. A conscience that defers to the judgment of another, it might be argued, is an erroneous conscience. This is so, it might be claimed, because there can never be good reasons or good grounds for accepting the moral judgment of another. In this way the gap is closed between doing what we privately think we ought to do and doing what we ultimately think we ought to do. He who is not mistaken in his judgment as to what he ought to do never defers to the judgment of another.

To meet this objection we shall have to consider whether there can be good reasons for thinking that one ought to defer to the judgment of another. I shall suggest that there are occasions when we are justified in believing that the judgment of others is better than our own or that others are in a better position than we are to form a judgment, and that, consequently, we are justified in following their advice even though we cannot agree with it and even though we cannot fully understand the basis upon which it is given. But before we consider these cases I wish to discuss two objections that might be advanced to what I have claimed hitherto.

An objector might concede that a person may be justified in deferring to the moral judgment of another and that when he does so he may be acting conscientiously, but maintain that such deference is incompatible with full moral responsibility. It is appropriate for a child to defer to a parent, but such deference cannot belong to one who is fully mature and responsible. In answer, it must first be noted that I am not claiming that all kinds of deference to the authority of another are consistent with morally responsible action; if the agent is to be justified in deferring he must have good grounds for believing that he ought to accept the decisions of another. Now, if it is the case that there can be good grounds for deferring to the judgment of another, we need to consider what responsibility requires in such instances. Does it require that we take all the relevant decisions ourselves and remain deaf to the suggestion that we should accept the advice of those whom we acknowledge to be wiser [3] than we are, or, where we have done our utmost to clear our minds and we still believe that the judgment of another may be more inspired than our own, does it allow that we may defer to that judgment? It would seem that being responsible sometimes not only allows but requires the humility to acknowledge superior judgment.

An objector might further claim that the position I am defending rests upon a false antithesis between what I have termed what I privately think I ought to do and what I ultimately think that I ought to do. It cannot be the case that at the same time I both think that I ought to do action x and that I ought to do action y, and that the performances of actions x and y are incompatible. If, therefore, I ultimately think that I ought to do action x, I can no longer privately think that I ought to do action y. Or, if I still privately think that I ought to do action y, it must be the case that what I privately think I ought to do is compatible with what I ultimately think I ought to do. There can be no resoluion of conflict because there can be no conflict.

This objection can be met by distinguishing carefully, as we did above, between (1) what I think to be my duty after I have considered the arguments that others have put forward to clarify the issue, but not before I have taken into account the fact that others disagree with me and the possibility that I should defer to their judgment, and (2) what I think I ought to do when I have taken into account not just the reasons adduced by others (which can become my reasons) but also the fact that others disagree with me and the possibility that I should defer to their judgment. Now conflict can remain at the moment

---

3. In what follows I discuss some of the reasons that may be given for believing that some men are wiser than others in moral matters. The position defended in this paper requires (a) that some moral judgments are better than others, (b) that, either in general or for a range of moral problems, the moral judgments of some men are better than those of others, and (c) that we can have good reasons for believing that the judgments of some men are better than those of others.

of action between (1) and (2). A man may say that he believes that he ought to do an action because others recommend it, but that for his own part he would judge that he ought to do otherwise. My conviction, all things considered, that I ought to follow the judgment of another can co-exist with my (private) judgment, based on the reasons which I have been able to make clear to myself, that I ought to do otherwise.

II

I now need to establish that it is consonant with our ordinary moral beliefs that we may have good reasons in moral matters for accepting the judgment of another, even though we cannot agree with that particular judgment and even though we cannot fully understand the basis upon which the judgment is made. For the purposes of my argument it is not sufficient to show that there may be circumstances in which our understanding is illuminated by the advice of another, or that after discussion we may come to change our minds as to the direction in which our duty lies; in these cases no conflict will remain between what we privately think we ought to do and the judgment of another, and no question of deference will arise. What we require are instances in which we would have good reasons for thinking that we ought to accept the judgment of another when we do not ourselves agree with that advice, or when we do not fully understand the grounds upon which it is based.

It is freely admitted that in technical matters there is a place for experts; the layman is justified in accepting their advice even though if he were sufficiently imprudent to rely upon his own judgment he would act differently. Of course, the prudent layman must be reasonably sure that the person who claims to be an expert is an expert, but the evidence that is required to establish reasonable confidence in an expert is different from the evidence that is required to support a particular judgment. We don't need to share his experience and skills to establish that it is prudent to act upon his advice. To what extent is this true in morals?

Perhaps the least controversial of the respects in which it may be claimed that one man may direct another in coping with moral problems concerns the probable outcome of actions. Some, it may be readily admitted, are better than others at estimating the probable consequences of actions and at prescribing what needs to be done to achieve desired results. Some will be better than others at foreseeing what will cause anxiety, pain and distress, and some will be better at predicting what will relieve suffering. And though the advised may not be able to appreciate in detail the force of the demonstration, he may be sufficiently impressed by the adviser's experience and past successes to come to think that he should accept his advice.

Further, the adviser may be well versed in the moral rules of a social group, and he may be particularly sensitive to the various degrees of seriousness attaching to them. If we grant that there is a presumption in favor of following the established rules of a society, especially those the violation of which occasions deep offense, there is a presumption in favor of following the advice of one who is well versed in those rules, and who appreciates with a fine discrimination their different degrees of importance. The adviser may have little difficulty in showing that a rule is observed, but it may not be easy for him to communicate the precise degree of importance which is attached to its observance. The person advised may thus come to understand what he is advised to do without being able to appreciate fully why he is advised to do it. As in the previous example, the person advised may well be in a position to satisfy himself that his adviser is qualified to advise, even though he is unable to determine for himself the validity of the advice he is given.

The further respects in which we stand to be advised in moral matters concern the specifically moral and non-empirical elements in the nature of the decisions we have to take. And here there are several points at which we may need the guidance of those with insight and experience. We may be advised as to the moral rules which are relevant to the situation and as to how they are to be applied. We may be shown how certain features of a situation either excuse or modify the application of

a rule. In cases where there is a conflict of duties we may be
shown how to assess the importance of a rule; where, to use
Ross's terminology, there is a conflict of *prima facie* obligations,
we need to estimate or weigh the degree of *prima facie* obli-
gatoriness or *prima facie* disobligatoriness which attaches to an
action, and those who are skilled in moral judgment may show
us how to determine what is obligatory in such circumstances.
The expert may also show us not simply what action we should
perform but the programme or policy we should adopt. Satisfying our obligations is not always just a question of performing
a single action, but is sometimes a matter of composing a plan
of action which will maximize the satisfaction of obligations; the
expert may be in a position to show how the programme which
will best satisfy various obligations can be devised and sustained. Lastly, the expert can show us not just what the situation
as we describe it requires, but also how to construct or to
describe a situation. He may be able to bring to our notice
morally relevant features which we have ignored, and he may
be able to suggest new interpretations of the situation which do
justice to relationships and claims we have neglected.

Now, if there *are* moral insights of the kinds I have indicated,
and if our moral judgments are corrigible, it is not unreasonable
to suppose that some men are more gifted and more skilled than
others in determining what duty requires, and it is not unreasonable to suppose that a man may come to think that he
ought to defer to the judgment of one who, he has come to
think, has a sharper discrimination and perception in respect
of at least some kinds of moral problems. If deference is to be
moral deference, it must be capable of justification; there must
be good reasons for accepting the judgment of another. The thesis
advanced here therefore requires that a man may have good
reasons for deferring to another even though he does not agree
with, and perhaps does not even fully understand, the judgment
which he is given. It needs to be shown not just that the moral
judgment of one man may be superior to another's, but that we
can have good reasons for believing that another's judgment is
superior to our own, even though on a particular occasion we
do not agree with it. If the agent does not have such good

reasons, the deference cannot be moral deference; on the other hand if the good reasons are those which support the particular judgment, no question of deference can arise, for the person advised will share the judgment of the adviser. What has to be the case for this thesis to succeed is that the person advised has good reasons for accepting the authority of the adviser. His respect for the judgment of the adviser must be such that it counter-balances the discrepancy between the particular judgments. In circumstances where the adviser and advised disagree as to what should be done, what kinds of reasons can the person advised have for thinking that he ought to accept the authority of the adviser? His reasons could be of the following kinds:

(a) He might have previous experience of the soundness of his adviser's judgment, of his ability to analyze a situation and detect the morally relevant features, and of his ability to determine what course of action the situation requires. It might be objected that I am crediting a person of inferior moral judgment with the capacity to evaluate the judgments of one who is his superior in judgment. But this is not so; what is required is that the person advised should be able to recognize a superior capacity, and it is not paradoxical to suggest that a person of inferior judgment can recognize that another has superior powers.

(b) Secondly, the adviser may have had considerable experience in advising upon the type of situation for which his advice is sought, and in retrospect there may be little to suggest that his previous judgments have been erroneous.

(c) Thirdly, the adviser may be of a saintly character or well adjusted personality, and the person advised may have no reason to believe that his judgment is in any way vitiated by flaws of character.

No doubt in many cases the adviser will be able to convince the person whom he advises that his judgment is correct, and where he does the problem with which we are concerned will not arise, but the capacity to form a judgment is not always accompanied by the ability to persuade and enlighten, and the person advised need not assume that his adviser's inability to persuade and convince lies to the detriment of his judgment.

It is necessary to say something about the limits of the view which is presented here. Throughout I have assumed that conscientiousness requires that where the agent defers to the judgment of another he believes that he ought to do so. It is not being claimed that, in the sense of "ought" to which moral praiseworthiness attaches, the agent ought to defer to the judgment of another, either where he does not believe that he ought to or where he believes that he ought not to. What is being claimed is compatible with the view that a person ought always to do what, when he has carefully considered the matter, he believes he ought to do. But there is a sense of "ought" in which it may be true that an agent ought to act in a way in which he does not believe he ought to act. This use of "ought" will arise in those contexts in which we wish to criticize the agent's construction of his duties. There will be certain contexts in which there will be good reasons for saying that the agent ought to rely upon the judgment of another rather than upon his own. In such contexts where the agent fails to defer to the judgment of another, we may claim that he has failed to do what he ought to do, but in doing so we shall not be impugning his conscientiousness but criticizing his construction of his duties.

Further, it is not being claimed that whenever the agent thinks he ought to respect the advice of another he is absolutely and unconditionally bound to act upon that advice. The presumption which he feels in favor of the judgment of the adviser may be defeated by other considerations, so that the *prima facie* obligation to accept the judgment of the adviser does not develop into an ultimate obligation. For example, the agent may come to think that the disobligatoriness of some aspect or element in the course of action which he is advised to take is of such a degree that it outweighs the presumption in favor of acting upon the advice given. What I am advised to do may be in some respect sufficiently morally abhorrent to counterbalance the respect I have for the judgment of the person who advises me. Or the agent might feel that in describing the difficulties he has to meet he has failed to present them with sufficient accuracy, so that he doubts whether the advice will be appropriate to the problem he has to solve.

Further, it is not being claimed that the deliverances of what we have termed private judgment are never sufficiently clear to preclude the possibility of any ultimate judgment differing from them. All that is being claimed is that there are some circumstances in which a person may be justified in coming to believe that he ought to defer to the judgment of another even where he does not agree with that particular judgment. And it is consistent with this view to hold that there are some deliverances of private judgment which are sufficiently clear and sufficiently definite to have final authority, i.e., that there are some deliverances of private judgment so clear and definite that they cannot be overborne by the advice of another however high the respect in which that advice is held. All that is being claimed here is that we cannot always assume that private judgment is definite and decisive.

III

Hitherto we have been concerned with those instances in which the agent comes to think that he ought to defer to the judgment of another because he believes that the other's judgment is superior to his. Now we need to take account of the other reasons a person may have for accepting the judgment of another. The agent may come to believe that his adviser is in a better position to make a judgment, not because he has more experience or greater insight but because he can more easily be impartial. For example, the agent may feel that his judgment is likely to be colored or biased in favor of his own interests, or even prejudiced by his being too scrupulous in avoiding favoring his own interest. Where he despairs of impartiality he may welcome the advice of one who is in no way interested in the outcome of the decision, and he may come to think that he ought to accept judgment from such a source even though it conflicts with his own private judgment.

A similar reason for accepting the judgment of another will

lie in the need to arrive at and accept *some* decision. This need
is likely to arise where there are differing moral conceptions,
and where conflict can only be resolved by some form of
arbitration. The agent may believe that he is morally committed
to pursuing a certain policy or programme, and that someone
else is also committed to following a policy which is incompatible
with his. He may indeed recognize that his opponent is as
deeply committed to his own programme as he is to his, and
though he does not approve of his opponent's policy he can
concede that his opponent ought to pursue it. He may believe
that, while he is morally committed to trying to realize his own
conceptions, his opponent is also morally committed to trying
to realize his. Reflection may lead both contestants to the position
where they see that their attempts to realize incompatible aims
and their continuous frustration of each other's programmes
will produce more harm than their acceptance of a settlement,
even though such a settlement would require both parties to
modify their original programmes. Each contestant will have
to sacrifice the realization of his own original conceptions in
order to avoid the frustration which would ensue if two or
more parties attempted to secure incompatible aims. In such a
context each agent might come to think that he ought to accept
the arbitration of a third party, even though such acceptance
would lead him to abandon the full realization of his own
private judgment. In these situations there is a duty to compromise; and along these lines of argument it is easy to see how
we may establish that there are duties to support institutions
which provide this type of arbitration. Though the obligation
to accept arbitration can derive from the superior judgment
of the arbitrator, or from the fact that the arbitrator can more
easily be impartial than any of the contestants, it can also
derive from the mere need to arrive at a settlement which will
avoid harmful frustrations. When the agent places his own
private judgment in its social context, when he takes account
of the fact that others think differently and construe their obligations differently, he is led to change his belief as to what
he ought to do. In these instances, the change in conception
is brought about not by discovering some moral feature of the

action contemplated, but by reflection upon the fact that others are committed to pursuing moral aims, and that not all of these aims are compatible.

I do not, however, wish to suggest that the man of enlightened conscience should always be prepared to submit his moral commitment to arbitration. In some cases, and this may be true for all contestants, the agent will believe that it is better for him to continue his own policy at the risk of much frustration rather than accept any compromise. He may see his duty so clearly and firmly that no benefit to be gained by arbitration can compensate for his failure to attempt what he believes it his duty to attempt, and in this course of reasoning he may be justified. Neither do I wish to suggest that all forms of competition between those of differing moral conceptions are morally undesirable. Nor do I wish to suggest that there is necessarily a basis upon which conflicting parties can justify the acceptance of arbitration. All I wish to suggest is that there are at least some cases in which different parties to a dispute can come to think themselves obliged to accept a settlement which resolves conflicting moral conceptions, even though the settlement varies and violates what each had taken to be their duty. Coming to see that I have a duty to accept an arbitration will, in these circumstances, not be founded simply on the merits of the policy which the arbitration sets forth, but will be a product of reflection upon what is required in situations where private judgments differ and conflict.

If the argument advanced here is valid, it will be seen that there are two different kinds of reasons which support moral judgments. There are those which support the private judgment and are grounded directly on the merits of the action proposed, and there are those which support the ultimate judgment and are concerned with the modifications which need to be made to the private judgment when it is placed in its social context. The reasons which support the ultimate judgment (where it differs from the private judgment) are those which derive from reflecting upon the quality of the agent's judgment, upon the quality of the judgments of other members of society, upon the claim that some are of superior moral wisdom or are in a better position to make a moral judgment, and upon the need to harmonize conflicting conceptions. Ultimate judgments have their place because we cannot be sure that our private judgment is always the best guide available to us; the reasons which justify our modifying our private judgments are those which demonstrate why we cannot always rely upon them.

XI

The Value
of Conscientiousness

P. H. NOWELL-SMITH

Is conscientiousness necessarily the best motive? To say that
conscientiousness is a good motive or a virtue is, among other
things, to praise the conscientious man and to encourage people
to be conscientious; and this is not to comment on the use of
moral language but to make a moral judgment. It would therefore be very strange if it were logically necessary that conscientiousness should be the best motive. It is, however, worth-
while investigating this question, since so many philosophers
have supposed that, while the value of other virtues is contingent, conscientiousness is necessarily good.

Sir David Ross uses the following argument to prove that
we must regard a man who acts from a sense of duty as a better
man than one who acts from any other motive. "Suppose that
some one is drawn towards doing act A by a sense of duty
and towards doing another, incompatible, act B by love for a
particular person. *Ex hypothesi,* he thinks he will not be doing
his duty in doing B. Can we possibly say that he will be acting
better if he does what he thinks not his duty than if he does
what he thinks *is* his duty? Evidently not. What those who hold
this view mean by "acting from the sense of duty" is obeying
a traditional, conventional code rather than following the warm
impulses of the heart. But what is properly meant by the sense
of duty is the thought that one *ought* to act in a certain way ....
And it seems clear that when a genuine sense of duty is in conflict with any other motive we must recognize its precedence.
If you seriously think that you ought to do A, you are bound

---

1. *The Right and the Good,* (Oxford: Clarendon Press, 1930), p. 164.

to think you will be acting morally worse in doing anything else instead." [1]

It should be noticed that Ross has loaded the scales in favor of the sense of duty by representing the only alternative motives as *impulses*, a word which suggests that they are sporadic, wayward, and capricious.[2] But sympathy, benevolence, patriotism, and ambition are not necessarily impulsive. A man can consistently adopt a policy of doing good to others, not because he regards it as his duty, but because that is what he most wants to do or enjoys doing. The word "wants" is, of course, far too weak a word to cover the pro-attitude of the non-conscientious altruist. But his altruism is not necessarily less consistent or more easily shaken than that of the man who tries to do good because he thinks it his duty.

Secondly there is an ambiguity in the phrase "acting better." If this means that what he does is better in some non-moral sense, for example that it brings about better consequences, it is extremely doubtful whether a man who acts from a sense of duty in fact "acts better" than one who does not. But if by "acting better" Ross means that a critic would necessarily regard the man who acts from a sense of duty as a morally better man, the argument begs the question.

Indeed the passage I have quoted is mostly an appeal to the self-evidence of the proposition that a man who acts from a sense of duty is a better man than one who acts from any other motive. It is only in the last sentence that an argument is used to support this view; and the argument seems to depend on a confusion between what an agent necessarily thinks about his own action and what a critic or spectator necessarily thinks. Ross's object is to prove that Jones necessarily regards Smith as a better man if he does what he (Smith) thinks he ought to do; but the statement at the end of the quotation is only true

---

2. Ross in fact gots on to describe instinctive affection as "wayward and capricious." But, though affection may be instinctive it can be cultivated and need be neither wayward nor capricious. Ross's view seems to be another example of a mistake due to thinking of all motives other than the sense of duty as "desire," "inclinations," or "impulses."

if "you" is taken to refer to the same person throughout. We must distinguish the following three statements:

(1) I think that I ought to do A but that I would be a better man if I did B.

(2) I think that you ought to do A but that you would be a better man if you did B.

(3) You think that you ought to do A, but you would be a better man if you did B.

Now there is an air of contradiction about (1) and (2), but not about (3). And the reason why (1) is logically odd is that "I ought to do A" expresses a decision to act in a certain way and implies that the decision is of a certain type, namely one based on reasons which, in a moral case, may take the form of a belief that A would be fitting or in accordance with a certain moral rule. A man who said that he ought to do A but would be morally better if he did B is in the same breath deciding to act on a moral principle and condemning himself for making this decision. But to condemn himself is to abandon the moral principle in question.

And (2) is logically odd for a similar reason. To say "you ought (morally) to do A" is to advise a man to adopt a certain moral principle and the force of "But you would be a better man if you did B" is to retract this advice. It is as inconsistent to recommend and to condemn a moral principle in the same breath as it is to decide to adopt and to condemn a moral principle in the same breath.

But (3) is not logically odd at all; it is the natural way for Jones to express his moral disagreement with Smith. Now conscientiousness is an extremely valuable motive and it is so valuable that we often wish to encourage a man to be conscientious even in a case in which we think that the principle on which he thinks he ought to act is a bad one. In such a case we might well wish to encourage him to do what he thinks right without wishing to endorse the principle on which he proposes to act. We should then say "I think you ought to do B; but, if you are really convinced that you ought to do A, then you ought to do it. For what really matters is not that you should act on the right principle but that you should act on the principle that you believe to be right." But I do not think it is logically necessary that we should rate conscientiousness as highly as this, nor that, as a matter of fact, we always do. Statement (3) is not logically odd except in the mouth of a man who has already accepted the very principle of the supreme value of conscientiousness which Ross is trying to establish.

The Value of Conscientiousness. The case of conscientiousness differs from that of other virtues in two ways. (a) The mode of conduct that the word designates is an artificial mode of conduct; and (b) the value of conscientiousness is artificial in a way in which that of other virtues is not.

(a) to be conscientious is to do what one believes to be right, not for the sake of bringing about a certain result nor for the sake of doing what is done, as such, but for duty's sake. And two different motives can lead a man to do the same thing. For example a man may be both altruistic and conscientious, and such a man will help a blind man across the road both because he wants to help him and also because he thinks it his duty to do so. But, in order to simplify the issue, I shall consider the case of a man who acts from the sense of duty alone and does something for no other reason than that he thinks he ought to do it and has a pro-attitude towards doing what he thinks he ought to do, as such. This certainly occurs; how has it come about?

I have incurred a debt and I pay it with no desire to part with my money, no thought of the welfare of the recipient, and no expectation of gain. My sole motive is the desire to conform to the moral rule "Pay your debts." It will hardly, I think, be argued that anyone has a direct, natural pro-attitude towards obeying this rule, or even the germ of such an attitude that could be fostered by education. It may be that men are naturally ritualistic, that they have an innate love of orderliness and doing things according to rule. Anthropologists are divided on this point; but in any case it is irrelevant, since conscientiousness is not the desire to conform to *any* rule, but the desire to conform to a rule which one regards as *right*. And it is therefore necessary to explain how I came to regard this particular rule, "Pay your debts," as a right rule to adopt.

As usual custom and education can explain much but not everything. In the case of any given man it is no doubt true that he adopts those rules which are customary in his society and to which he has been trained to conform. But these causes are not reasons and they cannot explain how the customary rules which a man has been trained to adopt came to be accepted as the right rules. There must have been some motive for establishing the rule in the first place and, in so far as men are rational, there must be some reason for adhering to it. Now the motive for adopting a rule cannot have been the sense of duty, since the sense of duty is the desire to do whatever is laid down by the moral rules we have adopted. A man who acts from a sense of duty pays his debts because he thinks it right to do so; he must therefore have some reason for thinking it right *other than* the fact that his sense of duty bids him do it.

This argument is equally valid whether we think of the sense of duty as a desire to conform to "objective" moral rules, to a customary code, or to those rules which a man adopts for himself. In each case, if he adopts the rule he must have some motive for adopting it, and this motive cannot be a desire to conform to it. It must be a direct or indirect pro-attitude towards doing what the rule lays down irrespective of the fact that the rule does lay it down.

(b) To say that conscientiousness is a natural virtue is to say that it is natural to praise (and therefore to have a pro-attitude towards) obedience to a moral rule. But this, although not logically impossible, seems very unlikely to be true. Here is a man who has incurred a debt and pays it for no other reason than that he thinks he ought to do so. Why should I praise and admire him rather than condemn and despise him? These questions sound odd only because "conscientious" is already a term of praise. If we are careful to exclude the praising force and to think of it as meaning only "acting from a sense of duty" it clearly makes sense to ask why we should praise the conscientious man.

And the reason cannot be found either in a regard for our own interest or in a regard for that of others. I may or may not have a pro-attitude towards the redistribution of wealth involved. This is immaterial, since the question is not "Why do I approve of his paying the debt?" but "Why do I approve of his doing this from a certain motive?"; moreover we approve of conscientious action even in cases in which we have no pro-attitude towards any element in the situation other than the motive of the agent.

Now the value of all good motives is, as we saw, artificial. We may come to have a direct pro-attitude towards the types of conduct designated "virtuous" and praise the virtuous man without any thought of the consequences of his action in this particular case; but the type of conduct concerned would never have come to be called virtuous if it was not believed to have good consequences. But the value of conscientiousness is artificial in another way also. For conscientiousness is not the disposition to do certain sorts of things that are, in fact, valuable, but the disposition to obey certain rules; and its value therefore depends on the value of the rules, which are themselves artificial devices for ensuring certain states of affairs that we wish to ensure.

Now to be conscientious is not to conform to an accepted moral code, but to conform to rules to which the agent himself thinks he ought to conform. But, although it is possible for some individuals to adopt rules that conflict with the accepted code, it is logically necessary that such cases should be rare. There could be no such thing as an accepted code if most people did not accept it. It follows therefore that, although there may be exceptions, in the majority of cases a conscientious man will do those things that are laid down in the accepted code more often than a non-conscientious man will; and since the code consists of rules which are believed to promote the interests of society, it follows that a conscientious man must be more likely to do what is believed to be in the interests of society than a non-conscientious man. This belief may be false; but, even if it is false, it explains why people are praised for being, and encouraged to be conscientious even in cases in which we do not endorse the rule which they adopt and deplore the consequences of their actions.

The Unique Position of Conscientiousness. Apart from the bad reason provided by the dogma that all non-conscientious action is impulsive or selfish, there is a good reason for allowing conscientiousness a special place on the scale of moral virtues. A man who displays some other virtue, for example courage or honesty or generosity, can be relied on to do just those things that belong to his special virtuous disposition; and these virtues can only be exercised in comparatively narrow ranges of situations. But conscientiousness is a substitute for all other virtues, and its unique value lies in this fact. The so-called "natural virtues" are dispositions to do certain sorts of things towards which we have, in general, a pro-attitude; and moral rules are rules enjoining these same things. Hence the conscientious man will do exactly the same thing that a man who has all the natural virtues will do. He does not do them for the same reason; and he is not brave or honest or kindly, since he acts for the sake of doing his duty, not for the sake of doing the brave, honest, or kindly thing. But he will do what the brave, honest, and kindly man does.

The value of conscientiousness is therefore not unlike that of money. Just as a pound note has no intrinsic value but is valuable because it can be used to buy any of a large range of goods, so the desire to do his duty, whatever it may be, will lead to a man's doing any of a large range of valuable actions. And the value of conscientiousness is like that of money in another way also. Just as a pound note is valueless except in a country where it is accepted in return for goods, so many of the duties of "special obligation," for example promise-keeping and debt-paying, are only valuable in a society in which the rules enjoining them are generally obeyed. The ends which these rules are designed to promote would not be promoted by obedience to them unless there was a general system of obedience, so that people could be relied on to keep their promises and pay their debts. Without such a system the very notions of a "promise" or a "debt" would be unintelligible.

To ask whether conscientiousness is the highest virtue is not unlike asking the question whether money is more valuable than other goods. The answer depends on how much you have. Moreover this is a question the answer to which is a moral judgment and it cannot therefore be answered either by observation or analysis of moral language. Aristotle held that a man was not really good unless he enjoyed doing what is good, and I am inclined to agree. The sense of duty is a useful device for helping men to do what a really good man would do without a sense of duty; and since none of us belongs to the class of "really good men" in this sense, it is a motive that should be fostered in all of us. But it plays little part in the lives of the best men and could play none at all in the lives of·saints. They act on good moral principles, but not from the sense of duty; for they do what they do for its own sake and not for the sake of duty.

XII

Conscience and Conscientiousness

A. CAMPBELL GARNETT

PROFESSOR Nowell-Smith tells a story of an Oxford don who thought it his duty to attend Common Room, and did so conscientiously, though his presence was a source of acute distress both to himself and others. This story is told in illustration of a discussion of the question whether conscientiousness is good without qualification. The philosopher's comment is "He would have done better to stay at home," and he reinforces this view with the historical judgment that "Robespierre would have been a better man (quite apart from the question of the harm he did) if he had given his conscience a thorough rest and indulged his taste for roses and sentimental verse." [1] The harm, in these cases, he points out, seems to spring, in part at least, from the very conscientiousness of these people, and he concludes that we have no reason for accepting the principle of the supreme value of conscientiousness and that there is nothing either self-contradictory or even logically odd in the assertion "You think that you ought to do A, but you would be a better man if you did B." [2]

This judgment, it should be noted, is a *moral* evaluation. "Better man" here means "ethically better." It explicitly excludes "better" in the sense of "more useful or less harmful to society" in the reference to Robespierre. Further, it is not restricted to the mere right or wrong of overt acts, saying, for example, that Robespierre would have done less that is objectively wrong if he had attended to his roses more and his conscience less, for it is a judgment on the moral character of the *man,* not merely on that of his overt acts, and moral judgments upon a man must take

---

1. P.H. Nowell-Smith, *Ethics* (London: Penguin, 1954), p. 247.
2. *Ibid.,* p. 253.

account of every feature of his personality concerned in the performance of his acts, i.e., his motives, intentions, character, beliefs, abilities and so forth. What we have here, therefore, is the contention that in some cases where conscientiousness would lead to more harm than good (as it may do in cases of mistaken moral judgments or other ignorance) a man may be a morally better man by stifling his conscience and doing what he believes he ought not to do. It is not claimed that this will always be true in such cases, and it is not denied that conscientiousness is to some degree a value. But it is denied that it is the only moral value, or a value with supreme authority above all others, or that it is an essential feature of all moral value.

These denials are not uncommon among contemporary moralists, but it should be noted that they constitute a rejection of the major tradition in moral philosophy, from Plato to the present day. They also conflict with the convictions of the common man expressed in such injunctions as "Let your conscience be your guide," "Do what you yourself believe to be right, not what others tell you," "Act on your own convictions," "Always act in accord with your own conscience," "To thine own self be true." Conscientiousness is firmness of purpose in seeking to do what is right, and to most people it seems to be the very essence of the moral life and a value or virtue in some sense "higher" or more important than any other. Among philosophers this view is notably expressed in Joseph Butler's doctrine of the "natural supremacy" of conscience and in Immanuel Kant's insistence that there is nothing good in itself, intrinsically good, save the good will, and that this consists in the will to do one's duty for duty's sake. There are, evidently, some complex issues and confusions involved in these sharply varying positions and to clarify them we shall need to begin with an examination of what is involved in conscience itself.

Analysis of Conscience

Conscience involves both a cognitive and an emotive or motivational element. The cognitive element consists in a set of moral judgments concerning the right or wrong of certain kinds of action or rules of conduct, however these have been formed. The emotive or motivational element consists of a tendency to experience emotions of a unique sort of approval of the doing of what is believed to be right and a similarly unique sort of disapproval of the doing of what is believed to be wrong. These feeling states, it is generally recognized, are noticeably different from those of mere liking or disliking and also from feelings of aesthetic approval and disapproval (or aesthetic appreciation) and from feelings of admiration and the reverse aroused by non-moral activities and skills. They can become particularly acute, moving and even distressing, in the negative and reflexive form of moral disapproval of one's own actions and motives, the sense of guilt and shame. In this form (indeed in both forms) they may have some notably irrational manifestations, but the sense of shame also has a very valuable function as an inhibitory motive upon the person who contemplates the possibility of doing what he believes to be wrong.

These are the commonly recognized aspects of conscience, and they frequently function quite uncritically. Because of this uncritical emotive reaction conscience all too frequently moves people to approve or disapprove actions and rules concerning which adequate reflection would lead to a very different verdict, and sometimes it afflicts people with a quite irrational sense of guilt. These deplorable effects of some manifestations of conscience are a large part of the reason for its devaluation in the judgment of many modern moralists. What these thinkers rightly deplore is the uncritical emotive reaction which the person who experiences it calls his conscience, particularly when the emotive element in it inhibits any critical activity of the cognitive element. But it is not necessary, and it is not usually the case, that the emotive element in conscience stifles the critical, and there is no justification for jumping to the conclusion that conscience should be ignored. For critical ethical thinking is itself usually conscientiousness, and conscience can be trained to be habitually critical.

For clarity of thinking on this question we need to distinguish between the critical and the traditional conscience. The latter is uncritical. Here the emotive element attaches to moral ideas accepted from the tradition without critical re-evaluation of them. Its strength lies in this perpetuation of tradition, but this is also the source of its errors. It is this blind but emotive perpetuation of an outgrown and mistaken tradition that contemporary critics of the supreme evaluation of conscience, for the most part, are concerned to deplore. And thus far they are right. But one would be unfair to such critics if one were not to recognize that their efforts to point out the errors of the tradition are usually also conscientious and are not merely the echoing of another tradition. Sometimes their critical ideas are boldly new and very commonly they are presented with persistent and painstaking care and in spite of personal cost. Nietzsche and Marx, Schweitzer and Gandhi, as well as Robespierre, were thoroughly conscientious men. Their ideas were new but were held with great emotive strength and tenacity. The same is true of the prophets of Israel and the great moral innovators of other religions. Indeed, the outstanding examples of conscientious men are not the mere sustainers of a tradition but the thinkers who try to improve the tradition.

This fact of the vitality of the critical conscience shows the superficiality of Freud's identification of it with the super-ego and of the explanation of it as an after-effect of early social conditioning as put forward by many psychologists and sociologists, and uncritically adopted by many philosophers. On this view the moral judgments which tend to arouse spontaneous emotions of approval or disapproval, shame and guilt, are those which we learned to make in our childhood and which we then heard expressed by those around us accompanied by strong manifestations of moral approval and disapproval. The child, it is pointed out, must naturally assimilate the tendency to feel similar emotions whenever he himself makes a moral judgment, and this emotive tendency remains with him in adult life together with the tendency to frame and express such judgments. Conscience is then said to be simply the inward echo of the emotionally expressed judgments of our childhood social environment. This may be accepted as part of the explanation of the emotive element in the uncritical traditional conscience, but as an explanation of how men come to feel the way they do about the results of their own original critical thinking, and of the motivational drive conscientiously to do original critical, ethical thinking, it is woefully inadequate.

It is not difficult to see how the cognitive element in conscience, the judgment of right and wrong, becomes critical. To some extent it must be so from the beginning. A favorite word in every child's vocabulary is "Why?" And especially does he ask for reasons when told that he *ought* to do something he does not want to do. If moral injunctions are accepted as such on mere authority it is because it is implicitly believed that the authority *has* good reasons for issuing them, or else that the demand or example of this authority is in itself a sufficient reason for obedience or conformity, as with kings and deities. Apart from authority, reasons for moral rules have to be found in their relevance to the needs and security and peace of the community and the well-being of the person himself. But always, it is a distinguishing mark of a *moral* rule that it is one for which it is believed that reasons can be given. Critical thinking about moral rules is therefore stimulated whenever the reasons presented seem inadequate, beginning with the child's "Why?" and whenever there is a conflict of rules.

This critical thinking at first accepts as its basic principles the sort of reasons customarily given for moral rules and injunctions—the traditions of the tribe, its peace, security, prosperity and honor, revelations from divine sources, and so forth. But at a higher level of critical thinking conflicts are found between these basic principles themselves, and man is directed to the philosophical task of thinking out the *most* basic of all principles—if any such can be found. The search may end in skepticism and confusion, but so long as the thinker is prepared to accept any reason at all as a reason why something "ought" (in the ethical sense) to be done he also feels conscientiously constrained to do that which his search for reasons has led him to believe that he ought to do. Further, the experience of finding reasons for rejecting old views and accepting new ones impresses upon him the need and value of the search. Thus, so long as he recognizes any moral reasons at all he must recognize a duty of continued critical examination of moral ideas. The critical conscience thus becomes its own stimulus to further critical thinking. Conscience takes the form of the firm conviction, not merely that one ought to do what one believes one ought to do, still less that one ought to do without question what one has been taught one ought to do but that one ought to think for oneself as to what one really ought to do and then act on one's own convictions. And the emotive drive is apt to attach itself as firmly to this last formulation of the cognitive element in conscience as ever it does to the other two.

Conscience, Love, and Personal Integrity

It is clear that the motivational element of conscience in its most developed form is not merely the continuing echo of approvals and disapprovals of specific rules and actions impressed upon us by the social environment of our childhood. Yet the emotive content is continuous through all the changes in the sort of action the contemplation of which arouses it. One can imagine a youth of the eighteenth century feeling strong moral approval of a man who challenges a dangerous opponent to a duel in defense of his wife's good name, and later, in his maturity, feeling similar moral approval of another man who faces social obloquy for his refusal to fight a duel in similar circumstances because he is opposed in principle to duelling. In both cases it is the manifestation of courage in defense of principle that calls forth the moral approval, but his judgment has changed as to the principle of action worthy of such defense. We see that what has changed is the specific sort of action that calls forth approval and disapproval, while what remains the same is the specific sort of reason that is held to be appropriate for judging an action to be worthy of approval or disapproval. And this we would find to be true in general (if we had space to demonstrate it) through the whole process of critical re-examination of moral judgment. Moral approval and disapproval attach to whatever we find to have reasons for approval. These reasons, in the course of thinking, become more and more specifically formulated and more and more highly generalized into abstract principles of moral judgment and they are only changed as change is seen to be needed to bring them into consistency with one another. Emotive unwillingness to accept some of the consequences of this process of ethical thinking sometimes inhibits and distorts it, but through it all the emotive drives of approval and disapproval tend to attach themselves to whatever lines of action are thought to be characterized by the recognized reasons for such attitudes.

On account of the complexity of all their implications the exact and proper statement of these basic ethical principles is a matter of very great difficulty. Yet there is a degree of agreement as to general principle which is really remarkable considering the complexity of human conduct and the diversity of traditional moral judgment with which we start. Thus, there is almost universal agreement that the fact that an act may have bad consequences for some persons is a good reason for disapproving it, and the reverse if it would have good consequences. Similarly there are certain rules of justice that are generally recognized, such as that of impartiality in the distribution of goods and burdens, the keeping of contracts and promises, the making of reparations, and the equitable application of the law. Questions arise as to how far the duties of beneficence should go, as to what to do when principles conflict in practical application, as to whether all principles can be comprehended under some one principle, and so forth. But the general trend is clear. Moral approval and disapproval are moved by the thought of the effect of our actions upon the weal or woe of human beings. This is the root of conscience. If some conscientious thinkers, such as Nietzsche, seem to be an exception to this rule it is because they have developed unusual or paradoxical views of what really constitutes true human weal or woe, or how it can best be promoted.

This connection of conscience with reasons for action bearing on the effects of action on human well-being enables us to understand the distinctive feeling-tone of moral approval and disapproval—i.e., their difference from mere liking and disliking, and from other emotions such as the aesthetic, and from non-moral admiration and its reverse. The moral emotions are often mingled with these others, but they are also different. There is in them a distinct element of concern for human welfare which is gratified by what promotes it and distressed at anything that seems injurious. For this reason the moral emotions have often been identified with sympathy, but they are not mere passive feeling states. There is in them an element of active concern for human values with an impulse to give help where it seems needed. For this reason these emotions are responsive to judgments about the effects of human action, bringing forth a positive response of approval to that which seems helpful and the reverse towards the hurtful. For this reason also moral approval is a gratifying emotion, inducing a favorable reaction, while moral disapproval is apt to become a source of distress and an occasion for anger. For moral approval, we can now see, is a specification in action of the most deeply satisfying of all human emotions, that of love, in its most general form of expression.

Moral approval, then, is a development of the basic social interest of man as a social animal. It is an expression of the general sympathetic tendency of concern for human values with special attention to those depending on the orderly life of the group. It is an expression of the desire to create and maintain those values. Its conflict with other motives is therefore, a conflict of desires. But this particular conflict, the conflict of conscience (moral approvals and disapprovals) with other desires (temptations) is not just an ordinary conflict of desires. It is a conflict in which the integrity of the personality is peculiarly involved. In an ordinary conflict of desires, in which there is no moral issue, the best solution is for one of the desires to be completely set aside and fade into oblivion without regrets, the opposing interest being completely triumphant. And, for the integrity of the personality it does not matter which interest gives way. But if the conflict be between "conscience" (the interests involved in moral approval and disapproval) and "temptation" (some opposed interest or desire) then it does matter which triumphs. The integrity of personality is involved. It tends to dissolve as a person slips into the habit of doing things he believes to be wrong. He loses his self-respect and his firmness of purpose. For a time the sense of guilt depresses. Later it tends to be repressed. With these psychological repressions the personality tends to manifest either general weakness or the over-compensations which give a false impression of strength as they manifest themselves in irrational drives. The guilty conscience and the repressed conscience are at the root of most of the disorders of personality, whether the guilt itself be reasonably conceived or not.

It is evident, therefore, that the emotive or motivational element that manifests itself in conscience is rooted in conative tendencies or interests which are of basic importance in the life of man. This psychological conclusion has, in recent years, been strongly emphasized by a number of workers in the field of psychotherapy, notably by Erich Fromm, who argues strongly that only in what he calls the "orientation of productive love"[3] can the personality of man develop continuously and with the integrity necessary for mental health. From this conclusion concerning the psychological need of this type of orientation Fromm also develops a most important theory of conscience. What we have distinguished as the uncritical (or traditional) and the critical conscience he distinguishes as the "authoritarian" and the "humanistic" conscience. The former he dismisses as the internalized voice of an external authority, but the latter, he maintains, is "the reaction of our total personality to its proper functioning or disfunctioning.... Conscience is thus ... the voice of our true selves which summons us ... to live productively, to develop fully and harmoniously .... It is the guardian of our integrity."[4]

If Fromm's psychological analysis of the growth and structure of personality is accurate in essentials, and if our account of the growth of the critical conscience out of the uncritical is also correct, then we must recognize that conscience at every stage is, as Fromm says of the "humanistic" conscience, "the

3. Eric Fromm, *Man for Himself* (New York: Rinehart, 1947), pp. 92-107.

4. *Ibid.*, pp. 158-60.

reaction of our total personality to its total functioning," its "voice" is the experience of the constraint of the personality as a whole, in its seeking of a growing creative expression with integrity or wholeness, upon the occasional and temporary impulses and desires which would tend to stultify its creativity and destroy its integrity. It is because doing what we believe we ought not is destructive of that integrity that conscience demands that we always act in accord with our own convictions; and it is because the fundamental orientation of human life is social and creative that ethical thinking tends, through the course of history, to clarify itself in the light of principles which tend to formulate moral judgments as expressions of impartial concern for human well-being.

The Authority of Conscience

It is time now to return to the question with which we started. Is it true that a man would sometimes be a better man (i.e., morally better) for refusing to obey his conscience rather than obeying it? It should be noted that the question is not whether the consequences to himself or to others might be better in general, but whether he would, himself, be a morally better man for acting in this way. This raises the question whether it is ever morally right to go against one's conscience. Is it ever right to do as you think you ought not to do? And this, again, is not the question whether conscience is always right in what it commands us to do, but whether it is ever right to disobey those commands, thus choosing to do what we believe to be wrong? The traditional answer is given by Joseph Butler in asserting the "natural supremacy" of conscience, which "magisterially asserts itself and approves and condemns." "Had it strength as it had right: had it power, as it had manifest authority, it would absolutely govern the world." [5] Against this we have the contemporary challenge voiced by Nowell-Smith.

---

5. Joseph Butler, *Five Sermons* (New York, 1950), p. 41.

One serious objection to this modern challenge to the traditional view is that it is necessarily futile and worse than futile, as a guiding principle of moral behavior. It is futile because, though a man may believe that *perhaps*, in some cases, it *may* be that he would be a better man if he did not do what he believes he ought to do, he can never believe this in any particular case, for that would be to believe that he ought not to do this that he believes he ought to do, which is self-contradictory. Thus this piece of ethical theory is so paradoxical that it can never function as a guide to action. Further, it is worse than futile, for it implies, not merely that moral judgment may be mistaken (and therefore needs critical examination) but that the very effort not to do wrong may itself sometimes be wrong—that the conscientious effort to try to find out what is really right and act firmly in accord with one's own convictions, is sometimes wrong and we have no way of knowing when it is wrong. From this state of mind the only reasonable reaction is to abandon the ethical inquiry and the ethical endeavor and make the easiest and most satisfactory adjustment we can to the mores of the community and the practical exigencies of our personal situation.

The logical alternatives, therefore, are either to abandon the moral standpoint entirely, or to affirm, with Butler, the moral authority of every man's own conscience. The fact that judgments conscientiously made may be in error does not imply that this assertion of the sovereignty of the individual conscience must lead to either conflict or chaos. It rather avoids conflict, for each person, in asserting the rights of his own conscience, and at the same time affirms the right of freedom of conscience for others. And it avoids chaos because, laying the injunction upon us to exercise continuous critical examination of our own moral judgments, it points us on the only possible way to consistency and order in moral judgment, by finding our errors and rectifying them. A community of people open-mindedly seeking the best formulation and reformulation of its moral rules, and abiding by its most intelligent findings, is more likely to maintain order with progress than one in which conscience operates in any other way, or in no way at all.

We must conclude, then, that if one were to accept Nowell-Smith's critique of conscience one could not apply it to the decision of any moral question in one's own conduct, and that its acceptance, if taken seriously, would be apt to have a deteriorating effect upon personal moral endeavor. But it is still possible to grant it theoretical credence and apply it to our evaluation of the moral value of the personality of others. This is what Nowell-Smith does in the case of Robespierre and the Oxford don: Robespierre would have been a better man if he had indulged his taste for roses and sentimental verse rather than follow the demands of his conscience that he strive by whatever terrible means seemed necessary to carry through the programme of the revolution; and the Oxford don would have been a better man if he had allowed his personal distaste for Common Room society to overcome his sense of duty which required him to attend it.

This is a judgment on the moral quality of the man as affected by his act of choice. The choice with which we are concerned is not that of his decision as to whether A or B is the right thing to do but his decision as to whether he would do what he believed to be the right thing or follow his personal wishes to do something that he found much more agreeable to himself. The latter act is the one he would do if he had not given any consideration to the effect of his actions on other people, or the needs of the social structure of which he is a part, except so far as his own interests were involved, and, coming as it does after he has considered these things and formed a judgment as to what they require of him, it is a decision to set aside the results of this thoughtful examination of the possible consequences of his conduct and do the thing he personally wants to do and would have done if he had never given the matter any ethical thought at all. When the issue is thus clearly stated it is very difficult to see how any thoughtful person could judge the unconscientious following of inclination to be the act of a better man, or an act that tends to make a better man, than the careful thinking and active self-determination involved in conscientiousness. It seems evident that those who have expressed the view that the following of personal inclination is sometimes morally better than conscientious-ness are confusing this issue with another to which we must next give attention.

Conscientiousness and Other Values

For Immanuel Kant there was nothing good in itself, good without qualification, except a good will, and a good will, he explains, is good, not because it is a will to produce some good, or even the greatest possible good, but simply by reason of the nature of its volition as a will to do one's duty, a will to do what is conceived as right. Thus, for Kant, an action only has *moral* worth if it is done from a sense of duty, not from any inclination, even that of an impartial desire to promote general human well-being. Kant does not deny that good-natured inclinations have value, but he insists that the will to do one's duty has incomparably higher value and that it alone is of distinctly moral value. Kant's position here is an extreme one. Conscientious-ness is regarded not merely as an essential part of moral value but as the only true moral value and supreme among all values. Against this Nowell-Smith is not alone in protesting, and it is this rejection of the extravagant claim for conscientiousness as compared with other values, that seems to him to justify the notion that here are some occasions when some other value should be preferred and conscientiousness rejected.[6]

It is true, as Nowell-Smith says, that "we normally think of moral worth as meaning the worth of any virtuous motive and we normally think of sympathy and benevolence as virtuous motives."[7] It is also true, that, contrary to Kant, we normally judge a right action done out of sympathy and good will to be morally better than the same action would be if done solely from a sense of duty but without sympathy or good will.[8] These normal judgments I think we must fully endorse, but they do

6. Nowell-Smith, *op. cit.*, p. 245.
7. *Ibid.*, p. 246.
8. *Ibid.*, p. 259.

not involve the implication that a man can be morally justified (i.e., can be a "better man" than he otherwise would be) in performing an act, even of sympathy and good will (let alone indulging an interest in roses), which, in the circumstances, he regards as wrong.

There is a story told by Mark Twain of two ladies who lied to protect a runaway slave even though believing it wrong to do so and fearing that they might suffer in hell for their sin. In such a case we see a conflict, not merely of conscience with desire, but of the uncritical or traditional conscience with the critical. The deeper level of conscience, which they might well have called their "intuitions," urged the protection of the poor, frightened slave. They were not sufficiently capable of philosophical thinking to formulate a philosophical critique in support of their own deeper insights, so they remained superficially of the traditional opinion that their action was wrong. But their choice was actually a conscientious one, true to the deeper levels of conscience, and we tend to endorse their decision because it is endorsed by our consciences too. But this example (and others like it) is not a case of judging that the motives of love and sympathy were here better than conscientiousness, but of judging that the will to do good, seen as the very root of righteousness, is better than the will to conform to rules uncritically accepted as right. Such a judgment is far from the same as judging that the Oxford don would have been a morally better man for indulging his reluctance to attend Common Room than he would for conscientiously fulfilling what he believed to be his duty in the matter.

If we accept a teleological ethics then we recognize that the purpose of moral rules is to protect and promote the more important aspects of social well-being. We then see that the motives of love and sympathy, if sufficiently strong, enlightened and impartial, would achieve the purposes of moral rules better than the moral rules do, and would also achieve other good purposes beyond them. A world of saints would be a better world than a world of conscientious persons without mutual love and sympathy. Seeing this, though there are no saints, we endorse such elements of saintliness as there are (i.e., love and sympathy expressed in this enlightened and impartial way) and recognize them as morally good and as expressions of a better type of personality than one in which conscientiousness is found without these motives. But this recognition of the greater value of enlightened and impartial good will, or love, can never involve a rejection of conscientiousness in favor of such love, for such love includes and transcends all that conscientiousness stands for. Such love is the fulfilling of the law and the fulfilling, not the rejection, of the conscientiousness which supports the law. Thus, while a teleological ethics rejects Kant's apotheosis of the will to do one's duty as the only intrinsic moral value it does not lead to an endorsement of the view that we should sometimes judge a man as morally better for neglecting his conscience to indulge some other inclination. If, on the other hand, we were to accept a deontological ethics we should find that to speak of a conflict between conscientiousness and an enlightened and impartial love and sympathy (or any other good motive) as a conflict between different moral values involves a category mistake. For conscientiousness and other good motives, on this view, are not moral values in the same sense. An act of love is not made moral by the kind of consequences at which it aims. The only moral actions are those which intentionally adhere to intuitively discerned principles. So whatever value is attached to love and sympathy, it is not moral value. Moral value belongs alone to conscientiousness. Thus a man could never become morally better by rejecting the morally valuable motive of conscientiousness for some other motive to which only non-moral value is attached. This de-ontological theory Nowell-Smith, I think rightly, rejects, but it is well to see that it, too, involves a rejection of his theory of the comparison of conscientiousness with other moral values.

Returning to the teleological point of view, and reflecting on the de-ontologist's claim, we can perhaps see the reason for the basic confusions that haunt people's minds on this question of the relative value of conscientiousness and impartial good will, or love. Conscientiousness is uniquely a moral motive in that its end is morality itself, the keeping of moral rules. All other motives, if without conscientiousness, are at best non-moral

(operating without concern for moral rules) or at worst immoral—consciously in opposition to them. This is true even of
love and sympathy, simply as such. But if the teleological point
of view is correct it is not true of love and sympathy *with a
concern for impartiality,* for this latter is the very basis of moral
rules and such love is of the essence of the moral life. Thus
conscientiousness and impartial good will share together the
unique character of being moral in the sense of being motivated
by a concern for morality as such, the former for the rules which
formulate it in lines of conduct, and the latter for the basic
principle of impartial concern for human well-being in accordance
with which the rules merely formulate the guiding lines. But
this merely means that impartial good will is a motive characterized by the critical conscience, while conscientiousness without love, sympathy or good will is an operation of the traditional
or uncritical conscience alone. Thus the motive that is of uniquely
moral value and of supreme moral authority is love finding
expression in the form of the critical conscience.

The main conclusions, therefore, of this paper may be summed
up briefly thus: (1) Conscientiousness, if it be properly critical,
is good without qualification, but an uncritical conscientiousness
is not. (2) Since we cannot be saints we need to be conscientious, and this includes both the effort to find out what
we really ought to do and the effort to do it to the best of our
ability. (3) We should also cultivate the motive of impartial
love or good will, for it functions as both an illuminating guide
and support to our efforts to be conscientious and is itself of
intrinsic moral value. (4) We can be righteous, and to that
extent good, men merely by being conscientious, but we can
be much better men by being not only conscientious but men in
whom, without conflicting with conscience, the effort to be
conscientious is made unnecessary by the out-flow of spontaneous
and impartial good will. These are very ordinary conclusions
but it takes clear thinking to keep them free from some very
extraordinary objections.

XIII

The Authority to Conscience

JOHN T. GRANROSE

IF you listen carefully to the ethical discussions of non-philosophers, it will not be long before you encounter the word "conscience" playing an important role. Appeals to conscience continue to play (as they long have) a major role in everyday thinking and talking about ethical matters. In very recent years, especially, reference to "the demands of conscience" has been frequently given by activists of the New Left. In view of the widespread use of the word "conscience," there has been surprising little effort on the part of philosophers to clarify the role (if any) which conscience might properly play in ethics.

Part of the reason for the lack of theoretical interest in conscience is the widespread belief that, in one way or another, modern psychology has "explained away" conscience. Briefly put, the conviction that psychological studies of conscience undermine the usefulness of appeals to conscience in ethics is due to two factors. In the first place, and most important, there seems to be no room in modern psychology for that mysterious and ethically infallible "faculty" which some persons have required conscience to be. The idea of conscience as an inner source of ethical knowledge simply does not fit in with what we now know of psychology. Along with this, psychologists find that the dictates of conscience vary from person to person and depend (at least to a significant extent) on parental training.

1. I wish to thank Professors Arnold S. Kaufman, Richard B. Brandt, and William K. Frankena of the University of Michigan for their helpful comments on earlier versions of this paper. The present paper is based in part on my dissertation, "The Implications of Psychological Studies of Conscience for Ethics." Unpublished Ph.D. dissertation, Department of Philosophy, University of Michigan, 1966.

All of this makes it highly implausible to claim infallibility for conscience. The second way in which psychology has tended to upset the role of conscience in ethics is through a variety of associations of conscience with non-rational aspects of human experience. For example, Freudians have pointed to various links between conscience and toilet training and infantile sexuality. Such connections, if true, would be understandably disturbing to many ethical theorists. It is small wonder, then, that psychological studies have tended to undermine the role of conscience in ethics.

In the present paper I argue that even in the light of modern psychological studies of conscience there is an important sense in which one always ought to follow his conscience. I take this claim to be at least part of the meaning of the traditional claim that conscience has "authority."

Infallibility vs. Authority

In order to clarify what is meant by the expression "the authority of conscience," we may begin by considering how this expression differs from and is related to "the infallibility of conscience."

It is popularly supposed that most religious and philosophical theories of conscience hold it to be infallible. Of course, if each man's conscience *were* infallible, this would be a strong reason for following the guidance of one's conscience. That is, if the actions against which one's conscience protested were always actually or objectively wrong (as opposed to merely thought to be wrong), then it would be easy to argue that a person has a moral obligation not to do those things which violate his conscience. But all the available empirical evidence suggests that there is hardly any reason to suppose that conscience is infallible, and substantial reason to suppose that it is not. It is the confusion between infallibility and authority which leads many persons to reject the claims of conscience entirely, simply on the evidence that different consciences conflict and are sometimes mistaken.

As a matter of fact, there have been relatively few persons who have ever claimed that conscience was actually infallible. The claim which has been more frequent is that conscience has authority, that is, that the demands of conscience should override competing demands. That conscience is infallible, if that were actually true, would be a good reason for accepting its authority. But is infallibility the *only* ground on which the authority of conscience could be based? My aim in this paper is to provide an argument for acknowledging the authority of conscience which does not require the assumption that the dictates of conscience are infallible.

Two Senses of the Term "Conscience"

A rough account of what is generally meant by "having a conscience" would be that one has the tendency to feel certain sorts of discomfort (guilt, shame, or remorse) just in virtue of the violation, intended violation, or contemplated violation of one's own moral rules.[2] This account would enable us, for example, to draw the distinction between pangs of conscience and fear of punishment. Conscience would necessarily involve one's *own* moral rules, while fear of punishment need not do this. But an even more important distinction must be made within conscience itself.

Conscience involves commitment to moral rules but there are at least two basic ways in which moral rules may be held. One way of holding moral rules would be that exemplified by the developmental psychologist Jean Piaget's stage of "realism."[3] This is a type of conservatism about the rules. Children who accept rules in this way are typically acquainted with only one set of rules and do not feel free to question their nature, origin, or authority. The rules are thought by the child to have always

2. *Ibid.*, pp. 29-64. This behavioral definition is based on an unpublished manuscript by Professor Arnold S. Kaufman.

3. Jean Piaget, *The Moral Judgment of the Child* (New York: Collier Books, 1962), pp. 50-60.

existed, to be unchangeable, to be absolutely correct, "above criticism," and so on. The important point for our present purposes is that moral rules are sometimes accepted as not subject to criticism or revision in the light of changing circumstances.

There is a second, and radically different, way in which moral rules are sometimes held, however. The distinguishing feature of this way of holding rules is that the rules are subject to rational criticism and possible revision. Of course, to provide some basis for this criticism and possible revision to take place it would seem that the point of the rules would have to be understood by the subject, at least to some extent. Also, it would not be necessary that the rules in question were *originally* accepted as a result of such rational deliberation, only that they be continually subject at present to such examination. This attitude toward rules is that which characterizes Piaget's stage of "autonomy." [4]

I propose to make this distinction between two ways in which a person may be committed to rules the basis for a distinction between two types of conscience which a man might have. [5] Borrowing a pair of labels from A. Campbell Garnett, [6] I wish to call these two sub-types of conscience "traditional" and "critical" respectively. With this distinction we are able to make a number of points easily which otherwise would have been cumbersome to express. For example, we can now say that many standard criticisms of conscience appear to be basically sound when directed against the traditional conscience, but not when directed against the critical conscience. Further, it is plausible to equate the Freudian super-ego with one's traditional

---

4. *Ibid.*, pp. 194-196.
5. Some distinction between two uses or senses of the term "conscience" has been fairly common. Perhaps the best known distinction of this sort is due to Erich Fromm. Fromm distinguishes what he calls the authoritarian conscience from the humanistic conscience. Although it is difficult to be certain, his basic distinction appears to coincide with the one I wish to maintain. Cf. Erich Fromm, *Man for Himself* (New York: Rinehart, 1947), pp. 143-159.
6. A. Campbell Garnett, "Conscience and Conscientiousness," pp. 205-220.

conscience but not with one's critical conscience. The sense in which I wish to claim that conscience has authority only applies to one's critical conscience.

Should One Always Follow One's Conscience?

Bishop Butler remarks at one point that the fact that conscience "tends to restrain men from doing mischief to each other, and leads them to do good, is too manifest to need being insisted upon."[7] But although it may be true that conscience tends to keep men from doing what they *believe* is wrong and in that way leads them to do what they believe is right, the main force of critiques of conscience is to show that what one believes is right or what one's conscience tells one is not necessarily what is actually right. Indeed, the rapid acceleration of change in society results in new situations in which acting under the old moral rules may suddenly be immoral. (Some of us consider the ban on birth control to be such a case.) As the song has it, "The times they are a-changing," and as an older song has it, "New occasions teach new duties, time makes ancient good uncouth." It may well seem that if there is no more to "conscience" than the "traditional" and "critical" senses suggested earlier, the whole notion of "the authority of conscience" should be scrapped.

In this section of the paper two main questions will be considered: 1) Admitting that even our critical consciences are fallible, have we an obligation to follow them nonetheless? and 2) Is this obligation absolute or only *prima facie?* That is, should one *always* follow one's (critical) conscience or may this obligation sometimes be overridden?

If we interpret the question of whether one should always follow conscience as asking whether conscientious action can

---

7. Joseph Butler, *Five Sermons Preached at the Rolls Chapel* (Indianapolis: Bobbs-Merrill, 1950), p. 26. *Ethical Theories: A Book of Readings,* ed. A. I. Melden (2nd ed.; Englewood Cliffs, N.J.: Prentice Hall, 1950), pp. 218-19.

produce harmful effects, the answer is clear. (It is, in fact, entailed by the admission that conscience is fallible.) Nowell-Smith's reply to this question is certainly correct: "Many of the worst crimes in history have been committed by men who had a strong sense of duty just because their sense of duty was so strong."[8] But Nowell-Smith not only claims that the effects on society might be better if a person did not follow his conscience in some particular situation but also that he might be a "better man" not to follow it.

I should myself have no hesitation in saying that Robespierre would have been a better man (quite apart from the question of the harm he did) if he had given his conscience a thorough rest and indulged his taste for roses and sentimental verse.[9]

Nowell-Smith's comments are understandable but nevertheless misleading. It is true that Robespierre, for example, would have been a better man in some sense if he had not done some of those things which his conscience prompted him to do. But the situation mentioned above must be described more fully if its crucial feature is to be brought out. Robespierre was doing what he thought to be his duty. Even if his beliefs about what he ought to do were mistaken, it still does not follow, without begging the question at issue here, that he ought not to have acted on his beliefs. Could one ever be a better man by refusing to do what he believes to be his duty? It does not seem obvious that the answer to this question *must* be "yes."

Nowell-Smith makes a comment which seems to indicate a misconception of the crucial point at issue. He suggests the sort of advice which a supporter of conscientiousness might offer to another person trying to reach a decision:

"I think you ought to do B; but, if you are really convinced that you ought to do A, then you ought to do it. For what really matters is not

----

8. P. H. Nowell-Smith, *Ethics* (London: Penguin Books, 1954), p. 247. Cf. Bertrand Russell, "The Harm That Good Men Do," *Skeptical Essays* (New York: W. W. Norton and Company, 1928), pp. 111-123.

9. *Ibid.*, p. 247.

that you should act on the right principle but that you should act on
the principle that you believe to be right." [10]

But this way of putting things suggests a crucial misunderstand-
ing, for it is *not* more important to act on one's own beliefs than
to act on the correct beliefs. This way of putting things suggests
that choosing to act on the right principle is an actual option in
such a case. It suggests that one can *know* what the right principle is. But acting on a principle believed to be right is not an
alternative which one might choose over acting on the principle
which *is right*. These two ways of acting are not in competition
with each other. This point has been made in some detail by
Kurt Baier in discussing what he calls "the paradox of subjective
duty." [11] It is not that following one's critical conscience is
superior to being right, but that the way in which one tries to be
right is by following one's critical conscience. It is a misunder-
standing of this point which leads to Nowell-Smith's comments
about Robespierre.

Nowell-Smith next remarks that he does not find the supreme
value of conscientiousness to be "logically necesary." [12] In this
Nowell-Smith is correct. The statement "One ought to do what
one ought to do" is logically necessary, but the statement "One
ought to do what one believes after critical examination one
ought to do" is clearly not *logically* necessary. The latter statement does appear to be true, however, and to be supportable
by convincing reasons.

Several lines of argument need to be examined in attempting to evaluate the nature and extent of the obligation to follow
one's critical conscience. The first line of argument concerns the
effects on the individual of acting contrary to his conscience.
Since it concerns only the effects of such actions on the agent
himself it may be called the "prudential" argument.

Briefly, put, this first argument is that following one's con-

10. *Ibid.*, p. 254.
11. Kurt Baier, *The Moral Point of View: A Rational Basis for Ethics*
(Ithaca, N.Y.: Cornell University Press, 1958), pp. 143-47.
12. *Ibid.*

science is necessary for maintaining one's psychological or mental health. The guilt feelings resulting from violating one's "principles" are claimed to be seriously disruptive of one's personality. Now this is obviously not the sort of claim which lends itself easily to experimental investigation. Nevertheless, the undesirable effects which guilt feelings may have on the personality have been dramatized in a great many works of literature. No doubt most persons have had their own experience of the disruptive effects of guilt. In addition, there are a number of psychologists who put forward clinical evidence on these matters. Some writers subsume these moral concepts under some more general concept such as "integration" or "consistency." Gordon W. Allport has been a chief spokesman for this view. Allport writes:

Psychology's chief contribution to mental health is the concept of integration, a term less Biblical, but meaning much the same as St. James' "single-mindedness." Integration means the forging of approximate mental unity out of discordant impulses and aspirations.[13]

Allport claims that integration is necessary to mental health. And the integration of one's sincerely held moral beliefs and one's behavior in those situations where these beliefs are relevant is what is known as moral integrity, conscientiousness, or following one's conscience.

The prudential argument for the authority of conscience may be summed up by saying that the violation of one's conscience tends to make a person miserable. (The rule of following conscience would be roughly parallel to that of preserving one's health.) To disobey society may make one uncomfortable. But so long as one can say, "I still have my self-respect," he need not be totally miserable.

But even if we accept the above argument, there does not seem to be any reason for saying that we *always* ought to follow our conscience. Even if following one's conscience were a

13. Gordon W. Allport, *The Individual and His Religion* (New York: Macmillan, 1950), p. 92.

necessary condition for mental health and the mental health of its members were necessary for the welfare of society, surely there might still be times when an individual was morally obligated to disobey his conscience, to sacrifice his (mental) health for the sake of others. This would seem to be just like those cases in which a person sacrifices his life or his own well-being for the sake of others.

This so-called "prudential" argument for the authority of conscience should, no doubt, not be overlooked. But neither should its defects. In the first place, it will apply equally well to obeying one's traditional conscience as to one's critical conscience. And in the second place, the above argument fails to suggest any sense in which one *always* ought to follow one's conscience.

There is a revision in the prudential argument, however, which would limit it to supporting critical conscience. To see this we must notice not only that doing what one believes to be wrong may lead to psychological disturbance but also that holding only rules which are subject to rational re-evaluation leads to holding a certain *sort* of rule. Briefly put, this sort of rule appears to be the sort which is conducive to an integrated, meaningful, and therefore satisfying life. It appears that deliberation is the only way in which one is likely to develop a set of commitments which is conducive to a satisfying life in this sense.

It is not just any sort of psychological integration which is advocated here—as though making one's actions consistent with one's beliefs, whatever they were, would be sufficient. The integration in question here is one which makes for a meaningful and satisfying life. It is obvious that not all rules which one might uncritically accept from tradition are conducive to such a life. Deliberation about one's rules tends to eliminate those which are not of this sort and to strengthen those which are.

It seems to me that something like the above must be the fundamental reason for obeying one's conscience in this sense. T. V. Smith puts the thrust of this argument well, I think, in the following:

...how do I know that it is better to do as conscience says than some other way? Well, as I said before, I've got to do something—something, too, that'll hold all these different ideas together into a sort of me....[14]

Consulting One's Conscience

In addition to the above prudential arguments there is an interesting line of argument which involves a rather different use of the term "conscience." This is the sense of the term as it appears in such expressions as "consulting one's conscience." It is this sense, and only this sense, in which it seems plausible to argue that conscience should *always* be followed.

When we speak of a person "consulting his conscience" before a major decision, we do not always mean that he asks whether a prospective action would violate one of his present (critically held) moral rules. Sometimes "consulting one's conscience" simply refers to critical moral deliberation about the particular situation at hand. When "conscience" is used in this sense, the question: "Should one always follow one's conscience?" becomes equivalent to: "Ought one always do what one sincerely believes, after rational deliberation, is right?" If the latter question can be answered affirmatively, the authority of conscience will be established in an important sense. Admittedly, this present usage of "conscience" has not always been the central one in ethics. It does, however, appear to be the sense most often appealed to in recent years by such groups as draft resisters. If the following argument for the authority of conscience in *this* sense can be sustained, it will provide one example of a sense in which conscience *always* ought to be followed.

One way to gain insight into the principle that one ought to do what one believes one ought to do after due rational deliberation is to consider the consequences of denying it. When one has evaluated all the available evidence in a particular situation as best he can and then must reach a decision and

---

14. T. V. Smith, *Beyond Conscience* (New York: McGraw-Hill, 1934), p. 257.

act on it, what is he to do if he denies that one ought to act in accordance with his deliberations? Basing one's decisions on rational thinking does not, of course, guarantee that one's moral conclusion will be correct (any more than it guarantees that one's scientific conclusions will be correct). There is *no* method by which a person can become infallible in his moral decision. Nevertheless, it does seem that if one wants to *try* to do the right thing, one ought to act on the basis of rational deliberation rather than on some other principle. If we make taking all the available evidence into account a necessary condition of rational deliberation, there will be, by hypothesis, no additional available evidence which might lead one to favor a different action. The crucial point in this argument, then, would be that since it is not possible to act on the rule, "Do what is best," the rational thing to do under the circumstances is to act on the rule, "Do what you have rationally concluded is best."

If one wants to do the right thing it would seem that the best he could do would be to deliberate about the particular situation and then act on his conclusion. If this is always the best general procedure for reaching a moral decision and if this is also what is meant by following one's conscience, then it follows that one *always* ought to follow one's conscience.

But at this point we are in danger of begging the whole question at issue here in favor of individuals and at the expense of society. Once the way is opened for an argument of the type which has been presented here by distinguishing between claims of infallibility and claims of authority, we must not simply assume that the authority of the individual conscience follows as the only option for the person who is trying to "do the right thing." Indeed, in an earlier version of this paper I suggested in a footnote that the Roman Catholic doctrine of papal infallibility might be re-worked along these lines. In such a revised view the Pope would not be claimed to be infallible, but simply to have "authority." Following his pronouncements would simply have to be argued to be "the best that could be done under the circumstances."

But is the authority to rest with the Pope, with the individual, or perhaps with society? The issue cannot be settled simply by the arguments so far presented. Those arguments reflect, in fact, what might be called a "protestant bias" (where "protestant" may be read in both the religious and social protestor sense). I have argued that "consulting one's conscience" in the present sense is simply the best general procedure for reaching a correct moral decision. But it would be perfectly understandable for a Roman Catholic to argue that consulting the Pope, who after all would have had the advice and council of bishops and experts in the field at issue, would be the best general procedure for reaching a moral decision. In the same fashion it would be perfectly understandable for a person who believed strongly in the wisdom of always acting on the basis of a group consensus to advocate this as the preferable method of moral decision-making.

Obviously, then, to speak up for the authority of conscience while it need not involve any reference to an infallible moral faculty does involve a commitment to an important and debatable principle of moral decision-making. How is our emphasis on the individual to be justified? (It is at this point that I must confess I do not see as clearly as I would like. The feeling persists that there is something repugnant about compelling someone to do something which he has conscientiously concluded to be immoral. I wonder, however, if the following justification is strong enough to justify this feeling of repugnance.)

In his writings on political philosophy John Stuart Mill argued that a major part of the value of democracy was that it fostered individual development in a way which no other form of government could match. Also, Mill defended freedom of speech by pointing out that it appeared to be a necessary part of the self-correcting process of arriving at the truth about any matter. Both of these considerations can play a role in justifying the claim that the final authority in ethical decision-making should be left with the individual.

When objections to the authority of the individual are raised they may, of course, be based on a number of different points. The major point which this paper has tried to expose thus far is the fallaciousness of the argument based on the possibility of error (that is, on the fallibility of individuals and their consciences). A second misconception, however, is at the basis of many objections to the giving of authority to the individual. Even if one has the right (or "authority") to decide for himself it does not follow that he must be permitted to do just anything at all, no matter how carefully he has arrived at the decision that it must be done. For example, if a person sincerely believes that he should handle poisonous snakes, assassinate the president, or chase Negroes with an axehandle, it neither follows that he is right in doing these things nor that he should be permitted by society to continue. Underlying all of this are certain pre-suppositions; for instance, that the person is not a child, is of sound mind, etc. It is clear that these issues require further analysis and discussion which must be omitted here. The criteria of sanity, for example, are surely normative in some sense and hence complicate the issue. The point here is simply that it may be right for a person to base his decisions on his own con-scientious reflection and at the same time right for society to restrain his resulting actions. There is nothing contradictory about this.

Among the many other factors which tend to support the authority of the individual conscience is the standard ob-servation that in such cases as conscientious objection to war, for example, it is exceedingly difficult (if not impossible) to force a person to those things to which he is conscientiously opposed. This simply indicates that the alternatives to allowing (or supporting) the authority of the individual conscience may be rather unsatisfactory.

All of this seems to me to constitute compelling reason for holding the view that one should always do what he sincerely believes is right after due rational deliberation.

But now let us return to conscience in the sense which involves the application of rules. It is critical examination of the *rules* one holds (not the critical examination of the partic-ular situation) which makes a conscience critical rather than traditional. So to appreciate the value of a critical conscience we must understand something about the potential usefulness of rules. One of the features of the human condition which is relevant here is that moral decisions (as opposed to certain types of theoretical decisions perhaps) have to be made within certain time limits. To postpone a decision on moral questions very often has the same effect as having decided one way or the other. To deliberate extensively about each situation which arises would normally be entirely too time-consuming to be practical. There is much to be said for accepting a number of general rules as time-saving guides to moral decisions. Moreover, our reflections in a particular situation are perhaps more likely to favor our own interests than a rule which we might have adopted as a general principle in a moment of "cool" reflection.

If we grant, then, the usefulness of guiding one's ordinary moral decisions by rules, and also the need for these rules to be continually subject to critical examination, we may conclude that people have at least a *prima facie* obligation to follow their critical conscience. To say that this obligation is *prima facie* means that in some circumstances it may be overriden by other obligations. In this respect it would seem to be analogous to the obligation to keep one's promises.

There is what might be called a "chain" argument which might be used to establish the obligation to follow one's critical conscience. We may begin by listing several very general rules of procedure in order of their apparent value, assuming initially that each is a rule on which decisions could actually be based in some way. The best rule of all to follow would be simply "Do what is right." Unfortunately, as was mentioned before, this rule is generally pointless in the absence of a means of determining what is actually right. The second best general rule appears to be "Do what you believe is right based on rational deliberation about a given situation." This is the rule which was discussed previously. But this rule is frequently (although not always) impossible to apply because in many cases we have insufficient time or opportunity for further deliberation. It is in such cases that the third best general rule becomes important. This last rule is "Do what conforms to one's rationally considered moral rules." It is because of the human limitations in wisdom (we are fallible) and time (we often lack it) that one is well-advised to follow this general rule. If one is trying to do what is right, then one has a *prima facie* obligation to follow his conscience in this sense. One should always do at least this, even though, when conditions permit more detailed consideration of the particular case, the critical conscience may be overridden.

We have now considered some ways in which two currently popular senses of the word "conscience" might be claimed to have authority. The one sense involved critical deliberation about a particular situation; the other, critical deliberation about one's moral rules prior to a particular situation. But what is the ground of this supposed authority? Consider first the statement "People should always do what they have carefully concluded is best." If this statement were *logically* necessary, to question it would make no sense. (Cf. "Why ought I do what I ought to do?" or "Why do you like what is nice?") This statement, however, is not self-evident or self-justifying. Further reasons for it may be given and are, in fact, called for, since there are many logically possible situations in which this statement would clearly not be true. These reasons involve an appeal to certain features of "the human condition" as such.

The principle features of the human condition to which I refer are two: human beings have no access to an infallible authority; human beings have the ability to deliberate and are generally committed to "rationality" in their decision-making. Under these conditions what rule should a person follow if he is attempting to do what he objectively ought? If he is committed to rational deliberation and is attempting to do what is objectively right, the only rational alternative open to him appears to be to act on the basis of his considered deliberation.

But one further aspect of the human condition is relevant here: the limits of time, information, and objectivity and the necessity to decide. Sometimes we cannot base our decisions on adequate deliberation about the particular situation. In these cases the best we can do is to follow our critical consciences. This may be a rather weak sense in which to speak of "the authority of conscience." It does, however, indicate some important ways in which "conscience" may be given a meaningful role in intelligent ethical discussion.

XIV

Some Paradoxes of Private Conscience as a Political Guide

WILLIAM EARLE

I. THE QUESTION

THOUGHT seems to thrive on crises to such an extent that when it can find none it either falls asleep or invents one. But surely most of the time it need only open its eyes; if there has ever been a substantial portion of human history without its crises, when was it? In any event, we hardly have to invent a crisis in the present day; one stares us in the face and it is indeed a crisis of thought. I refer of course to the conflict which some men experience between the demands of public law and those of their private consciences, to wit, whether to obey the law demanding their participation in the Vietnam war or their own consciences which may find that law morally intolerable. I should like to look into this question *without* raising the additional question whether *I* find the war a just one. That specific question is neither the premise nor conclusion to this discussion. And I should like to look at the question not from the point of view of those who approve of the war but only those who *disapprove* of it since only there can our question be posed. The question could still be raised even if no one at all actually raised it.

And again, the question raised here is the *moral* resolution to a moral conflict between public law and private conscience; it is not the question whether a dissenter can in *fact* dodge the penalties of law, or whether the law has in fact the power to compel obedience. The answers to those questions would leave the moral issue untouched. And so we shall confine ourselves to one problem: what is the moral resolution to the possible conflict between one man's conscience and the law.

This question is obviously not itself a purely legal question, for what is at issue is the moral authority of laws themselves of which I may disapprove; it would beg the question to invoke those laws once again in their own self-defense. Nor, I believe is it purely a question of my own conscience; for it is also the question of the absolute right of my own conscience against the laws which is raised. The laws give me no such legal right. If I begin by assuming the absolute authority of my own conscience, then I have also instantly come to the end of the problem and need only reiterate my principle at the conclusion. Neither simple answer is sensitive to the problematic character of the problem.

The problem is, of course, an ancient and recurring one; one need only recall the differing answers of Socrates and Aristotle, Galileo and Bruno, Thoreau and Emerson. My own little discussion will try to trace out dialectically and not historically the conflicting claims of private conscience and public law when each is taken by itself, put these claims into a dialogue, and then see what the conclusion might be, if there can be a conclusion.

II. WHAT CONSCIENCE SAYS

First, a few phenomenological remarks about what conscience is—"phenomenological" in the sense that these remarks only propose to discuss conscience *as it looks to itself*, not as it might look to a psychoanalyst, sociologist, historian, biologist, or to the faithful of any religion. Whatever else it might be, it primarily is a sense of right and wrong, of scruple that such a man without conscience, if one could be found, would regard himself as unscrupulous. Let us for the moment ignore the various things which men have regarded as right and wrong; we shall return to this later. But now we are looking at conscience itself no matter what moral language it speaks. And the first curious thing about it is that its *primary* word is "NO." Conscience is most itself when it forbids some action, to such an

extent that a "good conscience" approving my decisions looks
far more like a case of self-satisfaction, self-righteousness, and
moral smugness, which themselves could only be *disapproved*
by my own conscience. Socrates' "daimon" only said "no."

Second, the primary address of my conscience is to me. It
forbids *me* from doing certain things. Hence it is universally
regarded as the very personal center of a man his "inwit," as
Middle English called it. It is the very person of the man
and not some accidental or causal mental talent like a long
memory or a lively imagination. It is so very much myself
speaking to myself that radical conscientious self-criticism can
tear the self apart. My violation of my own conscience then is
hardly the same matter as making a mistake in arithmetic or mis-
calculating the practical effects of my decision. A violation of
one's own conscience is hardly a "mistake" at all; it is more
like the threat of dissolution of one's own deepest self.

And so, third, it is not difficult to understand why conscience
always speaks with final authority for each. Sometimes it does
not know whether to speak or not, the situation may be too
obscure; or it may speak hypothetically, falteringly, and without
blowing its certain note. But when it is most itself, it speaks
with an unquestioned authority; do I indeed have any thing
higher than my own conscience to consult? But that could only
be something which my own conscience might reject. The
authority with which conscience speaks when it does speak is
so absolute that many men suppose it to be the voice of God,
disobedience to which might carry with it eternal damnation.

The fourth note of conscience is that in its purity as a final
authority for each man, it is completely *abstract*. The conscience with which each man is born is nothing but a *sense*
of right and wrong; it is not also already provided with the
facts and the interpretation of facts necessary for its own exercise. If conscience then seems infallible, it is only because we
are taking it in its abstract purity. So if the difference between
right and wrong seems like a clear light, it is so only because
it has not yet been turned on the ambiguities of the concrete
domain where we must decide and act.

Now let us trace the course of the man of conscience in

public affairs. Fortunately we do not have to invent, since Thoreau has already stated the matter with perfect clarity in his essay on civil disobedience, an essay which, supplemented by the works of Herbert Marcuse, has already taken on the authority of a higher Bible with the New Left, and in any event an authority far transcending that of the Constitution and the Government together.

Thoreau puts the matter quite simply and plainly. He begins: "That government is best which governs least, or rather not at all." It is nothing but an "expediency" by which people exercise their will. And if this suggests a democracy, we are quickly disillusioned: "A government of majority rule in all cases can not be based on justice ... can there not be a government in which not majorities decide right and wrong but conscience?" He then asks: "Must the citizen ever resign his conscience to the legislator?" The answer comes immediately: "The only obligation which I have a right to assume is to do at any time what I think right.... A wise man will not leave the right to the mercy of chance nor wish it to prevail through the power of the majority." How does conscience react to laws when it regards them as unjust? "All men recognize the right of revolution: to refuse allegiance to, to resist the government when its tyranny or its inefficiency are great and unendurable.... If injustice is such that it requires you to be the agent of injustice to another, then, I say, break the law." "Breaking the law," he specifies, means "using your whole influence," which includes one's life. He has nothing but scorn for those who merely use the ballot.

As for alternatives, he says: "Unjust laws exist; shall we be content to obey them, or shall we amend them and obey until we have succeeded, or shall we transgress at once?" But to obey them of course is to connive with evil; as for amendment, that he says "takes too much time and man's life will soon be gone." Besides, he adds, "I do not care to trace the course of my dollar.... It is for no particular item in the tax bill that I refuse to pay it. I simply wish to refuse allegiance to the State, to withdraw and stand aloof from it effectually." He ends: "Authority of government to be strictly pure must have the sanction and consent of the governed. It can have no right over my person and property but what I concede to it . . . the State must come to recognize the individual as a higher and independent power from which all its own power and authority are derived . . . and must treat him accordingly." As for his fellow citizens—those who obey the law because it is the law—they serve the state, he says, not as men mainly but as machines, with their bodies; they are, he adds, of the "same worth as horses and dogs." When he emerged from his night in jail, he has a new vision of his fellowtownsmen; they now seem to him to be of a "distinct race."

No doubt not all of this is strictly relevant to our present question, but it does offer the dialectical unfolding of an intransigent conscience confronting the claims of law. And as must be obvious, its traditional name is anarchy, the withdrawal of allegiance from government and law in favor of the final accreditation by each man of his own solitary and ultimate conscience. Can any man of conscience do otherwise?

III. WHAT LAWS COMMAND

If this were the whole story, there would hardly be any problem at all. But it turns out to be *only* the voice of private conscience, opposing its intimate and final claims to *other* claims, namely, those of the government and its laws. What might they say on their own behalf? If Thoreau says they derive their only authority from the approval of his private conscience, perhaps the most striking feature of the law is that it makes no mention whatsoever of Henry David Thoreau or any other private citizen as authenticating them. Is this an oversight?

If we now shift our point of view to that of government and its laws, what claims may they advance on their own behalf? But let us make a distinction between two sorts of law; there are, first of all, the ordinary everyday enactments of an existing government. And second, there is law of a different sort, those laws such as the Constitution of the United States which define the government itself and its legal powers. Every-day laws of the first sort somehow never mention Thoreau or any other private citizen as giving them their authority; they claim authority from the government which enacts them. They lose authority if improperly passed or if in conflict with superior law, but never simply by virtue of being in conflict with Thoreau's conscience. Thoreau's conscience is then, from their point of view, strictly irrelevant to their authority. They are therefore morally or legally compelling upon Thoreau, whether he likes them or not. And to repeat, our question does not concern the obvious fact that the laws and their legal enforce-ment can *in fact* compel private obedience; it is whether they have any *right* to do so. If they derive their authority from the government and not from Thoreau, Thoreau can hardly repre-sent his own conscience as their sole authorization, even for himself. And on top of this, it is the government which has the moral obligation to *enforce* its own laws; it is commonly recognized that laws which are not even capable of being en-forced are but scraps of paper and not proper laws at all. But since Thoreau in his private person hardly has the means, let alone the right, to enforce those particular laws of his choice, by what authority can his private conscience claim to be the legislator of the world? In fact, the laws might continue (in this hostile vein), what initially looked like a beautiful appeal to conscience in analysis turns out to be the moral tyranny of one conscience over others and over the very government which it set up to adjudicate such problems.

Pursuing this last point, the laws might add the following. One would have to be very naive indeed to suppose that all con-sciences agreed. If each man's conscience speaks with final and absolute authority, what it is speaking about is concrete decision and action. Now on conscience' own terms, one must con-scientiously inform oneself of the very facts of the case being decided. No doubt in many cases these are sufficiently clear and agreed upon to offer no substantial problems; but surely not in all. A recent example might be the case of the *Pueblo;* an-other, the possibility of unidentified assassins of President Ken-nedy. On top of the difficulties of ascertaining the facts, there is

a deeper one of *interpreting* or *reading* those facts. The very
same facts can be put together in diverse ways, suggesting
diverse judgments about them. In the Vietnam war, surely most
of the dispute arises from this very source; if the question is
whether the United States is there upon invitation of South
Vietnam to prevent its invasion by North Vietnam and the
Viet Cong, or whether we are invaders in a territory to which
Ho Chi Minh can lay rightful claim, who could pretend that this
is a simple factual question? Is the dispute clearly not a case
of reading the facts very differently, such that, at this date,
no new *facts* will clinch the decision? On top of these sources
of difference in conscientious decision, there is the final existential truth that my conscience is rooted in and expressive of
my own deepest commitments; but so is the other man's. With
the ambiguity of fact, the differences of reading those facts, and
the final individuality of my concretely deciding conscience itself,
it is hardly surprising that nothing is commoner than conflicts
of conscience, not merely of one man with another, but the same
man with himself. Now if my conflicts with myself are strictly
my own business, my conflicts with others are not; at this
point I properly fall into the social and legal domain.

Now what can Thoreau do, armed only with the final authority of his own conscience, but declare one who disagrees with
him lacking in conscience, or stupid or malicious, definitely a
lower being; Thoreau saw them all as machines, dogs and
horses, a "different race." And with this particular species of
moral fanaticism, surely the very atmosphere in which there
might be a conscientious resolution to differences of conscience
disappears. On the other hand, the laws might continue to argue,
why were we, the laws, set up in the first place if not precisely
to give a moral solution to moral conflicts? It is not a case of
conscience versus the law but merely private conscience versus
public conscience. Private must cede to public conscience.

Which brings us back to that more basic law, that which
founds and authorizes government in the first place—in our
case, the Constitution. Thoreau declared the Constitution to be
not even worth thinking about from his higher point of view;
and indeed why should it be when he has his private conscience

to replace it? But perhaps the Constitution has something to say for itself. Since it supplies a primary justification for all consequent laws and authority, it can hardly be nothing. And yet in the ultimate probe, the founding law of any government is in what looks like a circle of justification. It is itself the authority for the government it sets up to uphold it. And so it is the authority for the authority of the very government it set up to enforce its authority. Here we have the possibility of a crisis in authority which becomes decisive in revolution.

And so chasing down final authority, now on the side of law and government, we may begin to see its own Achilles heel. The highest law, the Constitution, was itself the act of men at the Constitutional Convention operating not under the Constitution but under other agreements which were to be superseded by the Constitution. What moral right did such men have to bind us in the future? And here it is of no avail to say that there are provisions in the Constitution for its own alteration; the procedures of alteration themselves must be constitutional or not; and so we are bound in the end *by* the Constitution *to* itself. Further, not all governments and founding laws have arisen this way; some just grew up through practice, tradition, and custom. Surely a large portion of what passes for legal decision even in a law-ridden country such as ours, is and should be justified by custom, tradition, tacit understandings and the rest. In a word, both *final* authority in law and government, as well as a good deal of day-to-day rulings rest not upon law or government, but custom, which, looked at from the point of view of law, is unformulizable, notoriously subject to differences of interpretation, and even changeable with the personalities of the administrators. If law and authority then can be said to be reasonable, that reasonability is itself ultimately founded on the irrational, historical, even the arbitrary.

If Thoreau then elevates his own conscience to an authority higher than government and law and thereby ironically turns into a private moral tyrant, the opposite claim of government, seeking to stabilize and adjudicate private disputes by an authority higher than individual consciences, finally passes from an initial rationality to a nonlegal, arbitrary, and irrational basis in historical acts, customs, tradition, and mere *de facto* practice.

IV. CAN THERE BE A RESOLUTION?

I have tried to take two claims for ultimate moral authority seriously, and run both into the ground. Neither, all by itself, can sustain its claims to *moral ultimacy*. If some such thing is true, what is to be done about it? Perhaps admit a little bit of both? But so far as I can see, there is no theoretical resolution to the problem whatsoever; and if this sounds disastrous, I should finally like to point out why I think it is, on the contrary, of utmost value and importance.

Thoreau himself was a gentle man, and so his principle of private conscience might seem a good deal more acceptable than it would be if we compare two recent cases where violent men could appeal to the same principle. Both Lee Harvey Oswald and Sirhan Sirhan also employed their own consciences as their final guide, one to assassinate President Kennedy for his part in the Cuban crisis, the other to assassinate Senator Kennedy for his recommendations of aid to Israel. The reply that Thoreau was gentle and the latter two pathological only points up the paradox of private conscience as a political guide. All could justify their conduct by their private consciences, but on the other hand there is the case of Colonel von Stauffenberg, who, at least in my own judgment, very nobly tried with some associates to assassinate Hitler. All were cases of conscience at its extremity in conflict with officers of the government if not the government itself. In some cases we may approve, in others, disapprove, but all would be equally authorized by the general principle of private conscience and all equally condemned by government and law. Can these cases now be judged either by law or by private conscience? Their own private consciences approved them; the law condemns them all, yet surely there are decisive differences among them.

On the other side, law is in the same boat. Law and government must have some *prima facie* justification up to a point.

but revolution raises precisely that point. Law itself can hardly be taken as its own final justification. And yet no government and no law could possibly authorize each private citizen to pick and choose which laws he will obey and when and under what circumstances. Nor can any government regard itself as anything but the legal government; those who refuse to recognize its *moral* authority are not citizens of that country but in effect potential enemies of the State. And yet who would not have to recognize the possibility of a radically corrupt state, corrupt not in its own terms but in terms drawn from other sources, perhaps even finally private conscience?

I believe these paradoxes to be theoretically insoluble, that is, that there can be *no general principle* or method which we could consult to prove in all extremities, which side must be right, which wrong. And, far from being an intellectual disaster, on the contrary it throws into relief some existential points. First of all, if we could solve these paradoxes theoretically, once and for all, while we might take some thin pleasure in the fact, we would at the same stroke have removed all sense whatsoever from the historical struggles of men, from existence itself. Installing ourselves in the divine seat of judgment, that either of private conscience or law, we would be entitled to pronounce on the past and future course of history and would in effect be viewing it as a senseless struggle of either stupid or immoral men with wise and moral men who always more or less are pictured in our own image. Having solved in this room the problem of existence, it could have nothing further to teach us. Second, if any such attempted vision eliminates the essential moral *risk* of existence, it also prepares the atmosphere for that pseudo-discussion where neither side listens but each only speaks out of private moral or public legal certitudes. Conscience slips into fanaticism and criminality, becoming an enemy of the State; government and law can become enemies of the very conscience which defines each man. To ask for general criteria and standards is to ask for not merely what is impossible but, I am convinced also, precisely that which would obfuscate the problem by declaring it solved for life.

Meanwhile there are some interesting examples of the ultimately *insoluble* character of the conflict. Socrates, condemned by the law, declared he would not harm the laws themselves and drank the hemlock. Aristotle, also condemned on similar laws, declared he would not permit Athens to sin twice against philosophy and retired to a country estate. Bruno, condemned for his metaphysics and astronomy, went to the stake for them; Galileo recanted, adding, however, that he was still right. Thoreau went to jail for a night, an act incomprehensible to Emerson. And so the examples multiply. My inclination is not to pronounce judgment on these cases, but to point to the irreducible paradoxes of *both* law and of private conscience as final guides to anything; to retain the paradox then is to restore to our senses of existence its own paradoxicality and risk, where at last there can be nothing but listening. And after decision, even here, there are no final *guarantees* that any choice ever was right or wrong. To sum up briefly: I have tried to present something like an expression of the dialectic of listening. Listening, if it were nothing but a receptivity to diversity of opinions, could easily lead to paralysis of will. And, after having heard the possible options laid before me, I *still* have to decide; the options before me won't decide of themselves. And further, any decision whatsoever involves two matters: the course of action itself and the principle by which I justify that choice or authorize it to and for myself. My own discussion has involved this last factor, that by which I ultimately justify my political choices.

At first, the ultimate judge and moral authority looks simple: it is my own conscience. Here we met Thoreau. And we continue to meet his descendants in all those who without more ado simply bring each choice before their private consciences and rule upon that choice with a frightening finality.

But second, if conscience is conscientious enough, it will look into itself: what is it but an abstract sense of right and wrong, clear because empty of any particular information? And so a conscientious examination of conscience discloses that it has some unique disqualifications to rule on the world. As soon as it judges any particular matter of fact, it has descended into a domain where it loses its abstract majesty and looks like one more party to the quarrel, with incomplete information, faced

with a diversity of equally plausible readings of what information it has, and finally resolving the whole thing by a
pronouncement which inevitably reflects the personal situation
and biases of the person whose conscience it is. It is but one
conscience among many.

Having a sentiment of this from the beginning, men have taken
the next step: set up a public conscience, law, whose sole justification is to settle, by an agreed upon ethical procedure, differences among private consciences. At this stage of the dialectic,
private conscience which remains conscientious and not a blind
fist of power masquerading as moral, must cede to that moral
authority, the law, which it set up in the first place to resolve
these differences. At this stage of listening, the law has a moral
authority transcending any private conscience.

A third stage emerges when the man of private conscience,
having gone through the prior stages and not before, finds the
very foundations of the law under which he has consented to
live incompatible with his conscience. At this point, he has
chosen to be outside the law, cannot reasonably expect its
protection, and takes upon himself, in both his conscience and
his own particularity as a finite historical man, the authorization
and justification of his own social acts. In effect he has become
his own lawgiver or, following Nietzsche, is beyond good and
evil. If such a man rejects the principle of law as such, he is
simply an anarchist and has reverted to stage one, each for
himself. If he does not reject the principle of law but only a
particular set of laws, wishing to replace them with others, then
let him find his followers and let them collectively judge whether
they now have something better or worse, or just different.

In all of this, there is hardly any logical or purely rational
solution. The last stage is the stage of revolution; there are no
abstract principles by which to judge the worth of revolution.
And as for *particular* principles, it is exactly they which are
being revolved. At this point, the revolutionary is strictly and
eternally on his own; right and wrong in the domain of action
do not have the meaning of logically correct and incorrect or
valid. They refer to values, and the sole authority which values
possess is their ability to engage our deepest will. They are

neither correct nor incorrect, but affirmed or rejected. This dialectic of listening has only sought to indicate some stages of questioning which must be engaged in so that the deepest affirmation will indeed proceed from our existence and not some chance rage of the moment.